URBAN EDUCATION

Kansas City's Central High School
and the Enduring Legacy of Racism

BRADLEY W. POOS

M·P·P
www.MissionPointPress.com

Readers are encouraged to go to MissionPointPress.com to contact the author or to find information on how to buy this book in bulk at a discounted rate.

Published by Mission Point Press

 Mission Point Press

2554 Chandler Rd.
Traverse City, MI 49696
(231) 421-9513
MissionPointPress.com

Hardcover ISBN: 978-1-965278-70-3
Softcover ISBN: 978-1-965278-71-0

Library of Congress Control Number: 2025910044

Printed in the United States of America

To Central and all her people.

Dear old Central, far-famed Central,
Thou shalt never fail;
Round thy name there clings a tendril
Of tradition's tale.

Thou art victor; fame has followed,
Clad in dignity;
May thy name to all be hallowed
By our love for thee.

Every student soon or later
In his walk of life
Greets the thought of Alma Mater
As his strength in strife.

Contents

Preface

Let's begin with a basic, yet essential question: Why Central High School? It is an important question, after all. To answer this, I must go back more than a decade when, in 2010, I began my PhD program and was confronted, for the first time, with having to think deeply about education and formal schooling in the United States. Coming into my doctoral program, I had worked as both a middle school and high school teacher and counselor and had earned masters' degrees in both social studies education and school counseling. The field of education was not new territory, and I had already started carving out a career. Yet early in my doctoral studies, it was suggested to me that I take a look at *Race, Real Estate, and Uneven Development: The Kansas City Experience, 1900-2000*. This was the work of Kevin Gotham (2002), an impressively documented account of the relationship between the real estate industry and the Federal Housing Administration. Gotham's argument centers on the role of these two institutions in advancing the racialization of metropolitan space. In it, Gotham references the neighborhood racial transformation and subsequent school segregation around and within Kansas City's Central High School: all White in 1955; all Black by 1962.[1]

I was instantly struck by Central's swift and dramatic shift. This seemed like a big deal. It was certainly an intriguing and alarming change in demographics. I was also ashamed and embarrassed that I was completely unaware of it. Here I was, an educator, living and working in Kansas City, Missouri, and I was ignorant to the educational and racial landscape within my own city. I did not grow up in Kansas City, but this was not a sufficient excuse. As a White man living in an upper-middle-class neighborhood west of Kansas City's Troost divide (this will soon be explained), the reality was then and is now, that I walk through this world with certain privileges. One of those is that I can remain oblivious to racism by simply existing—thinking deeply about race is not something that I have been encouraged to do. In fact, I have been discouraged from doing so.

The messages I received were those that emphasized meritocracy and color-blindness, like: "everyone has an equal opportunity; it's how hard you work that makes the difference," or "racism is a thing of the past," or "school segregation ended a long time ago." It was not until I began my doctoral studies that I was confronted with the realities of education in the United States and specifically the ways in which race and schooling are rooted in a complicated historical, socio-political, and economic environment. This has driven me to better understand the Kansas City story, knowing that exploring what has happened in Kansas City, specifically around school segregation, desegregation, and resegregation, provides new and important insight into the American narrative. I have decided to focus on a single institution, which is a rather unique approach, but one that I hope makes a complex and messy issue like that of the American system of public education easier to digest. There is one school that illustrates the challenges faced in public education perhaps better than any school in the country. That school is Kansas City's Central High School.

A thorough search of the literature yields little in the way of comprehensive institutional histories of American high schools. There are very few—only a handful—out there. This is unfortunate, as the history of public education in the United States is complicated. There is potential in an institutional history for greater clarity and an opportunity for new considerations, as well as the possibility to provide a deeper understanding of that which is already known. The value lies in the thorough and comprehensive nature of the narrative, in that following a single school over time, especially a school as old and storied as Central High School, leads to greater insight, notably in how race and racism have affected individual schools, students, and communities.

As a mid-sized city in the heart of the Midwest, Kansas City certainly does not elicit the intrigue of larger coastal cities, nor does it get the attention that other Midwestern cities like Chicago, St. Louis, Detroit, or Denver do. And when it comes to the intersection of race and education, the focus is often on the South. The majority of titles that explore the history of race and education do so with a decided Southern angle, focusing on school segregation and desegregation as it unfolded throughout the South. This is not surprising, given the South's history rooted in slavery and segregation, but it is unfortunate and preserves a misconception that race is only a salient feature of the social structure in the South. Not so, and Kansas City's story serves as an exemplar and is among the most compelling and consequential. Race is and has been a prominent feature of Kansas City's educational history, as it has throughout many Midwestern cities, but it is under-explored. Case in point: There is only one title that explicitly approaches the topic of education and race in Kansas City, Joshua Dunn's *Complex Justice: The Case of Missouri v. Jenkins*, which explores the lengthy *Jenkins* school desegregation case in Kansas City, Missouri that unfolded between 1985 and 2003.[2] Additionally, there are a handful of books that consider education in Kansas City on the periphery of deeper analyses of race: Sherry Schirmer's *A City Divided: The Racial Landscape of Kansas City, 1900-1960*, examines the racial landscape of Kansas City; G.S. Griffin's *Racism in Kansas City: A Short History* details racism in Kansas City from an historical perspective; Tanner Colby's *Some of My Best Friends are Black: The Strange Story of Integration in America* looks at the failures of integration, specifically in Kansas City, as well as Vestavia Hills, Alabama; Margie Carr's *Kansas City's Montgall Avenue: Black Leaders and the Street They Call Home* considers the development of a residential block within Kansas City's Black community and the institutions that resided therein; and, as mentioned, Kevin Gotham's

Race, Real Estate, and Uneven Development: The Kansas City Experience, 1900-2000. Beyond these titles, there is little literature to be found.[3]

This book fills a void. It provides insight into the intersection of race and education outside the Deep South, and it does so from a unique perspective, by following a single school throughout its long and storied existence—Kansas City's Central High School. It is an important story. So much has changed over the course of Central's lifespan. Central's first eighty-eight years (1867-1955) were as an exclusive White high school, the premier institution of Kansas City's segregated school system. With the destruction of "separate but equal" and the *Brown v. Topeka Board of Education* decision (1954), Central quickly transformed into a predominantly Black school and has remained as such in *Brown's* aftermath. The post-*Brown* period has been anything but smooth, with great successes and epic failures. This book uncovers the history of Central High School and all the messiness and intrigue therein.

You will notice that, throughout this book, emphasis is placed on student and community perspectives, prioritizing student voice. For information about the early years, I relied on student newspapers, pamphlets, and yearbooks. Information about the later years was garnered through conversation and the use of oral history interviews. I owe a great debt to those who generously volunteered their time and shared their stories. I also relied on traditional archival research methods. The Missouri Valley Special Collections within the Kansas City Public Library, which holds most of the Kansas City Public School records, including yearbooks and student newspapers, and the State Historical Society of Missouri, home to the Arthur A. Benson Collection, were valuable resources from which to piece together Central's story. Countless articles in local newspapers provided great context as well. *The Kansas City Star* and *The Kansas City Times* were both founded in the early 1880s and eventually merged into *The Kansas City Star* in the 1990s. *The Kansas City Call* was the weekly Black newspaper that was founded in 1919 and is still in production today. All three newspapers played an important role in rounding out the story of Central.

I spent many hours in the archive and had numerous conversations with members of the Central community. It should be noted that I have employed a decided race perspective, in which I actively center race and racism as a primary lens through which to analyze the history of Central. This moves beyond the consideration of race as merely a demographic variable and leans into the idea that race is a systemic factor that has had a profound impact on Central High School and its community.

This book first explores the creation of the dual school system in Kansas City, Missouri. At the conclusion of the Civil War, in 1865, the State of Missouri ratified a new constitution, and by 1875 that same Missouri State Constitution included revised and specific language requiring that Black and White children attend separate schools. With specific constitutional language requiring a segregated school system, the Kansas City public school system began to grow accordingly. And as such, Central High School was born. This chapter describes the ways in which a dual, segregated education system was constructed in Kansas City, Missouri, and how Central High School became the premier institution within the dual system.

In Chapter 1, I examine the growth and popularity of all-White Central High School. Initial skepticism about public school in the late 1800s did not persist, and the popularity of public education in Kansas City grew, just as it did around the country. No school was growing faster than Central High School. Central occupied several buildings between 1867 and 1915, each one designed to hold more students than the building before it but all within the central city. In 1915, however, Central was destined for a new home in the growing southeast corridor.

Chapter 2 details Central's move to the new building and the extreme growth occurring within the Central attendance area in the early twentieth century. The school population nearly doubled in size in just a brief two-year period between 1920 and 1922. A brand-new building and record enrollment made Central and its surrounding neighborhoods particularly desirable, but notably only for White residents. Central's growth was solidifying a firm residential racial divide. Central was safely south of Twenty-Seventh Street, which represented a line of demarcation in Kansas City separating White residents from Black residents. By 1924, Central was not only the largest high school in Kansas City, but it was also the largest in the State of Missouri. Growth and popularity of schools like Central brought challenges to the district, including financial struggles and widening racial division.

Chapter 3 begins with challenges confronting Central in the midst of World War II, before moving into how the war ushered in a sentiment among the Black community that racial equality was within reach. The housing industry remained impenetrable, however, as Black families buoyed by wartime employment and increased wages looked for housing opportunities outside of historic Black neighborhoods. As Whites pushed a narrative that the presence of Black families in their White neighborhoods would result in declining home values, the real estate industry, banks, the federal government, and the courts fell in line making it nearly impossible for Blacks to penetrate White neighborhoods. Somewhat surprisingly, though, schools seemed to represent an opportunity for integration. The Brown decision would ultimately change the course of history and mark a new epoch in education—desegregation. Central High School would be among the first schools in Kansas City to welcome Black students.

In Chapter 4, I explore how desegregation unfolded at Central High School. Unlike the Deep South, initial desegregation in Kansas City, Missouri, began rather uneventfully, insofar as there was no violence accompanying the initial effort. But desegregation in Kansas City was most certainly not easy, nor was it clean and equitable. Central provides a clear example of the dramatic shift in student population following the 1954 *Brown* decision. During the 1955–56 school year, Central was 72 percent White; by 1960, it was 95 percent Black. Central and the neighborhoods around it swiftly shifted from all White to all Black as Black residents began to penetrate the Twenty-Seventh Street division and White families moved further south and west. Troost emerged as the new dividing line separating White from Black and ensuring neighborhoods and schools remained segregated even after court-ordered desegregation. Central was one of the highest-performing schools in the state through much of the 1960s, but there was growing frustration among the Black community around how the district was preserving racial segregation within its schools. Widespread conflict erupted.

Chapter 5 describes how Central remained among the highest-performing schools in the state through most of the 1960s. Central even became the subject of national intrigue, as interest grew around the school's Black students' academic excellence and its White principal, James Boyd. Yet, there were rumblings of discontentment, especially among the Black community regarding the school district's lack of commitment to meaningful desegregation. By the late 1960s, frustration with the school district had, for many within the Black community, turned to anger. This would all boil over in 1968.

Chapter 6 looks at the aftermath of the riot of 1968 and the challenges Central confronted in its wake. News stories about Central during this time devolved into extreme negativity, as Central became a primary target of media sensationalism. The riot in Maryville at a basketball game between Central and Raytown South, in which Central was blamed and punished for the incident, is a particularly salient example of how Central became a common target. While Central bore the brunt of it, all of the schools in the southeastern part of the district were segregated and facing negative publicity. Meanwhile, Whites were fleeing district schools in waves, subsequently leading to even greater segregation and ultimately leading to federal scrutiny.

Chapter 7 begins with the school district's attempts to find an interdistrict desegregation solution. Ultimately, the decision would rest with Federal Judge Russell Clark, who was given the case filed by the school district. The desire was to seek a metropolitan, interdistrict desegregation remedy. Judge Clark was quick, though, to remove such a possibility. Kansas City, Missouri School District (KSMSD) was forced to find an intradistrict remedy. While court proceedings were unfolding, Central High School was simply trying to survive. Despite innovative efforts like that of PUSH Excel and stable building administration, Central was hollowed out throughout the 1980s as the surrounding neighborhoods became less socioeconomically secure with middle class flight and students bused out of the school. Just when it seemed as though all hope was lost, the school district went all in on magnet schools, and Central High School became the Central Computers Unlimited/Classical Greek High School.

In Chapter 8, I explore the design and implementation of Central Computers Unlimited/Classical Greek Magnet. Construction on the new Central Computers Unlimited/Classical Greek Magnet School, which cost roughly $33 million, was completed in the summer of 1991, just in time for the 1991 school year to commence. The new magnet building was impressive. It replaced the building that was constructed in 1915 and was equipped with a natatorium and state-of-the-art indoor field house, as well as specialized computer labs for robotics, graphic design, electronics, and drafting design; in all, Central was said to have over one thousand computers with more than fifteen computer-equipped classrooms housing more than twenty-five computers in each of those rooms—certainly impressive in 1991. This chapter explores the planning and development of Central Computers Unlimited/Classical Greek Magnet and provides context by detailing the experiences of students who attended Central during the magnet years.

In Chapter 9, I examine the end of the magnet philosophy in Kansas City and the aftermath of the massive desegregation plan. By 1995, just four years after Central opened its brand-new building and just seven years after it implemented its magnet-themed curriculum, Kansas City's magnet experiment had already begun to fall apart. By 1999 it was effectively all over, though it was not until 2003 that the judge dismissed the court case and subsequently marked the end of a twenty-five-year process. After more than $2 billion had been expended to transform Central and the Kansas City, Missouri School District into magnet schools, there was not much to show for it in the way of academic outcomes or student demographics. Certainly an argument could be made that there were impressive and meaningful facility upgrades and that the overall student experience improved as a result, but the Kansas City magnet plan is largely remembered as a failure. In its aftermath, the district lost its accreditation (which it has now earned back) and continued to lose enrollment and shutter empty school buildings. Central was converted back to a neighborhood school in 2003, and the problems continued mounting. Student enrollment fell, building administrators—and teachers—came and left, advanced courses and electives were removed from the curriculum, and the top-notch facilities, like the natatorium, lay dormant. This chapter addresses the end of Central Computers Unlimited/Classical Greek Magnet and details the complex socio-political environment left in its wake.

In Chapter 10, I explain what has happened to Central High School and public education in Kansas City following the closing of magnet schools. I look at the growth of charter schools, which by 2010 had grown so substantially that it led to what is now the first of two rounds of school closures. The "Right Sized Plan" resulted in the closure of roughly half of the district's schools, twenty-six schools in all. Today, more than half of Kansas City, Missouri's student population attends one of its forty-one charter schools, and Kansas City Public Schools[4] ranks fifth in the country among school districts with the highest percentage of charter school enrollment. As charter schools continue to grow, the Kansas City Public School District suffers. This chapter elaborates on the public abandonment of Central and the complexities confronted by traditional public school districts in the contemporary educational landscape, especially with the growing popularity of charter schools. In particular, I consider the increasing influence on reform efforts of neoliberalism, which emphasizes choice and accountability. This ideology has subsequently positioned anything associated with White, private business ventures and policies as superior to those associated with public or social services and with Black and marginalized populations.[5]

In the conclusion to this book, I consider what comes next for the Kansas City Public Schools, Central High School, and its students. I look at how Central's institutional history impacts its current context and what we can learn from it. Particular emphasis is placed on positioning Central's story within the contemporary national narrative of urban schooling.

Introduction

"Need your I.D.," instructed the uniformed security guard as I was buzzed into the building and ushered through the metal detectors, a common process within contemporary urban high schools. It was an unseasonably cool and sunny late August morning in 2023. Kansas City, Missouri, can be hot during summer, so this was a treat. I had just arrived at Central High School to pick up a few documents from a staff member. Perhaps it was the weather, but I was particularly tuned in to my surroundings on this day.

The neighborhoods currently surrounding Central High School serve as a reminder that the area is decades beyond its prime, its neighborhoods and residents forgotten long ago. The middle school flanks the high school, built anew in 1991. The two structures are strikingly different. The middle school is the original building, completed in 1924, less than a decade after the original high school was constructed, and it reflects the architectural style of that era. Old Central High School was torn down upon the completion of the current high school that opened as a magnet school in 1991.

The current Central High School building has a decidedly modern look, especially when juxtaposed against the adjacent middle school. Although the high school is a relatively new structure, it looks dreary and tired now, even compared to the older brick middle school, which stands with large windows and a proud appearance. The high school has a very 1990s look, with tiny windows and sprawling stone features. It is almost prison-like in appearance.

As I entered the high school on this day, I was particularly intrigued. The 2023–2024 school year had just commenced, and a few months before, it looked as though Central would be permanently closed. While there is lingering uncertainty around the school's future and ongoing threats of closure, for now, it remains open for business.

Central is an urban school; defining what constitutes an urban school is no simple undertaking. The most common definition of "urban" relates to geographic location and population. Makes sense. Historically, the notion of "urban" did equate to city centers with heavy population density, but in the contemporary context, this definition can be problematic. Many city centers—Kansas City included—have experienced a population loss. Thus, relying purely on a population-only definition of urban is misleading. A definition that also considers the social context of an area is more appropriate. In applying such a strategy to schools, then, factors such as poverty levels, racial and ethnic diversity, achievement scores, facilities, and teacher quality are salient features to consider as well. Educational scholar H. Richard Milner's contemporary framework of classifying urban schools is most useful. Milner created three categories of urban: urban intensive, urban emergent, and urban characteristic.[6] Kansas City, by Milner's definition, is an urban emergent school district, characterized by a large city with a population under one million and a majority of students identifying as students of color and living in poverty.[7]

This book details Central High School's history, Kansas City's oldest public school. A recurring theme emerges: the issue of race. Race, rooted in Central's creation, has largely been the defining feature of the school's long and storied existence. This is more than a story of success or failure, though there are both. In particular, the narrative reveals the complex nature of schooling in the United States. Much has changed since Central ushered in its first class of students in 1867, yet to this day, Central's institutional history is not widely known. Central's story is arguably one of the most compelling of any school in the nation. While this is a unique narrative belonging to Kansas

City's Central High School alone, there are lessons here that have broader relevance.

Missouri's First Public Schools

Race was central to the development of the state's public schools. As a slave state, before 1865, the state of Missouri had prohibited the education of enslaved persons. Missouri was home to free Blacks too at this time, though White Missourians widely opposed the education of Black Missourians, whether free or enslaved. By 1847, the Missouri State Legislature passed legislation to restrict the teaching of reading and writing to "Negroes or mulattos."[8] Although an educated slave was potentially more valuable, it was reasoned by the White slave-owning class that an educated slave was also a more dangerous one. Training and education, many Whites feared, might aid in the organization and execution of a successful revolt of the enslaved. Toward the end of the Civil War, the Emancipation Act of 1865 passed in Missouri on January 11, 1865. The act abolished slavery and included the following language: "hereafter in this State there shall be neither slavery or involuntary servitude, except in punishment of crime, whereof the party shall have been duly convicted; and all persons held to service or labor as slaves, are hereby 'declared free.'"[9] With the declaration of freedom came a new state constitution, as well, which was ratified the same year and provided for the establishment and maintenance of free public schools for all persons in the state between the ages of five and twenty-one.[10]

While public schools were initially unpopular in Missouri and around the country, that would change by the turn of the twentieth century. By 1898, the total number of graduates at Kansas City's Central High School had ballooned to 250. This was impressive growth, considering Central's first graduating class—that of 1873—consisted of five students.[11] The number of graduates continued to increase. Of course, all 250 students graduating from Kansas City, Missouri's only high school in 1898 were White. Lincoln High School, the city's segregated all-Black high school, would not open until 1908, though as of 1880, Lincoln Elementary School was permitted to introduce a high school course of study. Once Lincoln High School was opened, it was routinely underfunded and under-resourced, yet it developed a national reputation for excellence. Like many all-Black high schools during the long period of de jure segregation,[12] Lincoln was staffed by excellent educators who cared deeply about the success of the school and its students.[13]

Vanessa Siddle Walker, education historian and leading expert on segregated schooling in the South, identifies four common themes among Black schools during the era of Jim Crow and segregated schooling that made them particularly strong: exemplary, dedicated, and demanding teachers; a rich curriculum and active extracurricular program; an involved parental and community support system whose members served as advocates; and an involved and active principal—a true leader. It is what she calls institutional caring. In her review of the research on segregated schooling, Siddle Walker concludes that the depiction of African American schooling as "unilaterally inferior" is misleading: "What emerges in these accounts is a particular kind of schooling born of the struggles associated with inequality, but nevertheless associated with successful schooling practices in the minds of constituents and on some limited objective criteria."[14]

The Black community's commitment to their schools and the education of Black youth was a result of the push during the post-bellum period of ex-slaves who had been denied such opportunities before the Civil War.[15] Black schools, like Black churches, served as backbones of the community. They were gathering places where community members often came together to exchange ideas and concerns.[16] But despite the successes of institutions like Lincoln High School in Kansas City, Black schools were a byproduct of an unequal system, one that relegated Black and Brown people to a secondary status.

The cherished gem of Kansas City's dual system was all-White Central High School. Its popularity among Kansas City's White residents was unrivaled. By 1921, Central was growing by 180 new students per year and would soon become the largest high school in the state of Missouri. White neighborhoods surrounding Central were booming in what was at the time the city's southeast corridor. Kansas City's White residents were seeking out Central; it was the prized possession of Kansas City's White community, or at least it was until the 1954 *Brown v. Board of Education of Topeka* decision, when the Supreme Court struck down the "separate but equal" doctrine. Once Central was integrated, it took White parents only six years to pull their children out of Central High School. By 1960, Central's student population was 95 percent Black, and the neighborhoods surrounding the school—the same neighborhoods that just several decades before were the areas of the city most desired by White residents—were over 80 percent Black.[17]

Central remains a segregated institution to this day. As more and more Whites left the city, the suburbs of metropolitan Kansas City exploded. White residents searched for homogenous White neighborhoods that would protect them from having to live and go to school with a growing Black population. By the 1950s, thanks to the avarice of the real estate and banking industries, White residents viewed any Black presence in their neighborhoods as a threat to their property values and pocketbooks. White residents were willing to do almost anything to avoid racial mixing in their communities, including leaving the comforts of their homes and neighborhoods. White flight was on. By 1970, the census tract around Central High School was 96.8 percent Black, a dramatic shift in neighborhoods that just two decades earlier were nearly completely White.[18]

There is nothing particularly unique about Kansas City's racialized landscape. Most American cities of at least moderate size have racialized spaces separated geographically. Of the more than one hundred cities within the United States with a population of two hundred thousand or greater, sixty-seven are classified as having "high segregation."[19] Kansas City is firmly in the top half of that list. Detroit sits atop at number one; Newark City, New

Jersey, Hialeah, Florida, Chicago, Illinois, and Milwaukee, Wisconsin, round out the top five. American cities are and have long been segregated, and so too have their schools. And though this has become somewhat "normal" or "expected," it is extremely consequential.

Racialized spaces did not (and do not) happen by chance, nor are they the result of innate preference. Racially segregated neighborhoods and schools, for example, are the product of careful and systematic planning. Power and economics are the driving forces. The foundation of racial inequity and White supremacy was solidified long ago, and the Black-White dichotomy and power structure were introduced by Black chattel slavery more than five hundred years ago. The vestiges of that system are profoundly relevant today. Our institutions have been structured in ways that advantage, above all, Whiteness. Schools are no exception. Race has always been centered within schools as institutions. In other words, race is unquestionably the most salient and important feature of education, past and present. Nothing about education in the United States can be fully understood without prioritizing the issue of race. This was true in the late nineteenth century as formal education developed, and it is true today in the twenty-first century.

A recent report by the United States Government Accountability Office (GAO) found that during the 2020–2021 school year, more than one-third of all public school students attended schools in which 75 percent or more of the students were of a single race or ethnicity.[20] The Midwest was the region with the most single-race majority schools—59 percent.[21] This is occurring during a time when the school-aged population is becoming increasingly diverse. Yet, students who are poor, Black, or Brown generally attend schools that have fewer resources and worse outcomes than those of their White counterparts. This is certainly true in Kansas City, where race continues to determine one's educational opportunities.

The Troost Divide

To the passer-by, Kansas City is a typical Midwestern city. The people are friendly; the food is good, especially the barbecue; and there is enough to do to keep one occupied and entertained. But buried below the surface and beyond the normalcy hides a terrible secret. Kansas City is deeply divided. The most striking division is not that of the state line, which separates Kansas City, Kansas, from Kansas City, Missouri. It is Troost Avenue.

To truly know Kansas City, one must understand the Troost divide. There is nothing striking about Troost Avenue, a nondescript street running north-south through the city. Look closely, however, and one will begin to see that Troost is the line of racial demarcation that separates Whites in Kansas City from the residents of color, and Troost has held strong for roughly eight decades.

Before 1950, very few of Kansas City's Black families lived south of Twenty-Seventh Street, the southeastern part of Kansas City at the time, making Twenty-Seventh Street the city's original racial dividing line. However, as the Black population in the southeast part of the city continued to grow in the mid-century and the White population in the area fell, the Twenty-Seventh Street divide began to dissolve. Nevertheless, when Black families began moving south of Twenty-Seventh Street, Whites pushed back. Someone bombed the house of the first Black family to move to Twenty-Seventh and Paseo in May 1952. The bombing resulted in only minimal damage, but the house became a target again in September of the same year. The second bombing caused considerable damage, and the Black family who had moved into the 2700 block of Paseo was under a constant barrage of threats and torments.[22] Eventually, many Whites left the city altogether and settled in newly developed and protected homogenous neighborhoods in the suburbs. Black families moved into the areas of the city Whites had abandoned. With Twenty-Seventh Street no longer the Black-White divide, Troost Avenue took its place.

Beginning in the 1950s, the shift from Twenty-Seventh to Troost resulted, in part, from the discriminatory actions of Kansas City,

Missouri School District leaders who used Troost Avenue as a school boundary between Black and White schools, with Black schools east of the avenue and White schools west of it.[23] Using Troost in this way resulted in the continuation of Black-White separation in the city's schools even after the *Brown v. Board* decision in 1954 and the deconstruction of de jure segregation; by 1970, all elementary and secondary schools east of Troost Avenue were 90 percent or more Black, and every elementary and secondary school west of Troost was less than 50 percent Black.[24]

By virtue of its location, just south of Twenty-Seventh Street and east of Troost, Central High School was one of the first schools to undergo a swift transformation from all White to all Black. Old and new residents began to associate neighborhoods east of Troost with Black neighborhoods and those west of Troost with White ones. By the mid-1950s, realtors began to follow suit, only showing prospective Black home buyers properties east of Troost, further solidifying the notion that Black neighborhoods were more unstable than White ones and thus needed to be kept separate. As the financial industry, federal government, and real estate industry developed the modern mortgage system, segregated neighborhoods—and, therefore, segregated schools—remained prevalent in the United States. As such, segregation—despite the destruction of Jim Crow and the legal end of the "separate but equal" doctrine—became entrenched in the social fabric of American cities. This fact of life was folded into a narrative that same-race neighborhoods and same-race schools are just the way things are and a result of personal preference. On the contrary, racial segregation is and has long been a result of a carefully planned and implemented system of racial inequity. This system has long plagued Kansas City's Central High School.

1 | Central High School's Origin Story

"Here's to dear old Central High. For her we'll live, for her we'll die. We'll always love the White and blue." This was written by Harold Slaughter, Class of 1913.[25] When Slaughter walked the halls of Central, it was still located downtown at Eleventh and Locust. But by 1913, the building could hardly support the school's growth. It was not just Central—public schooling had grown in popularity throughout the early part of the twentieth century, so much, in fact, that when Slaughter graduated from Central in 1913, it was one of four high schools in the district. There were three high schools for White students and one for Black students. It would not be long until the number would grow, as Kansas City's segregated school system was booming in the early 1900s. In the early days, however, Central was just getting established, and nothing was certain.[26]

All-White Central High School was originally named Kansas City High School when it opened in 1867 with a total of four students and only one employee, J. B. Bradley, who served as both principal and teacher for a "handsome" salary of $133 per month, plus three dollars extra for sweeping out the classrooms.[27] Central's first teacher was hired in 1869. Her name was E. R. Weeks; she was seventeen years old and was said to have been wrapped in a green woolen shawl as she arrived at the Kansas City, Missouri School District's Board of Education office for her interview. Her skills were rigorously tested. Mrs. Weeks was required to locate capitals, identify the bones of the body, recount the uses of the transitive verb, solve a radical equation, and explain the origins of America. Though there were

1

initial concerns about her age, Mrs. Weeks impressed enough to get the job, and so began the growth of the Kansas City, Missouri School District's secondary schools. From meager beginnings, Central would soon develop into one of the nation's best high schools.[28]

The Early Years

The school was originally opened in the basement of the Starke Building on the corner of Eleventh and Locust, which served both as the Board of Education and the office of the Superintendent of Schools.[29] There was no public school building in 1867 and little money for public education. In many cases, classes were held in unoccupied storerooms. The only accessible stairwell at the old Starke building was attached to the outside and exposed to the elements, a shaky flight of wooden steps sloping at a steep angle.[30] This, however, did not hinder the school's growth, despite opposition among those who opposed the idea of a high school altogether. The "pullbacks," as they were known, objected to the high school, as they claimed it pampered young, impressionable youth and emphasized foolish ideas about the need for higher education, a cost they alleged fell on poor taxpayers but benefited only rich people's children. The criticism was so widespread that the school board, upon Central's founding, left the word "high" out of the school's name, instead naming it simply the Central School.[31]

Central, however, was always a high school and was referenced as the Kansas City High School by the Board of Education, despite the reluctance among some to refer to it as such. The first graduating class, honored in 1873, consisted of only five students: four girls and one boy.[32] However, the number quickly grew; Central graduated more students than any other high school in the United States in 1898, with a graduating class of 250.[33]

Schooling was different in the late nineteenth century. In the beginning, Central offered courses in Latin and Greek, as well as German, French, Arithmetic, English, astronomy, mental and moral science, the derivation of words, and natural philosophy. Literary societies were particularly popular. One student recounted his first literary program and the apprehension that accompanied such an honor:

> I was elected into a Literary Society. Proud, of course. It was a great honor. I held up my head. From that time on, I was more of a man. It gave me a great start in school life. The first day that I was to appear before the society on the literary program, was a memorable one. I was very nervous, and though the committee had assigned a reading to me, nothing could be easier, but I was terrified. I thought each member of the society a cruel and careful critic. At last my name was called. I arose and read, my voice trembled, my head shook, but I read.[34]

Additionally, Principal J. B. Bradley emphasized the importance of hygiene, beginning each day by lining up students to inspect the cleanliness of their hands, and upon dismissal, he was known to watch the students until they were out of sight to ensure the boys and girls remained separated. Walking with the opposite sex was strictly forbidden.[35] Reverend W. G. Pratt, a Baptist minister turned principal who was known to prod his horse with a nail-tipped stick on their journey from his farm on Independence Avenue to school, succeeded Bradley. Pratt was widely recognized for his talent in Latin, gaining acclaim from universities nationwide for Central's students' preparation and training in the language.[36]

Growth in the Central School's student body required more space soon after it was opened. Thus, on June 9, 1868, a small lot at the southeast corner of Eleventh and Locust in downtown Kansas City measuring 240 by 132 square feet was purchased for $5,882.[37] This is where a two-story brick building of two rooms was erected. It would be Kansas City's first stand-alone public high school, Central High School. This facility underwent a greater expansion in 1872 and served as the high school until 1875, when a one-story frame building of three rooms was erected just south of it. The two buildings were connected by a passageway, the so-called "rope walk," which served as a thoroughfare that allowed students to access both buildings.[38]

Twelve-year-old Rollins Bingham, a small, self-described tow-headed boy, entered the city's only high school as part of the freshman class in 1873. In 1906, Bingham chronicled his days as a high school student, a time when gas lighting illuminated rooms, the telephone was yet to be known, mules hauled streetcars, and the phonograph and typewriter were future inventions. Yet, Bingham lovingly recalled his days in the "sturdy, plain, wooden-tailed brick" high school: "Whether 'Central High' was the official designation of the school in 1873 I do not know, but I do know that the pupils then never used the name, 'Central.'"[39] Bingham explains that as the only high school, Central was referred to at the time as simply "The High School," a designation that most certainly signifies that it was the city's only high school option but also indicates the high esteem the school was afforded—"[t]o those below it was in truth and in fact most high, so high as to seem almost inaccessible."[40]

The high school was indeed inaccessible to many, especially to Black children. Black students were not afforded a high school option until the creation of Lincoln High School in 1888. By 1889, Missouri made it a punishable crime in the state for Black and White students to attend the same school.[41] This was a time when the Black population of Kansas City was growing at a tremendous rate—increasing by almost 70 percent between 1880 and 1890. As the city's Black population grew, Lincoln's popularity did too. Lincoln was routinely underfunded, underequipped, and overcrowded. However, the quality of educators and education at Lincoln was superb despite the deplorable conditions under which Black students were required to learn. By the early twentieth century, Lincoln had become one of the nation's preeminent Black high schools.[42]

Meanwhile, like Black students at Lincoln, the number of White students seeking a secondary education at Central grew throughout the late nineteenth century and into the twentieth century. By 1875, the additional space created by the 1872 additions would no longer suffice. Central was growing, and so too was the district—the combined White and Black enrollment increased from a total enrollment of 2,150 in 1867 to 8,144 in 1875.[43] Subsequently, Central's frame building, constructed just a few years before, was torn down, and the original brick building was enlarged to accommodate nine additional rooms. Still, in 1884, a brand-new three-story brick structure was constructed to accommodate five hundred students. The new facility had wide halls, five classrooms on the first and second floors, and an assembly room that adorned the top floor.[44] Yet by 1889, the newly constructed building, built to house five hundred students, had to meet the needs of over seven hundred.[45] Student numbers were growing so fast that the total enrollment jumped by fifty-seven students between December of 1889 and February of 1890.[46] While Central's numbers were particularly impressive, the district as a whole experienced continued growth throughout the last two decades of the nineteenth century as more and more Kansas Citians began to embrace the value of education. This posed a problem for district leaders, who were confronted with an almost constant need for new buildings and building additions. The district, however, benefited from a supportive constituency willing to carry the burden, as shown in the continued support of tax levies:

> The fine equipment of the public schools, the buildings, the apparatus, the plentiful provision for doing all that schools are called to do represents a great expenditure of the peoples' monies and shows that the people are willing always to bear the burden, to pay the taxes if they are satisfied that the end sought is good and the expenditure therefore honestly made. There is no holding back, no grudging in regard to the support of the public schools of Kansas City.[47]

Year after year, tax levies for the purchase of ground and the construction of buildings found favor among the voters in impressive fashion. For example, in the April 1887 election, 6,472 votes were cast for the levy and a mere 197 against it.[48]

Unlike all-Black Lincoln High School, which received a mere sliver of the district's budget, Central was among the district's schools that benefited from generous taxpayers. In April of 1892, district voters approved a one-hundred-thousand-dollar initiative—the equivalent of $3 million in today's money—for a new high school facility.[49] Just months before, in October, a four-story addition had been completed, which added eight rooms. Even still, additional quarters were needed to serve the swelling population of students. Students eagerly awaited the completion of the new building. Anticipating that the new high school would result in greater educational opportunity, one student explained in 1893:

> The High School pupil of future years will have a much more pleasant time than does he of the present. A beautiful school building, well-equipped with every appliance for the best work, situated on a broad, well paved thoroughfare; opposite, a handsome park, a breathing place and a recreation ground. All these and many more will contribute to his happiness and to his soul's elevation. But will he be stronger, mentally, than those of the present and the past? We hope and believe so.[50]

These hopes became a reality for Central students when the new building was finished in December of 1893, a three-story building with a basement and large assembly hall. The new high school had a revolving copper-domed observatory atop the southwest corner and a 140-foot tower adorning the front.[51] The assembly hall seated two thousand, and it had excellent facilities for the natural sciences—it was most certainly an ornament and credit to the city.[52]

Central High School, 1893-1915

School Board President Robert Yeager claimed two years after the new building was constructed: "We think we can say without fear of successful contradiction that there is no high school in the country superior to the Kansas City High School."[53] Unquestionably, an atmosphere of confidence accompanied attendance at Central High School—a confidence carried forward by generations of students. Such pride led one student in a *Central Luminary* editorial to write:

> [E]very year in the history of Central High School adds something to its already brilliant record, every year brings forth achievements and accomplishments which make for her unsurpassed reputation. We of the present Central should congratulate ourselves upon our good fortune, for we have received a richer inheritance than any other class . . . does it not make you proud that the best of all high schools is your own?[54]

A sense of privilege can be seen routinely in the early years of the school newspaper, the *Central Luminary*. The pride that Central students took in their school was not unsubstantiated. Indeed, Central High School and its students had gained national recognition by the late nineteenth century as one of the best high schools in the nation. Central students were attending college in large numbers. In 1897, forty students were headed to college, including one to Harvard, four to Princeton, and five to Yale.[55] The publicity inspired one student to ask playfully in 1894, "[W]hat's the matter with Central?" only to offer a quick rebuttal, "[F]rom the vast number of visiting teachers, principals and departments that descend upon us every week we should judge that we are all right. Why not have a reception committee?"[56] Central welcomed educators from around the country interested in seeing firsthand the course of study offered at the high school. In February of 1897, Central received two visiting superintendents of public schools in New York who claimed that Central High School was "one of the finest in America."[57]

Central's early success largely resulted from several visionary and exemplary administrators, especially John T. Buchanan. It was under Buchanan that Central's student population grew from five hundred sixty-seven to nearly two thousand. Beginning his tenure in the nine-room building, Buchanan ended his principalship in the grand new building of 1893. As a true testament to his successes and Central's progress under his leadership, Buchanan left Central when the New York School Board appointed him as the Principal of the Boys' Latin High School in New York.[58] So impressed was New York by Buchanan that Dr. Murray Butler of Columbia University stated publicly in 1897, "[i]n Mr. Buchanan New York gains for its schools and for its citizenship the man who is in my judgment the best all-around public high school principal in the United States."[59]

The growing demand for high schools in Kansas City resulted in the creation of a second all-White high school, The Manual Training High School, which opened in September of 1897. The Central administration welcomed the opening of the new school. Conditions were so crowded at Central that Principal Buchanan had sent a report to the superintendent in 1896 suggesting that classes were "greatly in excess" of thirty students, as he claimed: "The new Manual Training High School is coming just in the 'nick of time.'"[60] Thus, Manual would relieve the crowding at Central and was designed to provide a broad course of instruction "for college or for the practical duties of life."[61] Manual was also to introduce students to certain trades but not to turn out skilled carpenters, machinists, or dressmakers.[62] Manual's opening did not impede Central's development, as Central continued to flourish at the end of the nineteenth century:

> Indeed few schools furnish such splendid opportunities for individual development. Our widely diversified course of study, our Thursday morning exercises, our society programs and open sessions, and our contests all afford facilities equaled only by schools and academies of much higher grade.[63]

The diversity of the course of study at Central included United States history and art, which were added to the curriculum in 1897 and 1899, respectively. Both courses were forward-thinking, as the addition of United States history made Central one of only a few in the country to offer such a course of study.[64] Moreover, an athletic association was formed in 1898, laying the foundation for organized sport in football, baseball, and track for boys only and establishing a connection between good health and scholarship.[65] Central was, as one student suggested at the turn of the century, fast developing "all of the symptoms of a college."[66] Central had gained a reputation for producing "well instructed, reliable pupils, supplied with an extensive stock of general information."[67]

In 1908, the same year that Westport High School opened, Central at Eleventh and Locust underwent construction yet again. This time, a new wing on the east side was added, and the building was remodeled and connected, providing a spacious sixty-two rooms.[68] To the students' delight, as part of the additional space, a basement gymnasium free of columns and rods to interfere with basketball was added, along with additional classrooms for art and business classes, as well as a dining hall:[69]

At last we are to have our new building. . . . A new building! No more will you be able to touch the top of the gym when you are jumping. No more will you be forced to study art in half the necessary space. Let us trust that next year we may have a new building, with more lockers for girls' wraps, etc., more halls for our enthusiastic floor walkers, more room for vocal aspirants, more breathing space for gymnastic experts or otherwise more space for prospective artists.[70]

However, the additions of 1908 would only offer relief for so long as the school and city continued to grow.

The district even employed a night school to meet the needs of children employed during the day despite the compulsory nature of education established in 1905.[71] In 1911, the night school was moved to Central High School because of its large numbers, more than two thousand students; this surpassed the aspirations of even the most ardent supporters of night school.[72] Thus, the night school began accommodating all students and offering courses in all commercial branches, including manual training, domestic science, elementary and higher mathematics, and additional elementary subjects.[73] In 1912, the *Kansas City Times* noted that four of Central's classrooms were not enough to hold the large numbers of students who desired to take mechanical drawing, and in 1913, the enrollment had grown to over three thousand.[74] Four additional night schools were added, including one for Mexican Americans and one for African Americans, segregated, of course.[75] Indeed, the numbers suggested that Kansas Citians were hungry for formal education and would take advantage of the public schools in both conventional and unconventional ways.

Central, with an enrollment of 1,200, was soon to occupy a new plot of land in the southeastern-most portion of the city—the southeastern corner of Linwood Boulevard and Indiana Avenue.[76] By 1911, Central, Westport, and Manual, the city's White high schools, were all enrolling record numbers.[77] Lincoln High School, still the city's only Black high school, was overcrowded as well, though judging by the media coverage at the time, this was not a concern. Meanwhile, talk of new schools to accommodate the growing popularity of public schooling for White students was getting louder, and calls for a new high school centered around an area east of Troost and South of Eighteenth Street—the southeast district. It was reasoned that Kansas City's population was moving toward the southeast part of the city, which necessitated a high school to house the increasing number of school-aged children.

In 1913, I. I. Cammack, former principal of Central High School turned superintendent, requested eleven new schools and eight additions to existing schools. Among the list of new schools was a new Central High School relocated to the southeast district.[78] That same year, Asa Earl Martin, a sociologist studying the Black population of Kansas City, noted that, as of the end of the year in 1911, Kansas City's Black schools were valued at just over $450,000 and White schools, close to $6 million.[79] Such discrepancies can also be seen in the upkeep and maintenance of the district buildings. Of the nearly $2 million spent on the maintenance of district school buildings, just over $100,000 was spent on Black schools.

By 1918, there were eight Black elementary schools and one high school in Kansas City, and by 1920, Lincoln High School was overcrowded and lacked equipment. Among some of the most egregious complaints included classes being held in stairwells, many teachers without desks, no gymnasium or library, and leaky gas lines to the stove of the Domestic Science Department classroom, which required windows to be open at all times.[80] Despite public recognition of these deplorable conditions in 1920, it would take fifteen years before Lincoln students would have a new home. Yet despite these circumstances, Lincoln provided a stellar education among the city's most experienced and credentialed faculty. While the physical conditions at Lincoln were poor, the quality of educators and students and overall education were not.

With bonds approved, the district initiated a massive plan that included both new buildings and additions to old ones. The money was going to support the district's White schools. One local journalist asked in 1915, "[D]id you know that Kansas City had spent nearly 5 million dollars on your little Johnnie and Susie in the last five years?"[81] Central High School and all-White Northeast High School were the two high schools where "Johnnie" and "Susie" would enjoy new lavish surroundings.

2 | Brand-new Central

While many welcomed the idea of a new Central, students at Central High School approached the news with some skepticism:

> The tidings have come from the Board of Education that Old Central is to live after 1913-1914 in a new habitation amidst new and happier surroundings. The incessant demand for a trade school will then probably be satisfied, and our present building will go for that purpose. What concerns us, however, is the removal of Central to Linwood and Indiana. All her trophies, her traditions, and, we hope, her faculty, will go with her. The name "Central" has always stood for the best in high school standards, and when she takes up her abode in what will be one of the finest high school buildings in the West, with all the modern conveniences and advantages, to what glories will she not rise? . . . Everything is propitious, and we predict a glorious future for a school that has had a most glorious past.[82]

After roughly $500,000 in expenditures, an equivalent to approximately $15 million today, the new Central High School that occupied the center of a tract of land at Linwood Boulevard and Indiana Avenue opened in 1915.[83] The old building would become the Kansas City Polytechnic Institute and Junior College, originally led by E. M. Bainter, former principal of Central High School, 1911–1912 and appointed Commissioner of Education for Puerto Rico by President Taft, 1912–1915.[84] The Polytechnic Institute and Junior College was an outgrowth of the teacher-training department founded at Central High School in 1911. The program enjoyed steady growth and, by 1931, became a four-year college awarding diplomas.[85]

As the reality of the move to the new building set in, nostalgic students proclaimed their affinity for dear old Central: "Lo, though the walls are old and dirty, and the stairways narrow and worn, we shall carry away the most cherished memories of old Central High at Eleventh and Locust."[86] The nostalgia, however, was soon washed away by the modernity and newness of the building in the southeastern part of the city. By December of 1915, memories of old Central were distant:

> Did you ever stop to think of the care the school board has taken to insure our health and comfort? Did you ever stop to think of the advantages we, the Central students, have over the students of other schools? Let us pause a moment and think about some of the comforts given us in our new building.[87]

Considering the extravagance of the new building, it is no wonder students were willing to embrace their unfamiliar surroundings.

The new building was fronted on Linwood Boulevard with a large athletic field and six-lap track. Elevated behind the field was the rectangle-shaped four-story school. The school itself was, as described by one journalist in 1915, "beautiful in simplicity and suggestiveness."[88] Indeed, the building was somewhat factory-like in appearance, but its amenities were far from pedestrian—it had a 1,432-seat ventilated and well-lit auditorium with a large stage, dressing rooms, and a drop curtain; it had spacious restrooms, a matron's apartment with hospital furnishings, a laundry room, intercommunicating telephone system with eighty-seven telephones, a large dining hall and kitchen, and a branch of the public library. The gymnasium, too, was designed to impress, with a twenty-four-lap indoor track in the balcony and enough room to accommodate indoor tennis matches, in addition to a large swimming pool.[89] With such lavishness, it is no surprise that in 1919, Central High School at its new southeast location led enrollment among the city's high schools, outnumbering Manual Training School, Westport High School, Lincoln High School, and Northeast High School.[90]

The new high school ushered in a new era, including a growing interest in sports during this time, especially basketball and football. While organized athletics at Central began with the formation of the boys' athletic association in 1894, interest in the community was hardly impressive.[91] Sports seemingly assumed a second-class citizenship, a backseat to the literary societies. But by the turn of the century, a girls' athletics association had been formed, and there appears to have been a growing interest, most generally, in the role of athletics at Central High School. Still, academics and society life reigned supreme: "In a purely academic institution like the Central High School, such training is especially required to give wise relaxation, and to so maintain the bodily health as to enable the student to use to the best advantage his intellectual attainments."[92] With the beginning of the principalship of H. H. Holmes in 1912, the athletic association had found an enthusiastic advocate: "[I]t is evident in our current principal," one Central student noted, "we have found a man who does not deem it beneath the dignity of a principal to get out and root at a basketball game."[93] To be sure, sports did grow in popularity during Holmes's tenure. Football was reintroduced at Central and to all Kansas City high schools after an eleven-year hiatus due to a Manual player fracturing his skull during a game in 1906. A successful basketball team gained a widespread following, and track and baseball also expanded for boys while girls continued to participate in club sports. Holmes was so instrumental in growing athletics at Central that after his untimely death in 1920, an athletic field was dedicated in his honor in 1922 just east of Central— Holmes Athletic Field. It was the first of its kind in Kansas City.[94]

However, the first years at the new building were not without challenges. World War I resulted in changes in the course of study. The sewing classes devoted their efforts to making Red Cross relief garments, and cooking classes, due to rationing, emphasized the use of cooking substitutes. German language courses were even formally suspended in 1918 at Central and all Kansas City, Missouri School District public schools following a vote by the board.[95] As if the war effort were not enough, the flu epidemic caused significant disruption in the lives of students and teachers. As was the case across the district, Central High School closed its doors during the fall period, and many would succumb to influenza, even claiming lives—Central's principal, H.H. Holmes, among them.

During this time, there was also a curricular shift, as the district began emphasizing the industrial arts over a more classical education. Greek was dropped from Central High School's curriculum, and Latin too faced the threat of termination: "It seems a pity that Central, after running an ancient language department for years that could bring forth jealousy from many a college, should allow these languages to drift away from it."[96] The domestic science department, however, was thriving, turning out "scores of housekeepers every year."[97] Central was not the only school shifting from a classical education to a more vocational one. Lincoln High School was as well. All Kansas City, Missouri School District public schools emphasized the industrial arts. Pre-vocational and vocational schools grew in popularity, making workers more efficient and preparing students for the workforce. Education was changing in light of the growing industrial sector, and the purpose of education had shifted from one that educated a few in the classics to a system that educated the masses for the occupations of a new industrial order.

The Southeast Corridor

In 1920, 270 students graduated from Central, and in 1922, the number of graduates had risen to 407.[98] Growth was occurring so fast that half-day school sessions were employed. As of 1921, the morning session housed 1,582 students, and the afternoon 821, for a total of 2,403.[99] While the two-session approach was not ideal, it was necessary to accommodate the considerable size of Central's student body. Students, however, expressed their displeasure with the organization of the double session:

> One of the evils existing in Central at the present time is the lack of proper relationship between students. This is a well known fact due to the double session. The students are not allowed to remain at school after they have finished their classroom work and do not even get to see each other except during school hours.[100]

With enrollment having increased by two hundred students annually since the new building was constructed in 1915, it had reached a critical juncture by 1922. Despite building a fifty-thousand-dollar annex in 1921, adding eight classrooms and one hundred eighty-two lockers, Central needed even more space to accommodate the increasing population of students. Overcrowding was not just a problem at Central; many district schools faced similar issues. Both Westport and Lincoln High Schools were forced to build annexes as well.[101] Yet, the growth at Central was particularly challenging due to the sheer number of students—four thousand.[102]

In 1922, the tremendous growth in the Central attendance area resulted in the design of two new junior highs, Central Junior High and Westport Junior High, as well as another new high school, Paseo High School, to relieve the crowding at Central High School and Westport High School. Central Junior High School was to be built just east of the high school building, and the new junior high impressed—it was designed with sixty-five classrooms, two gymnasiums, a swimming pool, and manual training shops.[103] The junior high school was necessary; the congestion at Central limited school activities, and Central High School qualified as one of the largest high schools in the country. Central exceeded Westport High School's enrollment by 971, Northeast High School by 1,263, and Manual High School by 1,942.[104] Lincoln High School experienced continued growth during this period as well, and while an annex was added to Lincoln just as it was at Central, Lincoln would not get a much-needed new building until 1936.[105] Under Kansas City, Missouri School District's racially segregated system, the White schools were a priority. But it was not only in education that Whites were enjoying great privilege; the housing boom in the southeastern corridor where the new Central High School resided was exclusively White.

Large-scale building by investment companies catering to White families looking for housing in the nearest open territory to town resulted in many families settling within Central High School's attendance zone, and led to rising numbers of Central students. Thus, the southeastern part of Kansas City south of Twenty-Seventh Street, the area immediately surrounding Central High School, quickly became an exclusively White territory.

Ninety houses a month were being built in the Central attendance area in 1921, and for every six houses built, one new student entered Central, equaling about one hundred eighty per year.[106] The area around Central was booming, in large part a result of available land that was nearest to town. New businesses accompanied the area's development, many lining the streets surrounding the new Central High School, and the growth was evident by the thriving commercial industry that sprang up around Central.[107]

Black Population Growth

The families who funneled into the neighborhoods surrounding Central High School were exclusively White, yet the Black population of Kansas City was increasing as well. The Black population grew from 23,566 in 1910 to 38,754 in 1930. Still, the indices of Black isolation increased as well, from roughly 21 percent in 1910 to just over 30 percent in 1930, signifying a distinct separation of the residences of Blacks from Whites.[108] Racial tension in Kansas City was rising in the early 1920s, and much of it concerned housing. The Anti-Ugly Movement was a local initiative but mirrored a broader trend in the early 1900s throughout the country. The movement involved city planning aimed at improving the aesthetic quality of the city.[109]

Kansas Citians were increasingly concerned with their property values. As the Black population's numbers continued to swell, the Black east side neighborhoods began to expand and press closely to the White east side neighborhoods. The Black commercial center near Eighteenth and Vine, an area known as Lincoln-Coles, was attractive to arriving Black families. Still, it was crowded, with an average of four and one-half families per residence, and it was plagued by increasing health and sanitation problems. Death rates climbed, and sickness spread.[110] Thus, middle-class Black families began seeking to relocate out of the crowded Black east side and turned to realtors for assistance.

As Kansas City's Black population increased, White residents of the southeast side began to associate the presence of Blacks with declining property values and neighborhood instability.[111] Ambitious blockbusting realtors capitalized on Whites' fears and Blacks' desire for more spacious homes. Blockbusting was a technique whereby profit-driven realtors introduced Black families to previously White neighborhoods to play on White fears and encourage White flight. These realtors rightly speculated that they could scare Whites into selling their homes by escorting Black families into White neighborhoods. As soon as one White family sold their home to a Black family, realtors would work quickly to create a narrative in which Blacks' presence in White neighborhoods would result in declining home values. The plan often worked.

When neighborhood blocks on Kansas City's east side fringe were "busted," Whites fled. But by 1926, improvement associations had been formed among White residents on the east side to restrict the sale of their homes to "Negroes."[112] In 1927, The Linwood Association, an improvement association headquartered near Central High School, met to discuss making the association national in scope. A reporter recounted the events of the evening:

> At the meeting which was sponsored by the Linwood Improvement Association steps were taken toward the formation of a national

protection association whose purpose is to be to improve property of the members and protect it against encroachments. The real purpose of the new organization, however, is the restriction of property against sale, lease or rental to Negroes. Speakers at the meeting Friday night urged the necessity of restriction against Negroes, asserting that property values would go down if Negroes were allowed to buy there. Hence, the "protective association" members of the organization in KC hope to make the association a national one "to keep Negroes where they belong."[113]

In the 1920s, Black families struggled to find adequate housing near or in White residential neighborhoods. The National Association of Real Estate Boards (NAREB), founded in 1908, set out to convince Whites that all-White, racially homogenous neighborhoods were "a superior atmosphere for residential life and a requisite for protecting the homeowner's investments."[114] Such a line of reasoning became official policy by 1924. It was institutionalized with the publication of real estate textbooks, the first of which surfaced in 1923 and stated: "Colored people must recognize the economic disturbance which their presence in a White neighborhood causes and forego their desire to split off from the established district where the rest of their race lives."[115] Whites seemingly took heed of the warnings and began protecting the homogeneity of their neighborhoods with fervor. Between 1921 and 1928, bombings of Black-occupied homes became commonplace, with seven bombings occurring within a single year.[116] Lines were being drawn, and where deed restrictions, homeowners' associations, and scare tactics were unsuccessful in keeping Blacks out of White southeast-side neighborhoods, violence would follow. Whites were becoming increasingly insistent on the homogeneity of their neighborhoods, just as they always had been about their schools.

Era of Construction

Meanwhile, Central High School continued to grow. Like the school, the White neighborhoods surrounding Central were also steadily expanding, safely south of Twenty-Seventh Street, which in the 1920s came to represent the division between White and Black residential areas. In 1924, Central became the largest high school in the state, welcoming ninety-four new students from eleven different states and averaging nearly forty students per classroom.[117] Westport was the only other high school that came close to Central's numbers, and it was almost five hundred students shy of Central's mark.[118] Such expansion led Otto F. Dubach, principal of Central, to remark in 1925 that the greatest progress Central had made during his tenure was the "tremendous increase in enrollment."[119] In Dubach's five years as principal, from 1920 to 1925, Central had grown from 1,300 students to 2,400.[120]

The new Central Junior High, targeted for a 1925 opening, would relieve some of the crowding. It was to accommodate 1,500 and, in 1924, was predicted to be the most modern school in the city. The stand-alone junior high school concept had, by 1924, gained widespread approval, as it was seen as most necessary to isolate the seventh-grade student from the child-like atmosphere of the grade school and the more adult atmosphere of the high school.[121] The acceptance of the junior high model and the continued growth of the district led the school board in 1924 to begin plans for five new secondary schools: three high schools and two junior high schools—Paseo High School at Forty-Eighth Street and Paseo, East High School between Seventeenth and Eighteenth Streets at Van Brunt, Southwest High School at Sixty-Fifth Street and Wornall, Northeast Junior High School on Independence Avenue east of Van Brunt, and West Side Junior High School with a location that was yet to be determined.[122] This was news welcomed by Centralites, as the new Paseo High School would further relieve crowded conditions by taking roughly five hundred Central students.

The period between 1913 and 1925 became known as the "Era of Construction," as the Kansas City, Missouri School District built thirty-nine school buildings and made additions and equipment to forty-three buildings. Moreover, the schools of Kansas City,

Missouri, had increased at a rate of one room-full of pupils each week in this same twelve-year timeframe: "The schools of Kansas City," Superintendent Cammack announced in 1926, "are now on par with those of other American cities."[123] The prosperity of the 1920s would be tested, as the Great Depression in the 1930s would challenge the Kansas City, Missouri School District.

Kansas Citians continued to support public schools, routinely approving tax levies and bond initiatives that both contributed to and assisted with the tremendous growth of the district and the constant need for new buildings and additions to existing ones. However, toward the end of the 1920s, the district faced cutbacks. In 1928, automatic increases in teacher salaries were suspended, the bonus system was cut, and necessary building maintenance and repair were restricted.[124] The demands on the Kansas City, Missouri School District had become a long-term problem.

By 1930, Superintendent Melcher submitted an editorial to the *Kansas City Star* to outline the changing responsibilities of the schools to taxpayers, an attempt to justify an increase in taxation. In the editorial, Melcher explained that the district's valuation had grown to $27 million, a far cry from the $7 million valuation in 1915. Moreover, he explained that the number of pupils over the same period had increased from 43,000 to 70,000, and the annual cost to run the schools had gone from $3 million to $7 million. The reference to "mills" is language used to describe the amount of tax payable per dollar of the assessed value of property. Government entities set mill rates based on the total value of property within their jurisdiction to cover expenses, such as schools, roads, and other costs. Melcher made his case for the necessity of generating additional revenue for Kansas City's schools by increasing taxes:

> In spite of this increased expenditure, tax rates in Kansas City have not increased. From 1914 to 1918 the tax rate was 12 mills; from 1919 to 1921 it was 13 mills; and for the last five years it has been 11½ mills. This rate has yielded revenue sufficient,

when supplemented by state and federal funds, to meet the needs, including retirement of bonds . . . The increase in enrollment, of course, increases the task greatly, but there are also added duties from new kinds of services demanded.[125]

The "new services" referenced the 1913 law requiring public schools to supply free textbooks and the Smith-Hughes law of 1919, which placed greater emphasis on vocational education, in addition to the dedication of a small portion of the budget for special education classrooms, open-air classrooms, a school for the deaf, a school for the so-called "crippled," a teacher's college, and a junior college. However, the costliest undertaking was the modernization of school buildings between 1912 and 1927, which included the construction or improvement of roughly seventy buildings at a cost of approximately $15 million. Only two of the seventy buildings, however, were Black schools.[126]

There were 19,910 high school pupils in Kansas City, Missouri, as of 1932, and district-wide daily public school attendance was 60,025, an increase of nearly 15,000 students in ten years. Additionally, by 1930, the Kansas City, Missouri School District's course offerings had expanded. Industrial arts courses for boys and home-making courses for girls became more readily available, and fine arts courses, such as drawing, sketching, design, band, orchestra, and piano, were added.[127] At Central, 1930 ushered in new high school requirements whereby a student could choose one of two lines of study: making a living or going to college.[128] A student's elective course selections were thus determined by his or her future aspirations. Moreover, a comprehensive health and physical education system had been supplied to the schools by the early 1930s, requiring school nurses, gymnasiums, and playgrounds.[129] Even though the district was attempting to keep costs low, it had also incorporated special schools and a junior college.

Money Troubles

Kansas City, Missouri School District, for the first time in the 1930s, was confronted with a dilemma—the unenviable task of trying to reduce expenditures while sustaining the high standards for which it had become widely recognized. The Depression initially hit the district hard, leaving district leadership with the task of attempting to save money by increasing class sizes, combining small schools, eliminating certain services, reducing the number of supervisors, decreasing the quantity and quality of school supplies, postponing repairs and improvements of property, and using reserve funds.[130] But despite these efforts, the district continued to face fiscal challenges. The cost to the district of educating Kansas City's school-aged population had increased by 31 percent in the ten years between 1922 and 1932, but the district was somewhat successful in reducing costs:

> The reduction made by the Board of Education of Kansas City, MO, in per pupil cost and in the total cost of schools for the year 1932-1933 is relatively greater than the reduction made by any other agency having taxing power over the property and people of Kansas City or any other agency having spending power over the revenues of Kansas City.[131]

By 1934, district expenditures averaged 20 percent less than what other cities of comparable size were spending, and the tax rate or mill for school purposes was inadequate. At nine mills, Kansas City, Missouri, ranked at the bottom in the state, with 262 other towns and cities having a higher levy rate than Missouri. Compared to other cities of comparable size, the levy rate for school purposes in Kansas City, Missouri, was alarmingly low. Even Kansas City, Kansas, schools were levying over twice as much—twenty-two mills.[132]

Despite the district's shortage in revenue, Centralites were dreaming of a new gymnasium and cafeteria, and plans were drawn for a two-story extension. Such improvements became a reality in 1938 when Central benefited from a federal government-authorized school improvement plan and got the eighty-five by fifty-one-foot extension that had been in the works since 1935.[133] In addition to the Central Annex, a new all-Black Lincoln High School was finally completed in 1936. Also during the second half of the 1930s, Southeast High School was constructed, as was the R. J. DeLano School for "crippled" children located across Linwood Boulevard from Central High School. The Kansas City, Missouri School District was a beneficiary of New Deal efforts and public works projects, partly because "Boss Tom" Pendergast, chairman of the Jackson County Democratic Club, held significant local, state, and national political influence. Pendergast had given Franklin Delano Roosevelt early support in his presidential bid, and FDR rewarded him with control of virtually all federal relief expenditures in Missouri.[134] Kansas City profited from the connection, as a disproportionate amount of relief money made its way into the city.

The Great Depression did not hit Kansas City as hard as many other cities, yet the school district continued to struggle financially.[135] The board recognized in 1935 that failure to reduce salaries would soon leave the school district insolvent.[136] In 1936, teachers' salaries, for the first time, were significantly reduced as a cost-saving measure. Cuts ranged from 5 percent to 12 percent depending on one's salary. According to a survey by the University Women's Club, part of an educational project sponsored by the state Department of Education, the situation in Kansas City had reached crisis proportions:

> Something must be done to raise Kansas City from its low rank of eighteenth in a list of twenty-one cities of comparable size in median salaries paid elementary class room teachers and seventeenth in median salaries paid in high schools. . . . This is a matter not only for the board of education to consider but parents of every child in the public schools.[137]

Most certainly, the fiscal problems confronted by district leaders throughout the 1930s would create problems in future years. Yet despite the financial obstacles, the Kansas City, Missouri School District, including Central High School, continued to grow steadily during the 1930s as student enrollments increased. Throughout the 1920s and 1930s, the district evolved into a large urban school district with Central High School as its premier White institution.

3 | In the Midst of Change

In 1940, the Kansas City, Missouri School District had a new leader, Dr. H. C. Hunt. By 1942, Hunt faced cuts in maintenance and building repairs, educational supplies, and teacher salaries. Moreover, students faced a shorter school year—a six-month term, due to the district's financial problems—which resulted in students having to extend their schooling to meet graduation requirements. Resolution of the crisis hinged on a ten-mill tax levy, which required a vote every four years.[138] Voters approved the levy on March 31, 1942, saving the schools from impending financial ruin, at least for the moment.[139]

In 1942, the financial woes of the Kansas City, Missouri School District were secondary. World War II and the war effort took its toll on the secondary schools of Kansas City, Missouri. Air-raid drills were occurring with some frequency, pictures were taken down as an air-raid precaution, a ration on typewriters made it impossible to purchase new ones, and repairs of broken typewriters were difficult as well. Food substitutes were used in cooking classes, food prices for school lunches had increased, and even fuel rationing and oil quotas were having an impact.[140] Individual schools were feeling the weight of the war as well. In January 1943, Central High School suffered its first casualty of the war when Wyatt Hundley, a Central student, was killed in action in the Southwest Pacific, and Hundley would not be the last Centralian to lose his life. By 1944, twenty-one Central alums had been killed in action; that number grew to sixty-nine by April of 1945.[141]

World War II had disrupted the lives of high school students all around the country, and not just those who were deployed for combat. Many high school students entered the labor force to fill the void left by soldiers who were called to duty. Hundreds of Central students had entered the job market between 1942 and 1945. By the close of the 1945 school year, however, the war was finally drawing to a close, and so too were the concerns about conflict that had occupied the minds of young people all over the world, including students at Kansas City's Central High School. Central's well-respected principal, O. F. Dubach, who in 1945 was finishing up his twenty-fifth year as principal, made some interesting remarks at the conclusion of the 1944–1945 academic year:

> One year ago, all of us were quite uncertain about the future of our war efforts. Now, with ultimate victory a probability, we need to be reminded that wars do not settle the problems that brought them on. For example, it was Missouri's own Champ Clark who forty years after the Civil War said, "The Civil War did not settle the Negro problem. It created it." Eighty years after that war we are still searching for a solution. The postwar period ahead is a vital one for you. You cannot become too familiar with life and the history of all the peoples of the world. You need all the education you can possibly get. My hope for each is that you will measure up to the abilities and opportunities which are yours. Then you can really share intelligently in the discussion of the tremendous world issues we older folk unfortunately are bequeathing to you, because we haven't been as smart as we hope you will be.[142]

Dubach's commentary in 1945 appears to acknowledge the racial inequities in existence within Kansas City during the time and seemingly calls on Central's students to work to find a solution. This is rather ironic, given that when Dubach made these comments, Central had just concluded its seventy-eighth year as a strictly White institution. Nevertheless, Dubach's statement represents quite the premonition, as only a decade after his remarks, Central would welcome its first Black students.

Indeed, World War II had aroused a spirit of change in Kansas City, as it had across the nation, although the process was occurring slowly. In 1942, thirteen thousand Black Kansas Citians gathered at Municipal Auditorium to protest discriminatory practices of the war, an action that contributed to the adoption of the Fair Employment Practices Committee.[143] The protest did effect change, but by 1946, as war production fell off, nearly all Black employees had been laid off, and employment percentages had reverted to 1940 levels. Considering that there were nearly one million more Black workers in civilian jobs in 1944 than in 1940, that the numbers had reverted to those of the pre-war years was troubling. An editorial in a 1946 issue of the *Kansas City Call* asked, "Is Kansas City North or South?" and responded to the rhetorical question with the following:

> In some matters, tax-paying for instance, Negroes are 100 per cent, full fledged citizens. In other matters, housing for example, they are definitely second-or-third class citizens. In still other matter [sic] such as eating and entertainment, Negroes do not know where they stand. Sometimes they are treated as citizens and human beings and at other times they are not welcome to a drink of water.[144]

Kansas City, Missouri, was an anomaly of sorts. Unlike cities of the Deep South, Kansas City never legally mandated Jim Crow laws. Kansas City, Missouri, public schools had been segregated through a de jure process since their creation in 1867. Segregation, however, was the standard in both the public and private sectors. Yet, there was a sense of optimism among Kansas City's Black community in the aftermath of World War II:

> Little by little since World War II, our growing city has thrown off the shackles which have burdened its citizens of color for generations. First employment policies at the City Hall were broadened and Negro applications were given an opportunity to fill a greater

variety of jobs. There is still much to be desired along this line, but the first and hardest step has been taken.[145]

World War II ushered in a new era in the struggle for racial equality with President Truman's ten-point civil rights plan and Executive Order 9981, issued in 1948, which mandated the desegregation of the armed forces. However, further steps toward racial equality would not come quickly or easily. This became evident within the housing industry, wherein White neighborhoods were nearly impenetrable for Kansas City's Black residents in the first half of the twentieth century. With the destruction of Kansas City's segregated school system, the indelible link between housing and schools would become foremost in the second half of the century. The impact would be significant for all of Kansas City's schools, but it would be particularly so for Central.

Adequate and fair housing had long been a struggle for the Black population in Kansas City, Missouri. The 1940s, however, set the tone for later decades. By 1940, J. C. Nichols[146] had effectively used deed restrictions since he had first put them into practice in 1913 with the Mission Hills Homes Company.[147] Racially restrictive clauses within Nichols's deed restrictions created intentionally segregated spaces for Whites to live in exclusively White spaces. This was not accidental, and Nichols was among the first of the real estate giants to use such tactics successfully. Nichols built dozens of racially restricted subdivisions around Kansas City for upper- and middle-income Whites, and all of them specifically prohibited housing sales to Blacks. Nichols also protected his residential developments by implementing mandatory homeowner associations to enforce racial restrictions. Such an organization created a base for maintaining neighborhood cohesion as a means of preventing breaches of restrictive covenants.[148] By 1940, 94 percent of the 41,574 total Black residents of Kansas City, Missouri, lived in the Lincoln-Coles community, but between 1940 and 1950, many Blacks looked to escape its confines, a result of inadequate housing and the fact that roughly 60 percent of the rentals in the area lacked a private bath and a toilet that flushed.[149] Moreover, the influx of Black workers to Kansas City during World War II contributed to further crowding, and wartime wages and high employment meant that some Black families could afford better housing and began to look outside of the established neighborhood jurisdictions. Thus, racial tensions were heightened as Whites perceived such movement as a threat to their homogenous neighborhoods.

Shelley v. Kraemer signified a turning point, as the Supreme Court ruled that explicitly racially restrictive covenants were unenforceable in court.[150] Yet the damage had been done, at least in the minds of Whites who had become convinced that a Black presence in a White neighborhood would lower the value of their homes. Soon after the Supreme Court's decision, *Shelley v. Kraemer* would be tested in Kansas City, Missouri. A case was filed that involved fourteen owners of eight properties on East Twenty-Ninth Street who alleged the sale of property to a Black family, Mr. and Mrs. Rueben S. Street, lowered the value of their homes. As such, the fourteen homeowners sought over $100,000 in damages from James Leaon and his former wife Erma Leaon, the White family who sold their property to the Streets.[151] The case, which eventually made its way before the Missouri Supreme Court, was significant. The state Supreme Court ruled that the Leaons could be sued for breach of contract, in effect suggesting that the restrictive covenant was not enforceable against the Streets, but the Leaons could be sued for selling the property to the Streets in violation of the restrictive covenant: "under the facts of this case, we hold that according to the law as we now understand it, the trial court may hear and determine an action for damages for the breach of the restriction agreement in question between plaintiffs and defendants without violating any provision of the federal or state constitutions."[152] Following the Missouri Supreme Court's ruling, Carl R. Johnson, president of the Kansas City, Missouri, NAACP, suggested that Whites would refuse to sell their homes to Blacks out of fear of being sued by their neighbors. Just days after Johnson's comments, a White woman, Miss Flinn, brought suit against another

White woman, Mrs. Clark, on the grounds that she was in breach of the Santa Fe Place neighborhood agreement when she sold her property to a Black family, Mr. and Mrs. E. S. Dottrey.[153] In this particular case, the sale of the property to the Dottreys was upheld, but this did not deter Whites from continuing to protect White neighborhoods with fervor, often turning to violence. Violence and intimidation continued as some Whites stopped at nothing to prevent Blacks from undoing the homogeneity of their neighborhoods.

Further complicating the Black quest for fair housing was downtown redevelopment or what was otherwise known as "Black removal," which destroyed Black-owned small businesses and Black residences and displaced Blacks into crowded and deteriorating housing.[154] In 1948, the City Plan Commission recommended redevelopment.[155] Spurred by the Housing Act of 1949, which provided federal financing for slum clearance and urban renewal, Kansas City was, as were many American cities, swept into the redevelopment fervor. It became clear soon after the passage of the Housing Act of 1949 that there were no houses available for persons displaced, a group consisting almost entirely of people of color whose access to housing was severely limited.[156] Kansas City redevelopment resulted in bulldozing low-income housing and replacing it with new public facilities and middle-income housing. After the first eleven urban renewal projects, over eleven thousand persons had been displaced from their homes, and more than half of them were low-income Blacks. The Office of Housing and Community Development, a local government agency, noted that housing difficulties resulting from urban renewal were never satisfactorily decided: "The failures of urban renewal redevelopment projects are the personal and family histories of people who were forced out and could find no better place to live."[157] As part of the redevelopment, Kansas City subsequently used public housing—segregated public housing no less—to accommodate the displaced downtown residents. Thus, Blacks were placed primarily at T. B. Watkins Homes at Thirteenth and Vine and Wayne Miner on East Eleventh Street.[158] These were public housing projects, consisting of several multi-story, mid-rise, and high-rise structures. Wayne Miner, in particular, would become infamous for its dilapidated features and crime-ridden existence; it was a vertical slum of sorts.[159] Housing would remain a profoundly problematic domain for Kansas City's Black residents for decades beyond the Housing Act of 1949. Still, by the early 1950s, there was hope among many in the Black community that the public sector, including schools, might be ripe for change.

Brown v. Topeka Board of Education

During the first Kansas City Conference on Human Relations in March of 1953, a topic under serious consideration was how to work out the smooth transition to integrated schools in advance of court order or legislative enactment.[160] As part of the discussion, "subordinate problems" were many and varied, such as considering how to integrate all Black teachers into the integrated school system and how to prepare both White and Black children for integration.

The early 1950s saw the beginning of significant societal changes, not all of which went unchallenged. In 1952, a *Kansas City Call* article covered the opening of public facilities to Blacks:

> In granting that Negroes have the same right to enjoy public facilities as other citizens, the decision is another in a growing list of court rulings against the "separate but equal" philosophy. It is another indication that there is no practical method by which separate facilities can achieve actual equality.[161]

However, the integration of the Swope Park Pool reveals the struggle and resistance among White residents to desegregation of Kansas City's public facilities. Though the pool eventually desegregated, the initial response of the Board of Park Commissioners was to close the pool for the 1952 season rather than admit Black residents.[162] The following year, 1953, the pool was opened to Blacks and Whites on an integrated basis, and the Swope Park Pool operated without incident, eventually leading to the integration of all of the city's swimming and wading pools "to all persons of all races."[163] So with the integration of the swimming pools, the last of the public facilities to integrate, all public-owned facilities in Kansas City were theoretically open to all races. During this period, Kansas City, Missouri's public schools were also transforming from a segregated system to an integrated one following *Brown*.[164]

In the run-up to the landmark *Brown* decision, under the leadership of Legal Defense Fund director Thurgood Marshall, the NAACP in the 1940s began fighting to end the segregation of American educational institutions. But even within the NAACP leadership, the thought of confronting segregation in the White-dominated courts met with some resistance, and questions lingered: What would desegregation of schools mean in practice? Would desegregation destroy Black teachers and Black institutions, including schools?[165] Such thinking largely stemmed from the notion that the NAACP should challenge inequality and not segregation, instead working to ensure the equal part of separate but equal. W. E. B. Du Bois, founder of the NAACP, was initially in favor of integration, but by the mid-1930s, he had come to question the logic of combating segregation, which he expressed in *Does the Negro Need Separate Schools?*

> The question which I am discussing is: Are these separate schools and institutions needed? And the answer, to my mind, is perfectly clear. They are needed just so far as they are necessary for the proper education of the Negro race. The proper education of any people includes sympathetic touch between teacher and pupil; knowledge on the part of the teacher, not simply of the individual taught, but of his surroundings and background, and the history of his class group.[166]

Du Bois's ideas about schools, however, never commanded majority support, and the NAACP committed itself to fighting, emphasizing that segregated schools featured glaring inequalities.

In *Gaines v. Canada* (1938), *Sweatt v. Painter* (1950), and *McLaurin v. Oklahoma State Regents* (1950), the Supreme Court essentially banned racial separation in state colleges and schools of law, suggesting that the practice violated the Fourteenth Amendment's equal protection clause.[167] Yet there was uncertainty about whether such a principle could be applied to elementary and secondary education. In 1952, however, five cases—originating in Kansas, Delaware, Virginia, South Carolina, and the District of Columbia—challenged segregation within school systems that required segregated schools by constitutional or statutory mandate or provided for permissive segregation at the behest of local school boards.[168] Each of the five cases was appealed to the Supreme Court, and in 1952, the cases were combined into one, *Brown v. Board of Education* of Topeka.[169] The named plaintiff, Oliver Brown, had a daughter, Linda Brown, who had to walk blocks through a railyard, across a busy road, and onto a bus just to get to her segregated elementary school in Topeka, Kansas. This, even though there was a White school four blocks from her home. When Oliver Brown pushed for his daughter to be admitted into the White school, she was denied entry. This occasioned *Brown v. Board of Education* of Topeka.

On May 17, 1954, Chief Justice Earl Warren read the Court's unanimous opinion, in which he stated: "Does segregation of children in public schools solely based on race, even though the physical facilities and other 'tangible' factors may be equal, deprive the children of the minority group of equal educational opportunities? We believe that it does."[170] It was a decision that gave credence to the NAACP's trial strategy, in which they relied mostly on the testimony of social scientists to bolster the claim that separate schools were harmful in various ways. The arguments stemmed from the harm and benefit thesis and the work of Kenneth Clark, which included the following: self-esteem of Black children was low in segregated schools and that segregation led Black children to be prejudiced toward Whites; segregation had adverse effects on learning, as Black children achieved at lower levels than White children; segregation placed a physical burden on Black children, as the distance traveled to attend school was often far; segregation was psychologically damaging for Black children because it caused frustration, apathy, and hostility; segregation established a necessary precondition for prejudice; and, classifying students by race was not justifiable.[171] With the High Court's ruling that segregated education violated the Black citizens' constitutional right to equal protection of the laws under the Fourteenth Amendment, the segregated school systems of more than half of the United States, including Missouri, were drastically altered.

The Deep South began to criticize the *Brown* ruling almost immediately following the Court order. Southern governors, in anticipation of public school desegregation and well before the Supreme Court ruling, were vowing to defy Court orders. Upon the Court's decision, Georgia Governor Herman Tallmadge assumed a clear stance of non-cooperation, stating, "I am calling the State Education Commission into immediate session to map a program to ensure continued and permanent segregation of the races."[172] In South Carolina, lawmakers had been empowered by a public referendum to convert the public schools to private schools where they saw fit. Governor Hugh White of Mississippi said he was "sad" and "disappointed" with the Court's ruling. Walter Sillers, speaker of the Mississippi House of Representatives, suggested the state get out of the education business altogether. An Alabama lawmaker recommended that a television be used to teach Alabama children to avoid the physical integration of White and Black students in Alabama.[173]

The so-called Solid South's general reaction to *Brown* was open disobedience. *Brown II*, in which the Court convened to order its directives, did little to enforce compliance in the South, leaving implementation to be settled by local federal district courts—courts that native White Southerners operated.[174] Moreover, a vague and ambiguous timetable was presented, in which the Court suggested desegregation be done "with all deliberate speed."[175] The flexible implementation standard resulted from the Court's recognition that local circumstances varied considerably. Still, by leaving it to the discretion of the states, reactions varied from immediate compliance to complete obstinacy. In the South Carolina case *Briggs v. Elliott*, a South Carolina District Court stated the following:

> It is important that we point out exactly what the Supreme Court has decided and what it has not decided in this case. It has not decided that the federal courts are to take over or regulate the public schools of the states. It has not decided that the states must mix persons of different races in the schools or must require them to attend schools or must deprive them of the right of choosing the schools they attend. What it has decided, and all that it has decided, is that a state may not deny to any person on account of race the right to attend any school that it maintains . . . if the schools which it maintains are open to children of all races, no violation of the Constitution is involved even though the children of different races voluntarily attend different schools, as they attend different churches. Nothing in the Constitution or in the decision of the Supreme Court takes away from people freedom to choose the schools they attend. The Constitution, in other words, does not require integration. It merely forbids discrimination.[176]

Freedom of choice plans would surely prove to be an effective means by which many states in the South were able to avoid actual desegregation.[177] It became clear almost immediately following the *Brown II* implementation decision that the South was going to resist desegregation, whether through outward resistance or more covert methods veiled in misleading language, such as freedom of choice.

The response outside of the South was decidedly different, most notably in the Border States. The Southern border states that did not secede from the Union included Missouri, West Virginia, Maryland, Kentucky, Oklahoma, and Delaware. Baltimore, Maryland's Board of Education took only two weeks to approve a desegregation plan unanimously, and Washington, D.C., and Wilmington, Delaware, also commenced desegregation almost immediately following the *Brown* decision.[178]

Missouri State Commissioner of Education Hubert Wheeler began planning for the *Brown* ruling before it was decided. In March 1954, Wheeler wrote a memo in which he said:

> In Missouri we shall most certainly want to examine carefully the ruling of the United States Supreme Court in regard to white and negro education. Any statement previous to the study of the ruling of the Court must be general in nature. Should the Supreme Court rule that the states may continue the segregation of negro and white students, our Constitution and statutes now make provisions for such segregation. If the United States Supreme Court rules against segregation, it would, I suppose, nullify that portion of our Constitution and our state laws as now established in Missouri.[179]

Then, just following the Supreme Court's decision, on June 15, 1954, in a letter to county and district superintendents, Wheeler expressed the board's desire to implement the *Brown* decision "to the fullest extent of its authority and jurisdiction" but cautioned that a decision by Attorney General John M. Dalton would be necessary before proceeding.[180] Just days after Wheeler's letter, Attorney General Dalton stated the following regarding desegregation in Missouri:

> [I]t is the opinion of the office that the provisions of the Missouri Constitution and statutes, relating to separate schools for white and colored children are superseded by the decision of the Supreme Court of the United States and are, therefore, unenforceable, and that school districts may at the present time permit white and colored children to attend the same schools.[181]

For most Missouri towns with small numbers of Black students, the decision to desegregate did not involve any major realignment. The cost of maintaining a segregated system for these small rural towns was often burdensome, so from a sheer financial position, the *Brown* decision was a bit of a relief. For larger cities, particularly St. Louis and Kansas City, desegregation would require much forethought and planning. St. Louis was especially quick to announce its desegregation plan, which it began implementing in September of 1954 and continued in phases through September of 1955.[182] As St. Louis announced its plan, the Kansas City, Missouri School District Research Department began considering its options.

A July 15, 1954, report titled *A Study of the Problems Involved in the Desegregation of the Public Schools in Kansas City* presented district leadership with three possible options: Delay desegregation until further word from the Supreme Court, desegregate all schools beginning in September of 1954, or initiate a program of gradual desegregation in September 1954 and proceed systematically over some time.[183] At the time of the report, the Kansas City, Missouri School District had already desegregated summer school classes. Although summer school was only offered at two schools, Westport and Lincoln High Schools, and the vast majority of Black summer school students—all but three—would attend Lincoln, the act was a symbolic one for the district, suggesting that Kansas City was going to take the *Brown* decision seriously.[184]

Regarding the larger desegregation plan, the district opted for a gradual approach and consequently initiated a desegregation plan with two phases. The first phase was to commence with the 1954–1955 school year, in which students at the previously all-Black Lincoln Junior College would be transferred to the Kansas City Junior College at Thirty-Ninth Street and McGee. Additionally, the vocational divisions of R. T. Coles Vocational School would be transferred to the formerly all-White Manual Vocational School. The R. T. Coles building then would become the site for an integrated seventh- and eighth-grade junior high.[185] The district decided to phase in desegregation, no doubt, knowing that immediate integration would result in just shy of half of the district's Black students attending different schools in the fall of 1954. Thus, phase one of the plan, being extremely limited in scope, provided Superintendent Mark W. Bills an opportunity to declare success, which he did in his annual report for 1954–1955. The second phase was planned to begin in September of 1955, meaning the 1955–1956 school year would be the first official year of full-blown desegregation. Phase two, therefore, was to include the desegregation of the entire Kansas City, Missouri School District. Lastly, the school district emphasized the need to establish and publicize boundary lines of all schools "as soon as possible."[186]

Not everyone was satisfied with the district's course of action. Lewis Clymer, chairman of the Education Committee of the Kansas City Urban League, and Lee Reader, chairman of the Commission on Human Relations, made several suggestions to the Kansas City School Board, and both individuals offered their respective organization's services only to be told that they were not needed. In a letter dated May 25, 1954, from Lewis Clymer to Ray Joslyn, president of the Kansas City, Missouri School District's Board of Education, Clymer formally offered support in designing the desegregation plan, but city school officials declined. It appears that district leadership relied solely on their own people, all of whom were White, to devise the desegregation plan, a strategy that would routinely be employed and a policy that continued to especially anger Black Kansas Citians. Whether the pressure of the moment was too much, or he had accomplished what he had set out to do, Superintendent Bills resigned in 1955 and was replaced with respected Kansas Citian James A. Hazlett.

Hazlett had a reputation for understanding White interests and for having broad support among White elites but who nonetheless supported the High Court's desegregation decree if it did not inconvenience White families. To this end, Hazlett was a strict proponent of neighborhood attendance zones, which all but assured schools residing within White-Black racial borderline areas—like that of Central High School—would experience a degree of racial integration. Just how much, however, remained uncertain, at least until the fall of 1955, when students like Gwendolyn Adams became one of the first Black students to step foot in Central High School.

4 | *Brown's* Aftermath

As Gwendolyn Adams prepared for her first day of school in September 1955, her sophomore year, a feeling of dread overcame her. This was not the sense of uncertainty or trepidation often accompanying a first day of school. This was different. Adams was angry. She was angry because she felt forced to leave a school and community that she knew and enjoyed only to attend a different school that seemed ever so distant. Adams was among the first of Kansas City's Black students to enter a formerly all-White high school, as she was transferred from Lincoln High School to Central High School in 1955. The importance of the moment was of little concern to the fifteen-year-old Adams. Foremost on her mind was the school, as well as teachers and friends whom she would have to leave behind:

> When you are outside of it now and looking in that was, well . . . a piece of history. My mother talked to me, you know, and she told me how to behave and how to, you know, what it was all about and this is a big step for you. That went in one ear and out the other because I was of the mindset I don't want to be here; I don't want to go. So all of the positives that were given to me, they weren't registering at all. And I'm used to all Black teachers and people that I know and I could go to Mrs. Fox—I remember this one teacher. She was just . . . I loved her to death. She would send out for lunch to get French fries and hamburgers and stuff. You're not going to get that at Central. Come on! But the first year I was very angry, and my grades failed. But I wasn't a failing student. . . . And so my

mother sat down and she talked to me again about it and she had been talking to me all along. . . . But my life was too peaceful—I was happy where I was, you know.[187]

Adams described what many Black students felt at all-Black institutions: a genuine comfort and belonging, a sense of community. It was the institutional caring she became accustomed to at Lincoln High School that she feared losing when she was transferred to Central in the spirit of desegregation. Adams noted feeling uncomfortable or out of place at Central during her first couple of years, and it had much to do with her teachers:

> I don't think it was just me, but I didn't feel a lot coming from my teachers . . . I'm not used to teachers being aloof and just handing paper and do this. No communication. No nothing outside of school . . . I think that there were teachers who were there that did not want to because of the way they interacted with us.[188]

As early as 1954, the district began preparing for teacher reassignment and a reduction in teachers due to the district's impending desegregation effort. It was apparent from the beginning that White teachers would be prioritized over Black teachers. The board, in both subtle and overt ways, protected contracts for White teachers and dismissed many Black teachers without cause. In 1954, Black teachers were hired per diem like a substitute teacher, whereas White teachers were given year-long contracts. This did not go unnoticed, as was editorialized in the *Kansas City Times*: "Can you tell me why many White teachers were hired on a regular contract basis this year while no Negro teachers were hired, except on a day-to-day basis?"[189] Superintendent Bills, just prior to his resignation, attempted to appease the Black community by offering an explanation. Bills effectively side-stepped the question and justified the practice by blaming a reduction in enrollment. The messaging did not resonate. Shortly thereafter, Superintendent Bills was gone. Enter Hazlett, and among the first challenges he faced was addressing the plight of the Black teacher. This occurred while the district confronted a teacher shortage, which infuriated many in the Black community. As Hazlett was publicly claiming there were not enough teachers to fill Kansas City's classrooms, Black teachers were having great difficulty in finding work in the newly desegregated Kansas City, Missouri School District.

Following the *Brown* decision, Black teachers across the country lost their jobs. Many of these teachers were better educated and more experienced than their White counterparts, yet Black teachers were the first to be dismissed and the last to be hired. In Kansas City, a flurry of articles and editorials were written in the *Kansas City Call* in 1955 addressing the Black teachers' struggle. One such article in January of 1955 posed the question, "How much longer is the Kansas City board of education going to fail to employ new Negro teachers?"[190] Another such article stated the following:

> The Kansas City board of education is not being fair. For more than a year now, it has failed to hire new Negro teachers on a regular basis, although hundreds of new white teachers have been brought into the system. The excuses given this time last year for not hiring Negro teachers was that a large number of regular teachers were on leave and their places had to be held open for them. New Negro teachers brought into the system were given "reserve" status and served all year without contract. . . . Apparently, the board has adopted a policy of hiring no more Negro teachers, no matter how well qualified they might be.[191]

A variety of tricks were employed to keep Black teachers out of classrooms. In the South, particularly in Virginia, thirty-day contracts were implemented, whereby a teacher would have to sign a new contract every month, empowering the school district to get rid of Black teachers at will. A similar technique, though not a thirty-day contract, was used in Kansas City, Missouri, where many Black teachers were placed on "reserve" and thus not offered a contract. In many cases, however, Black teachers were simply dismissed.[192] By 1961, the Missouri Advisory Committee to the United States Commission on Civil Rights estimated that 125 to 150 Black teachers in Missouri had, as a result of initial desegregation, lost their employment.

Despite this, Kansas City, Missouri School District emerged as one of the examples of successful desegregation—though there were fears that Kansas City would erupt in violence. A Kansas City police sergeant suggested that Kansas City's Central would be "a lot worse situation than [Central High School] in Little Rock."[193] Desegregation at Central, however, as was described in the local press, had "proceeded smoothly:"[194]

> The public schools of Kansas City, Missouri are more integrated than it was anticipated last spring they would be. Forty-three out of a total of 92 schools have both white and negro pupils enrolled. The Kansas City school board has done well as far as the integration of students is concerned."[195]

No doubt, desegregation in Kansas City avoided a major incident and did unfold uneventfully throughout the fall of 1955, but this is largely a result of how Superintendent Hazlett and the school board designed and implemented the desegregation plan.

James Hazlett was hired in 1955 after serving as Director of the Kansas City, Missouri School District's Research Department from 1951 to 1955. Hazlett's rise to the superintendency was described by a 1955 article in the *Central Luminary* as a "success story."[196] A Kansas City native, Hazlett attended Kansas City, Missouri, public schools from kindergarten through junior college before obtaining his master's degree at Kansas City University. Hazlett then served as a teacher and principal in the Kansas City, Missouri School District. He taught at various elementary schools between 1938 and 1945 and then served as a principal from 1945 to 1951. As a result of his intimate relationship with the Kansas City, Missouri School District as student, teacher, and building-level and central office administrator, Hazlett understood the problems Kansas City schools were facing. Hazlett had been honing his leadership skills from an early age, having participated as Paseo High School's senior class president, student council president, and member of the National Honor Society.[197] Hazlett's approach to initial desegregation was cautious. Hazlett's plan affected only a small portion of White Kansas Citians—those who lived near Black residential areas, and even then, White families found ways to navigate around sending their White children to schools with Black children. This was done most notably through student transfers.

School officials in Kansas City determined that desegregation could be most readily achieved through the dissolution of the dual attendance zones,[198] which, under de jure segregation, kept Black and White students separate. Often, Black students lived closer to White schools than to Black schools, but of course, Black students would have to walk past the White schools to get to their respective Black schools. Alvin Brooks, a pillar of the Black community in Kansas City, vividly vividly recalled his days walking past the neighborhood White school, only several blocks from his house, to get to Dunbar. He described how he and his Black friends would often walk to school with White kids from the neighborhood: "They'd [White students] stop, and we'd keep on going . . . and catch the Thirty-First Street car and then go to Vine and catch the bus."[199] With the destruction of the dual system and the insistence of the Kansas City, Missouri School District to keep a neighborhood concept intact, theoretically, Kansas City, Missouri's Black students would attend the school nearest their house. As with Brooks, many Black students would attend formerly all-White schools, and conversely, many White students would be slotted to attend former all-Black schools. While the district did spend months considering and re-drawing district attendance lines, much of it was veiled in secrecy. In the end, however, the Kansas City, Missouri School District relied on geographical zoning to integrate the schools. This decision upheld the *Brown* mandate to dissolve the former system of segregation and provide assignment of students on a non-discriminatory basis. Such an approach, nevertheless, seriously limited the effectiveness of the effort.

The district desegregation plan included the continuation of the longstanding and liberal transfer policy: "The Board approves the continuation of the established practices of granting transfers, provided that no transfers shall be issued to schools where, in the judgment of the Superintendent of Schools, capacity of the building has been reached."[200] Transfers were subsequently granted for a variety of reasons, including to take a course of study not offered at the school of the resident district, to take advantage of convenient transportation, to complete one's senior year or part of any year where a pupil was previously enrolled, to avoid dangerous traffic situations, to make for a better pupil adjustment, and to permit continuation in the junior high school.[201] Indeed, the district closed schools that were above capacity, but students who wanted to transfer to schools that were below capacity were free to do so, regardless of race. The school district did not inquire about a student's race on the application to avoid preferential treatment.[202] As such, the transfer policy became the primary vehicle by which White students avoided initial desegregation efforts. Although the *Brown* decision seemingly ushered in a new age in American schooling, the transfer policy, coupled with the district's shifting of boundaries and growing residential segregation, all but guaranteed that the students in Kansas City, Missouri, schools would remain segregated. Central High School, which went from 100 percent White during the 1954–1955 school year, the last year of segregated schooling, to just under 98 percent Black during the 1961–1962 school year, reveals the complexities of the situation and the importance of the schooling-housing nexus, in particular, in the southeastern neighborhoods of Kansas City, Missouri. [203]

Desegregation at Central

Year	Black	White
1954-1955	0%	100%
1955-1956	11%	89%
1956-1957	17%	83%
1957-1958	28%	72%
1958-1959	42%	58%
1959-1960	70%	30%
1960-1961	90%	10%
1961-1962	97%	3%

Table 1: Central High School Enrollment by Race, 1954–1962[204]

The rapid transformation of Central from a majority White to a majority Black high school occurred in only five years. Table 1 shows the dramatic demographic shift. The Census data between 1940 and 1960 for the Central High School census tract, an area that extended one-half square mile and included a population of nearly nine thousand people, mirrored that of the school, which can be seen in Table 2.

Year	Black	White
1940	0.4%	99.6%
1950	0.2%	99.8%
1960	82.1%	17.9%

Table 2: Population of Central High School Census Tract by Race, 1940–1960[205]

Alvin Brooks was a police officer and resident of the Central High School attendance area in 1960, at 3336 Agnes, just several blocks from Central. He remembered how Whites reacted in fear of Blacks moving into the area. He specifically recalled a meeting at an all-White church at Twenty-Ninth and Prospect in 1960, which he estimated attracted some four hundred people, mostly Whites, to discuss the neighborhood transformation. Brooks explained that he had endured enough. He was tired of listening to his White neighbors insist that the arrival of Black families was causing their property values to fall. Brooks went to the microphone to address the crowd, a bold move considering he remembered being only one of fifteen Black residents at the meeting. But he was fed up:

> Let me tell you what . . . you are accusing us, what, twenty-five or thirty percent of us causing your property values to go down. May I see the hands of those of you who a Black person knocked on your door to buy your house? May I see your hands? How about was there a Black person who came and said I'm going to shoot you with gun in hand unless you get out? . . . We didn't cause your property values to go down. You caused it to go down. . . . You fell right into the racist trap. And when they said to you "look who's coming in. You better move out." We didn't tell you "you better move out." None of us knocked on your door and said we're going to sell your home or you got to sell your home. Nobody knocked on your door with a gun in their hand and said you better get out.[206]

Of course, Brooks was right. White residents were not being forced out; they were choosing to leave, but their decisions were being influenced by the tactics of realtors looking to make fast money. And despite the efforts of those like Brooks, who were willing to confront Whites seeking to leave the area at any cost, the flight continued at a rapid pace throughout the 1950s and 1960s.

In 1954, Thomas L. Gillette, a graduate student in the Department of Sociology at the University of Kansas City, wrote a master's thesis titled, "Santa Fe: A Study of the Effects of Negro Invasion on Property Values." Gillette stated the impetus of the study as the "recent and quite rapid expansion of the Negro population in the city and the accompanying increase in awareness of intergroup hostility."[207] The Santa Fe neighborhood of Kansas City is currently and was historically bound by Twenty-Seventh Street to the north, Linwood to the south, Prospect to the east, and Indiana to the west.[208] In the early 1950s, as it had for decades previously, Twenty-Seventh Street served as a division between White residents and Black residents. Very few Blacks lived south of Twenty-Seventh Street before the 1950s, but in the 1950s, the Twenty-Seventh Street divide began to dissolve.

Year	Black	White
1950	24%	76%
1960	45%	55%

Table 3: Population of Southeast Kansas City by Race, 1950–1960[209]

As Whites fled the southeast area of the city and Blacks moved in, Twenty-Seventh Street no longer served as a dividing line. In its wake, however, a new and equally stringent line of demarcation occupied its place: Troost Avenue.

As the first Black families moved south of Twenty-Seventh Street and into southeast Kansas City, White residents reacted with violence. The house of the first Black family to move to Twenty-Seventh and Paseo was bombed in May of 1952. The May bombing resulted in only minimal damage, but it set an obvious precedent. The house became a target again in September of the same year. The second bombing caused considerable damage, and the Black family who had moved into the 2700 block of Paseo was under a constant barrage of threats and torments.[210] The White response to Black families crossing Twenty-Seventh Street was one of racism and prejudice, in which Whites viewed homogenous White neighborhoods as superior. The fear, then, among Whites that Blacks would devalue their property resulted initially in pushback—violence and threats. Then, Whites simply left the area.

Troost Divide

Beginning in the 1950s, Troost Avenue became a racially identifiable boundary between Whites and Blacks. This was, in part, a result of the discriminatory actions of Kansas City, Missouri School District leaders who used Troost Avenue as a school boundary between Black and White schools, whereby Black schools were located to the east of Troost and White schools to the west.[211] This separation occurred almost immediately following the *Brown* decision in 1954. By 1970, all elementary and secondary schools east of Troost Avenue were 90 percent or more Black, and every elementary and secondary school west of Troost was less than 50 percent Black.[212] Because of its location, just south of Twenty-Seventh Street and east of Troost, Central High School was one of the first schools to transform swiftly from all White to all Black. With the school district's use of Troost Avenue as a racially identifiable school boundary in the post-*Brown* period, residents began to associate neighborhoods east of Troost as Black neighborhoods and neighborhoods west of Troost as White neighborhoods. Realtors, too, in the mid-1950s, began using Troost as a racial dividing line and thus marketed houses for sale east of Troost to Blacks only, further solidifying the notion that Black neighborhoods were more unstable than White neighborhoods and thus needed to be separate. It was the use of blockbusting techniques among Kansas City realtors, however, that ultimately led to large numbers of Whites leaving the neighborhoods of southeast Kansas City, Missouri.

Realtors went door to door to encourage Whites to sell their homes and flee the impending Black movement into the neighborhood. Almost immediately following the sale of a single house to a Black family, the entire block of Whites would follow, vulnerable to realtors' fear tactics as a result of prejudice and racism. Whites genuinely believed that the presence of a Black family in a White neighborhood would result in declining property values, crime, and general neighborhood malaise. Blockbusting proved to be a useful and lucrative tactic, and it was no secret to residents of the southeast area. A 1955 editorial in the *Kansas City Call* claimed that the over-zealousness of realtors was a central factor in the inability to build interracial neighborhoods.[213] And while blockbusting and panic selling were having a profound impact on neighborhoods throughout the southeast area in the 1950s and 1960s, some residents decided to take on the real estate industry themselves, including one neighborhood around Central High School.[214]

In 1955, a pastor of the Southeast Presbyterian Church, Pastor Earl T. Sturgess, attempted to halt White flight from his neighborhood near Central High School by placing a sign in his yard and his neighbors that read "not for sale."[215] The "My Home is Not for Sale" campaign, which promoted interracial neighborhoods, gained appeal in various neighborhoods around Kansas City and even received national notoriety at one point. Still, the forces of racism and prejudice were too great.[216] Sturgess's campaign was relatively short-lived, and despite efforts of opposition to panic selling, Whites continued to leave the southeast area in search of homogenous White neighborhoods in the suburbs. Blacks kept moving into the area in search of better and bigger houses. Thus, Central High School, situated prominently in the southeast side of Kansas City, Missouri, just beyond Twenty-Seventh Street, became the first school to undergo a total resegregation: all White in 1955, Central was all Black by 1962.

Post-*Brown* Central

It was business as usual at Central during the 1955–1956 school year. Interestingly, the student newspaper, the *Central Luminary*, covered very little about desegregation over the entire academic year. The only mention of race in the paper occurred in the March 1956 edition, in which a section titled "Human Relations Ledger" was introduced. The ledger was seemingly created to cover both the good and the bad, or so-called "liabilities" and "assets" of the school.[217] The March 23, 1956, ledger includes four separate "liabilities," each occurring on a different day and having to do with a racial incident involving Central students: a junior high student had thrown a firecracker that exploded near a White boy, which then led to a fight on school grounds; a group of White male students who resented the presence of Blacks at Central and tried to organize a strike to protest integration; unknown persons affixing a "Ku Klux cross" to Central's flagpole and setting it ablaze; a group of Black students, both boys and girls, allegedly tried to "cause trouble" as students left Central at the end of school.[218] The "asset" portion, like the "liability" section, includes separate incidents involving Central students, but this time, they are celebratory: a Black student in the Girls' Choir performed a solo performance and was applauded by Central students; Black and White band members at Central cooperated to make the Annual Band Festival a success.[219]

The absence of substantial coverage regarding desegregation in the student newspaper at Central High School is interesting and most likely a deliberate effort to downplay its significance. Presumably, Central's White administrators, faculty, and student body were not interested in highlighting stories about Central's new Black students. A certain hysteria had gripped the White community, and a quick exodus from Central and its neighborhoods was already underway among White families, so it is no surprise that stories about the growing Black population were silenced.

Meanwhile, Central's Black students, a mere 11 percent of the student population during the 1955–1956 school year, were trying to adapt to their new and unfamiliar surroundings. Lyle Davis, Jr., a freshman in 1955 and one of the pioneering Black students at Central, recalled the peculiarity of his new, mostly White school: "I walk in that first day, and I see all these White kids. They look so much older. Here I am a little Black kid walking in there."[220] And while Davis, Jr. did settle in at Central and befriend White classmates—friends with whom he formed lifetime bonds—he did not have a single Black teacher during his four years at the school and remembered the first couple of years at Central as "tough."[221] Indeed, the social and emotional support that Davis, Jr. received from his Black teachers at the all-Black R. T. Coles School before desegregation, he explained, was lacking among the White teachers of Central. About his experiences at all-Black schools with Black faculty, Davis, Jr. said: "You knew the teachers [and they] seemed to be more interested."[222] But the academic instruction at Central was "excellent," according to Davis, Jr.;

Central students had long prided themselves on academic excellence, and the spirit of such continued after 1955.

By the late 1950s, however, the press began to paint a bleak picture of life at Central, a trend that has persisted. Accounts of "gangland rule" and students wielding switchblades, beer can openers, and razor blades culminated in an account of Black students assaulting two White teachers.[223] Whites were already leaving the school and the area en masse, but such coverage no doubt expedited the process. This was occurring despite Central receiving accolades for its graduates' academic performance. In 1960, Central was graduating more students who were going on to get doctorate degrees than any other school in the state of Missouri.[224] Moreover, in 1959, three Central alumni placed among the highest ten thousand scores in the National Merit Qualifying Test given to more than one-half million students. Central graduates were making names for themselves at Harvard, Yale, MIT, and other top colleges.[225] This continued success led to a student editorial, which stated:

> How does Central rate? Let's look for ourselves: . . . Central High School is the oldest in Kansas City, and as far as campus goes, it is one of the prettiest. The school's equipment and facilities are more than adequate. It also has a wide range of subjects. We offer four languages and six courses in English. Scholastically we rate in the top five in Kansas City and can hold our own in the state as well. Forty percent of our students attend college although a great many more have the entrance requirements, thanks to our marvelous faculty. Forty scholarships were awarded last year out of a class of 390, as compared to ten years ago when three or four scholarships were awarded out of a class of 500.[226]

Despite the doting students, White students continued leaving "dear old Central" rapidly. Central was one of only a few schools in the Midwest offering four years in Latin, German, and Spanish and courses in college-level chemistry, math, biology, and drafting. However, this was not enough to entice White students to stay.[227] As Black families moved into the Central attendance area and Black students into Central High School, White families either found ways to transfer their children out of Central High School or left the area. On average, Central lost White students at roughly 20 percent per year between 1957 and 1960.[228] The district explicitly aided in Whites' effort to leave as well, adopting in 1959 a district policy whereby families had the option to have their children either remain at Central High School or attend one of two other high schools, which consisted of all-White student bodies. This was done under the veil of overcrowding, as the board cited Central's overcrowded building as the reason for the transfer policy. It is no wonder, then, that Central went from an all-White student body to an all-Black student body within just seven years of the *Brown* decision.

5 | Success to Frustration

In September 1958, Central's first Black administrator, Girard T. Bryant, took up his new post. Bryant was a former vice-principal at Manual High School. He had also taught in Bangkok, Thailand, and came to Central with impressive credentials. Bryant had a bachelor's degree from Chicago University and a master's from the University of Kansas. When he took the position as vice-principal at Central, Bryant was working toward his PhD at Washington University in St. Louis.[229] Bryant joined Central's new White principal, James Boyd, and vice-principal, Allis Keith. Boyd, a former chemistry teacher at Central who had left to become Northeast High School's vice-principal, returned to Central to assume the principalship in 1959, the same year that Central lost twenty of its teachers to transfer.[230] There is no documented reason why the teachers left, except that "three teachers retired; three have taken a year's leave of absence for advanced study; and 20 have transferred to other schools in Kansas City or further away."[231]

Loretta Stewart, a proud graduate of Central's class of 1963, fondly remembered her time at Central High School, but Stewart's path to Central was far from easy. Her first years in Kansas City's desegregated school system were extremely isolating. In her first year, Stewart remembered how she was the only Black student in her fifth-grade class during the 1955–1956 school year immediately following Kansas City, Missouri School District's desegregation effort:

It's just the memory of the isolation, of not having anyone like me to talk to. I'll never forget the one thing that really made me understand that I really wasn't part of that school. They had a Girl Scout troop and I had made friends with a young lady and she and I would go to the library. She would come to my house and I would go to her house, and she was in girl scouts [too] . . . And, so I was like, I was all excited about joining girl scouts. This was something totally new to me. We didn't have girl scouts in my church. So, you know, I was like okay. Great! Well, a few days later she came back to me and she said: 'I'm sorry, my mom said you can't be in the girl scouts.' . . . She told me because I wasn't White.[232]

In striking contrast to her first year in a mostly all-White classroom and school, Stewart's years at segregated Kansas City, Missouri's Charles Sumner Elementary School were anything but isolating:

I had great teachers. Everybody was concerned about us. They made sure that we understood that we were expected to give our best and to do our best. . . . And you know, we were all sort of family. Even though we might not have been actually related, there was a family atmosphere to that time.[233]

Stewart also explained that the collective, family atmosphere extended beyond the school walls and enveloped the community. She described that all members of the community—teachers, church leaders, parents, and neighbors—were responsible for watching out for children in the neighborhood. As a child, Stewart envisioned attending Lincoln Junior High School and Lincoln High School, the one-time segregated junior high and high school, and continuing to benefit from the robust neighborhood community she so cherished. But like many Black families in the mid- to late-1950s, Stewart's family moved to a bigger house on Twenty-Ninth Street, which had long been off-limits: "[W]e were not allowed to move to past Twenty-Seventh Street until I guess I must have been in seventh grade. And then we moved to Twenty-Ninth Street, which was wow!"[234] Stewart's move to Twenty-Ninth led the family to Central High School instead of their beloved Lincoln. The Stewart family was not the only Black family moving south: "[A]ll of a sudden we looked around and all of the White people were gone. And it was a Black neighborhood. . . . in a blink of an eye."[235]

Referencing her time at Central and the changing demographics, Stewart claimed that "there were White kids all over the place" during her freshman year in 1959, but by 1963, her senior year, she remembered two.[236] Stewart admitted that she was not thrilled about attending high school at Central, largely because, despite her family's move, she still hoped to reunite with her friends at Lincoln. Yet, her time at Central, she explained, proved to be enjoyable, and she remembered a few staff members by name who had an impact on her life. One of those for whom Stewart expressed fondness was James F. Boyd.

Central's National Reputation

Central's principal from 1959 to 1969, James F. Boyd, was appointed Director of Secondary Education for the Kansas City, Missouri School District in 1969.[237] Boyd was recognized as a progressive educator by those inside and outside the Kansas City, Missouri School District. In 1962, Boyd was one of sixty administrators chosen to receive the John Hay Fellowship at Colorado College.[238] Additionally, that same year, Boyd was invited to speak to a Dallas, Texas, school administrators' group regarding his success in leading a high school with a predominately Black student population. The organization's president, Mr. S. A. Cain, said that Boyd was sought due to his "unusual accomplishments" with Black students.[239] The recognition was not lost on Central's students: "Because of the wonderful record that Central students have made, Central has become nationally known. For Mr. Boyd to have been chosen to speak before this organization is an honor that all in the Central-Linwood Community should be proud."[240]

Most certainly, by the early 1960s, while Boyd served as principal, all-Black Central High School, just as it had done when it was all White, was proving itself to be one of the best high schools in Missouri. Two national publications in the spring and summer of 1961 explored the successes of Central High School: *Harper's Magazine* with the article "The Good Slum Schools" and *Time* magazine with "Everything's Up to Date in Kansas City."[241] Both articles were based on the premise that there was something uniquely intriguing about Kansas City's Central High School, a school that went from all White to all Black and not only maintained its record of excellence but exceeded it:

> In its last years as an all-white school, Central never sent more than 15 per cent of its graduates to college, and only four or five Central kids won scholarships in an average year. Now, despite the great drop in socioeconomic level, 150 out of 350 graduates go on to college, 50 of them with scholarships . . . In recent years, Central has sent its Negro graduates to Yale, Vassar, Smith, Oberlin, Northwestern, and Chicago, among others.[242]

Forestal Lawton, a member of the 1962 graduating class, was one of the successful Black students at Central mentioned above. Lawton had been class president at Central Junior High School, carrying his leadership aspirations forward to high school. At the high school, Lawton was forced to choose between class president and student council president. He chose student council president and Richard Tolbert filled the class presidency. Lawton and Tolbert were selected as Victor Wilson Scholars and subsequently had the opportunity to attend Yale University. Tolbert did attend Yale, but Lawton, due to family obligations, never made it to New Haven, instead staying close to home and attending Kansas City University. Upon graduating from college, Lawton spent thirty-four successful years with the juvenile justice system, from 1968 to 2002. He describes his time at Central High School as formative, shaping him into the person he has become.

Lawton credits his former Central teachers for his accomplishments, most notably a teacher by the name of Dr. Jeremiah Cameron.[243]

Dr. Cameron was highlighted in the Harper's article "The Good Slum Schools." Dr. Cameron was described as "handsome" and "athletic," wearing a "white shirt and tie under a half-zippered Eisenhower jacket."[244] Dr. Cameron eventually became known as the "dean of Kansas City's Black intellectuals," having had a successful career as both a social critic and educator.[245] Loretta Stewart described Dr. Cameron as "exceptional":

> Dr. Jeremiah Cameron was my English teacher. He was the roughest, hardest teacher I ever had in my life. He would embarrass us in front of everybody . . . He would use words that we would have to go look up in the dictionary. Because, I mean his vocabulary was that expansive.[246]

Like Stewart, Lawton remembered Dr. Cameron with great affection, claiming that "Jeremiah Cameron . . . had a lot of impact on me."[247] Both Lawton and Stewart, however, explained that Dr. Cameron was just one of many teachers at Central who excelled. Stewart claimed that many of her teachers, Black and White alike, exhibited characteristics like those of Dr. Cameron: "[t]hey [the teachers] were hard on us. They really pushed us . . . I never really had a problem with my teachers. . . . there was a good mix of non-White instructors, which makes a difference."[248] Lawton, too, explained how his teachers, Black and White alike, were focused on academic preparation and maximizing student potential—"I attribute some of the things that I have accomplished in life to the background that I had at Central."[249] Central students' success led to yet another write-up, this one in *Time* magazine, which proclaimed: "Central's youngsters are marching not only into junior colleges but also to Yale, Smith, Vassar, Oberlin, and Chicago."[250]

As a result of Central High School's progressive reputation, it was selected as the American Field Service host school for foreign exchange students in 1963. This was a remarkable feat, especially considering that when Enzo Benedusi, Central's first foreign exchange student, arrived at Central in the fall of 1963, the school was all Black. Benedusi, an Italian, was White, and all of the foreign exchange students who attended Central between 1963 and 1969 were also White, which led one Central student, upon Benedusi's departure in 1964, to remark:

> Enzo Benedusi has set a milestone in America. He was the first American Field Service foreign student to be sent to a predominantly Negro school and live with a Negro family in a Negro community without incident. Alongside of him Centralites have proved that students recognize no racial barriers. Central has taken a great initial step not only for Central but for all schools in the United States.[251]

White foreign exchange students from Switzerland, Germany, Finland, and Denmark succeeded Benedusi. By all accounts, the foreign exchange students held Central in high esteem. Hans Jaeger, a foreign exchange student from Switzerland who arrived at Central the year after Benedusi, stated that Central was a "great school" and that "the students are so kind-hearted and friendly. They make you feel like you are one of them."[252] In 1969, Central welcomed its first Black foreign exchange student, Evans Awalime, from Africa.[253] This coincided with the appointment of Central's first Black principal, Cornelius Settles. It appears that 1969 was the last year of the program at Central, as there is no mention of another foreign exchange student after that year. This, rather predictably, coincides with a period in which Central's public perception began to fall out of favor, and media reports characterizing Central as one of Kansas City's dangerous and low-performing Black schools became the dominant narrative.

Growing Discontentment with Desegregation

According to the Kansas City, Missouri School District's report of faculty integration, in July 1963, White teachers began "pleading" for transfers from Central Junior High and Central High School.[254] The report also stated that eleven Black teachers would be transferred from the junior high and high schools of Central and Lincoln— teachers who had expressed no desire to be transferred.[255] Among the teachers transferred, particularly the Black teachers, were individuals who truly cared about Central High School and Central's students. Meanwhile, Central High School's student capacity was 2,176, but its enrollment was projected to reach over 3,700 students by 1972.[256] The student population was growing fast, and nearly all of the incoming students were Black. This led desegregation proponents to question the district's efforts toward integration.

Angry patrons representing the Paseo, Southeast, Central, and Manual areas appeared before the district's board of education in June 1963 to protest boundary changes, which the committee alleged "followed the unwritten law that Troost be the boundary separating the White population and Negro population."[257] Such apprehension led to a 1965 article in the *Kansas City Star*, "A Danger of School Resegregation Grows," which suggested that "school systems in many northern and border cities [Kansas City included] are in danger of becoming resegregated Negro school systems."[258] Central was indeed resegregated by 1965, and so were other district high schools. The majority Black high schools in 1965 included Lincoln at 99.9 percent and Paseo at 62.4 percent. [259] The high schools' feeder schools, too, were resegregated, beginning to follow a predictable pattern that became more pronounced over time: schools east of Troost were majority Black, and west of Troost, majority White. So despite the destruction of Kansas City's de jure segregated school system, the district, just ten years after *Brown*, was firmly resegregated.

It is important to remember that Missouri's history is rooted in the "separate but equal" philosophy, especially in schooling. Though public accommodations were never mandated as separate, they were customarily so. As late as 1960, the Missouri Commission on Human Rights stated:

The problems of human rights for minority groups in Missouri reside today in the area of rights not specifically delineated in constitutional, legislative or judicial provisions, i.e., the right of equality of opportunity in the obtaining of employment, upgrading and promotion on the job; specialized education apprenticeship training, public accommodations, housing, health and welfare facilities, recreation and entertainment.[260]

Blacks were prohibited in most Missouri hotels, motels, resorts, restaurants, dining rooms, cafes, soda fountains, and drug store and department store eating facilities.[261] It was not uncommon for a Black family traveling from Kansas City to St. Louis to struggle to find a single café, restaurant, hotel, motel, or resort to accommodate them because there were no state laws in Missouri prohibiting discrimination in public accommodations, at least not until the Public Accommodations Law of 1964. The law was part of the broadest and strongest civil rights legislation since Reconstruction, the Civil Rights Act of 1964.

Less than a year after the March on Washington for Jobs and Freedom, on July 2, 1964, the Civil Rights Act secured passage.[262] The Civil Rights Act of 1964 prohibited segregation and other forms of discrimination in public accommodations, barred segregation in state and locally owned facilities, and gave the attorney general new powers to end school desegregation.[263] Perhaps most importantly, the Civil Rights Act of 1964 gave the attorney general the power to withhold federal funds from segregated school systems.[264]

It was widely assumed in the South that the Civil Rights Act would cause the general destruction of education. Considering that as late as 1965, only 2 percent of Black students were enrolled with White students in the public schools of the Deep South, the carrot-and-stick philosophy of the Civil Rights Act was most certainly designed to force the South to finally desegregate, and in parts of the South it worked well.[265] By 1966, the largest percentage of Black pupils attending school with White pupils was occurring in Texas, Tennessee, and Virginia—Southern states.[266] Border States, including Missouri, proved that desegregation was elusive, as described by United States Commissioner of Education Harold Howe in 1967:

> In addition to the problem of dual school systems, other forms of discrimination may arise in the northern school situation. We are precluded by the language of the Civil Rights Act and by amendments to the Elementary and Secondary Education Act from dealing with the massive problems of segregation resulting from housing patterns (so called "racial imbalance"), but there are additional problems, such as gerrymandered school boundaries, racially determined teacher assignments, and many inequalities in the educational programs that may constitute violations of Title VI.[267]

Kansas City school leaders, in fact, routinely suggested that resegregation was a result of residential segregation. While this is true, it is also clear that the school district engaged in practices, as referenced by Howe, such as gerrymandering of school boundaries, racially determined teacher assignments, and inequalities in educational programs and course offerings, all of which contributed significantly to the separation of the races within schools. Eventually, the school district would fall under the watchful eye of the Office of Civil Rights (OCR). Still, they first would have to answer to the increasingly vocal and numerous local civil rights groups collectively frustrated with Superintendent Hazlett and the district's board of education.

In August of 1964, the Citizens Coordinating Committee (CCC) was formulated with representation from all major civil rights groups, and it became one of the most influential and outspoken critics of the school district's efforts toward desegregation.[268] But it was the Kansas City chapter of the Congress of Racial Equality (CORE) that initiated efforts to effect change with their march to protest resegregation on July 2, 1963.[269] At the march, Dr. Robert Farnsworth, chairman of Kansas City's chapter of CORE, succinctly explained not only what his organization stood for but what many in the Black community were feeling at the time:

> We feel that the school Board of Kansas City, Missouri, has failed to comply with the Supreme Court decision of 1954. The School Board of Kansas City has not actively attempted to undo a history of wrong committed against the Negro citizens of this community. The School Board has not actively planned to provide integrated educational experiences wherever possible. On the contrary, the School Board has acted tardily and grudgingly to permit integration in some instances, but seldom to foster it. Since the Supreme Court decision we have frequently seen White students, in wholesale numbers, permitted to transfer out of integrated schools, thus creating resegregated schools. New school construction has not been planned with the Supreme Court's decision in mind. Boundaries have been shifted . . . and, in many cases, the boundary changes have clearly worked against the Supreme Court's ruling. There has been only token integration of the faculties. There are no Negroes in central administrative positions which affect the problem areas I have just mentioned. . . . Classes of Negro children are bused from the Ladd School to the Humboldt School but are not permitted to join in the integrated activities of the school. We have walked the parade route here to demonstrate publicly our concern for these problems.[270]

In particular, it was the busing of Black students to White schools and their treatment and total segregation within those schools that seemed to elicit particular frustration from both the Black community and their White allies.

As early as 1960, parents of the all-Black Ladd Elementary School called for a new building to alleviate crowded conditions. With the school well beyond capacity, even cloakrooms were used as classrooms.[271] A new building would have to wait, as the district's solution to the overcrowded nature of its majority Black schools in the central city was to bus Black pupils to White schools. Busing, however, did not equate to integration. By 1964, the Kansas City, Missouri School District was busing 1,300 Black students from overcrowded Black schools to under-utilized White schools. In nearly all cases, the Black students were kept separate from the receiving White students.[272] The CCC took issue with the district's busing plan, citing the numerous deprivations that were experienced by bused Black students.[273] When Superintendent Hazlett finally succumbed to the demands of the CCC and announced in October of 1964 that Black students bused to White schools would be integrated within the receiving school, he faced considerable push-back from White parents. White parents did not want their White children "mixed" with Black children, claiming that in other cities, "White children from the homes of a higher cultural level were retarded because of the slower learning of bused-in pupils."[274] Ultimately, White opposition to the busing of Black students resulted in the passage of a $17.5 million bond initiative to build three new elementary schools and a junior high school, all within the area of Central High School.[275] However, it was the district's construction plan that would erupt in controversy and widen the growing rift between the Black community and district leadership.

Havighurst and the Middle School Controversy

"My people are ready to die for the middle school," said one Black individual at a public meeting in 1967.[276] The middle school controversy between 1965 and 1967 fueled racial tensions. Upon passage of the school bond issue in 1965, Superintendent Hazlett immediately began advocating and planning for the construction of three elementary schools in the congested area around Central High School. By 1965, the elementary schools in the Central High School area were "critically overcrowded," with approximately 1,700 elementary pupils being bused out during the 1965–1966 school year.[277] The district estimated in 1965 that the elementary overload in the Central High School area would increase to over four thousand by 1967 and well over six thousand by 1969.[278] Not all schools were similarly overcrowded. The Central High School area was the only "severely overloaded" attendance area at the time, as it was estimated that there were roughly eight thousand available spaces in Kansas City elementary schools in other parts of the district.[279] As such, it was clear that something needed to be done to relieve the overcrowding; the issue was whether the construction of three new elementary schools in the Central High School area was the best approach.

Despite Superintendent Hazlett's assurance in 1965 to a group of parents that the work to build three new elementary schools was "proceeding rapidly," Kansas City's local civil rights organizations were increasingly concerned about the district's construction plan. In July 1965, the Citizen's Coordinating Committee told Hazlett it could not endorse the three school sites where the district board of education had planned to construct the new schools.[280] Thus, an already precarious relationship between Superintendent Hazlett and Kansas City's civil rights organizations grew even more strained. The CCC had concluded that the plan outlined by the district would offer no substantial relief and would only represent a continuation of existing patterns of segregation in Kansas City:

> We are appalled that the public statements emitting from the superintendent's office persist in the claim that an end to bussing will come after the new schools are opened in 1967 when, in fact, the figures compiled by their office show an expectation of drastically increased over-crowding. This appears to be deliberate deception and distortion in fact.[281]

In September of 1965, the CCC and the Kansas City, Missouri Board of Education reached a consensus in which the board agreed to suspend all building activities until after a study was conducted by three outside consultants led by Dr. Robert Havighurst. Dr.

Havighurst was selected as lead consultant in Kansas City because of his work with the Chicago Public School system, where he had conducted a similar study in 1964.[282]

Dr. Havighurst, Dr. William Cobb, and Dr. Norman Drachler released their report, *Problems of Integration in the Kansas City Public Schools*, in November 1965, listing various recommendations.[283] Havighurst's Kansas City study included several major recommendations that took into consideration that the overcrowded nature of Black neighborhoods was about to push into the upper grades and secondary schools. Consequently, the primary recommendations included the following: five or six sites for a junior high school as a way of achieving some "racial mixing," a new senior high school in the Manual area, additional educational services given to the Paseo High School and its surrounding elementary schools to help preserve integration, the appointment of a director of community relations, greater faculty integration, attention to issues of student transfers and busing, and the abandonment of the school district's plan to build a de facto segregated elementary school at Fortieth and Park Avenue and instead to construct an integrated middle school— a new concept at the time—in the area of Brush Creek Boulevard and the Paseo.[284]

The proposed middle school became the foremost issue for local civil rights groups fighting for meaningful integration in the Kansas City, Missouri School District. At the same time, it also symbolized the board of education and Superintendent Hazlett's indifference to it. Upon release of the Havighurst Report, local civil rights groups immediately supported it. However, Superintendent Hazlett was unconvinced, stating that the recommended middle school "pays temporary homage to integration."[285] Hazlett's statements indicated that he assumed that the balanced enrollment that Havighurst projected was inaccurate. Moreover, Hazlett questioned the cost of the middle school project. In 1967, Hazlett made his recommendation to the Kansas City, Missouri School District Board of Education concerning the construction of a middle school in the vicinity of Brush Creek and Paseo:

> Charged with responsibility of as prudent management of funds as possible, I cannot recommend this school simply because we do not have the money to build it without materially affecting other sorely needed projects which were a part of the original building plan. . . . The construction of a middle school from a practical standpoint, therefore, becomes academic. True, land could be acquired and construction delayed until money is available in another bond issue but I cannot propose doing this because of the pressing need to take care of overcrowding and to finish other projects subjected to increasing costs.[286]

Civil rights groups scoffed at Hazlett's statement. They were further angered by his recommendation that the district consider the third elementary school, either to build the school or redeploy to build space elsewhere."[287] Having positioned themselves firmly behind the integrated middle school recommended in the Havighurst Report, Kansas City's civil rights groups, particularly the CCC and the Council for United Action (CUA), stood vehemently in opposition to another elementary school built in the inner city that would only contribute to the segregated nature of the school district.

Ms. Thelma King of the CUA, in particular, became an outspoken critic of Superintendent Hazlett's policies regarding desegregation. His decision against the middle school angered her. In July 1967, King addressed the school board:

> It should be clearly understood that the middle school is but a part of a much larger problem which reflects the failure of our present system of education to provide quality education for all children within the Kansas City School District. It should also be understood that the Council for United Action will not participate in any trading or "dealing" with this board or its superintendent based

solely on the question of whether or not a middle school is to be built or not. . . . The board should clearly understand that we will no longer "compromise" the future of our children. Specifically, we are asking this board, not only to meet its commitment to provide quality integrated education by building the middle school—but to provide a master plan for the integration of all schools in the Kansas City School District.[288]

Charging a betrayal of trust, King and the CUA did not stop at the school board. Following Hazlett's decision and the school board's three-to-two vote in support of the superintendent, the CUA threatened a federal investigation of segregation practices in the public schools of Kansas City, Missouri.[289] On June 23, 1967, Thelma King, in a letter to the OCR, submitted a formal request for an investigation of the Kansas City, Missouri School District. By June 30, 1967, a team of investigators were en route to Kansas City.[290]

Federal Involvement

A federal team of eight OCR educational specialists investigated the Kansas City, Missouri School District between July 17 and July 21, 1967, to determine if the school district complied with Title VI of the Civil Rights Act, which required school systems receiving federal aid to operate without racial discrimination or segregation.[291] The investigators examined teacher and administration recruitment, transfer and promotion, course offerings, and student transfers. Their findings were troubling.

The investigation team discovered that twenty-four Kansas City, Missouri School District schools' faculties were all White, and ten were entirely Black. Moreover, teachers in 1967 signed open contracts whereby the district would hire a teacher and then place them. Eighty-one percent of the Black teachers for the 1967-1968 school year had been assigned to majority-Black schools, while 78 percent of the White teachers had been assigned to majority-White schools. Concerning the administration, the federal investigators suggested "no area of the Kansas City, Missouri School District situation reflects more tellingly its tradition as a dual school system than its allocation of administration. Negro Administration, it appears, are assigned to exclusively Negro schools."[292] In 1967, there were no Black principals at schools where Black students comprised less than 97 percent of the student body, and there were no Black head principals at any of the district high schools. Students, they found, were given a battery of tests at the conclusion of their eighth-grade year to determine their ability group and subsequently were classified as A, B, or C level. Determinations were made based largely on achievement and teacher recommendations. It was concluded that the process and the tracking were not done equitably. Manual High School, roughly all Black by 1967, had no A or B level students and did not offer a single advanced class. Considering student transfers, the investigators explained that if a pupil wanted to transfer, a parent called the board and asked for a list of open schools; no requested applications, they noted, were investigated by the school district.[293] In conclusion, the federal team of investigators stated: "It is undeniable that the graduates of Negro schools in the Kansas City, Missouri, system are at an inferior educational level."[294]

The Department of Health, Education, and Welfare (HEW) sent a different team of investigators to Kansas City in early March of 1968 and found that little had changed since their previous visit roughly eight months before. It must have been clear to Superintendent Hazlett and the board of education that the Kansas City, Missouri School District had caught the eye of federal investigators. It was no surprise, considering Title VI enforcement began pushing north and west from the Southern states late in 1967. The Border States, therefore, would come under heavy scrutiny for years to follow, including Kansas City, Missouri. Hazlett surely anticipated as much, mainly because federal investigators had made two trips to Kansas City in less than a year by the spring of 1968. It is little wonder, then, that Hazlett released his own desegregation plan, "Concepts for Changing Times," in the aftermath of the middle school controversy.[295] The plan coincidentally was released to the public just days after the federal investigators had departed Kansas City for a second time. It dealt with pupil integration at the elementary and secondary levels, faculty integration, and curriculum. Hazlett suggested clustering and pairing elementary schools; creating magnet secondary schools in vocational-technical, performing and fine arts, and science; revising teacher and principal assignment policy; and broadening the curriculum to include pluralistic viewpoints.[296] Having laid out his vision, Hazlett established a so-called "council of thirty," consisting of civil rights organizations, business and real estate groups, organized labor, teacher organizations, PTA representatives, and other citizen bodies. Superintendent Hazlett had already established a reputation among civil rights groups as anti-integration, and it was unlikely that his vision for the future would be welcomed by those who had already lost trust in his leadership. His fate was all but sealed with the district's mishandling of the Dr. Martin Luther King, Jr. funeral service on April 9, 1968, and the events that unfolded in its aftermath.

Riots and Violence

On the morning of Tuesday, April 9, 1968, Alvin Brooks was at the Grace and Holy Temple Cathedral. At the time, Brooks was working for the Kansas City, Missouri School District coordinating efforts involving Title I programming with parents and schools.[297] Sitting among the congregation on Tuesday morning, Brooks remembered how his day was interrupted by an emergency phone call: "They hand him [the minister] a note, and he says 'Is Al Brooks in the congregation?' I said, 'Yes.' He said, 'You have an emergency call.' That was the call that three schools had walked out."[298] The walkout included the majority of students at Manual High School, Lincoln High School, and Central High School, as well as many students at Paseo High School, Southeast High School, and Westport High School.[299] The students were angered by the district's failure to recognize the importance of April 9, 1968, the date of the funeral service for Dr. Martin Luther King, Jr. Still, it was clear that the student walkout ran deeper than it seemed on the surface. Dr. Martin Luther King, Jr.'s funeral service was the initial spark. Yet, the riots that subsequently enveloped the community resulted from longstanding inequalities, many of which involved the Kansas City, Missouri School District.

The Mayor's Commission on Civil Disorder, completed in August 1968, suggested the failure of the district to act on the Havighurst Report was a matter of which the Black community was "acutely aware."[300] Several incidents were a prelude to the April 9, 1968, walkout. One incident, in particular, occurred at Central High School and involved both students and non-students. In November 1967, a disturbance broke out that ended with the involvement of thirty-five policemen. Before it was over, bottles and rocks had been hurled at police officers and their cars; the police had made twelve arrests. The *Kansas City Times* covered the incident, reporting that "three seventeen-year-old boys and nine juveniles were arrested yesterday afternoon following a second day of disturbances outside Central High School, 3221 Indiana."[301] A history of complaints already existed within the Black community against the police department for their treatment of Black residents. Most generally, there was a feeling that Kansas City's White residents favored discrimination against Blacks and gave merely nominal support to the 1964 Public Accommodations Law. That law was granted under Title II of the Civil Rights Act and prohibited discrimination in places of public accommodation (any place that offers goods or services to the general public).[302]

On Friday, April 5, the day after the assassination of Dr. King, the Kansas City, Missouri School District lowered the schools' flags to half-mast and reported that all was quiet; there appeared to be no indication of trouble. Meanwhile, on the Kansas side of the state line, in the immediate aftermath of the assassination, the Kansas City, Kansas School District was busy assisting in a planned student march that would be accompanied by Black police officers, as well as local clergy and the city's mayor.[303] Kansas City, Missouri School District leadership planned no such march. Superintendent Hazlett left for Washington, D.C., on Sunday, April 7, to fulfill his duties as chairman of an advisory committee. Before he left, however, Hazlett announced that school was to be held on Tuesday but that a one-minute moment of silence was to take place in honor of Dr. King.[304] The same day that Hazlett announced Kansas City, Missouri, would hold classes on Tuesday, the Kansas City, Kansas School District—across the state line—announced that schools would be closed, a result of pressure from civil rights groups. At 7:30 a.m. on April 9, the Kansas City public radio station announced open and closed schools, and almost immediately upon hearing that school was open in Kansas City, Missouri, students planned a walkout from Lincoln High School, intending to walk to Central High School.[305]

J. Anthony Snorgrass, a sophomore at Central High School in the spring of 1968, vividly recalled the evening of April 9, the day the riots began:

> I do remember leaving school . . . and things were bubbling, and then getting off work coming back home it suddenly hit pretty hot and heavy. I remember that night, I remember . . . there was a post office, Gates, and my barber shop; it must have been Twenty-Seventh and Indiana back towards the school. I remember seeing all that in flames. I remember, you know, chaos, mass chaos.[306]

In the beginning, though a few cars were overturned and windows broken, the student walkout was mostly peaceful. Alvin Brooks joined the student protest and marched with them to the steps of City Hall, where he and others addressed the crowd. But as Brooks explained, things suddenly turned violent: "Somebody had thrown a Coca-Cola bottle at the feet of the police officer directing traffic at Twelfth and Oak, and that's when the tear gas gets thrown. And the city manager and I hit the ground."[307] The scene was, as Brooks described, "mayhem."[308] There was a report of a priest being struck by a patrolman and another priest, who was coming to the downed priest's aid, being pushed off his feet and overcome by tear gas.[309] Later that day, many student protesters reconvened at Holy Name

Catholic Church around Twenty-Third and Benton. The church was a gathering spot for teens, a safe place for them to hang out on Friday and Saturday nights.[310] As the students proceeded to the basement of the church for a dance on Tuesday evening, April 9, police used tear gas both outside and inside of the church. Eight canisters of tear gas were found in the church.[311] The mood changed to anger. By Wednesday morning, April 10, ninety-four fires had been set, and extensive looting had taken place. Nine people had been wounded, and one person had been killed.[312]

By dawn on Thursday, April 11, 1968, the riots were over, but not before the death of six people, all of them Black, and another thirty-six wounded. Ninety-eight fires had been set in the predominately African American east side neighborhoods, and 312 buildings had been damaged at an estimated cost of nearly $1 million.[313] Those among the dead were Maynard Gough, Charles Martin, George McKinney and his son George McKinney, Jr., Julius Preston Hamilton, and Albert Miller.[314] Four of the individuals had been killed by police officers, and unknown persons had shot two. Many in the Black community were angered by the way the police handled the situation, which was covered in a *Kansas City Star* article, "Negroes Still Angry at Police":

> The Negro community, following the disturbances here, has never been more united in its opposition to the police. While the police are a constant point of friction in almost every lower income Black community, police-community relations in the inner-city area have been [sic] suffered immeasurably.[315]

Moreover, several Black parents suggested that they could never forgive the police for their use of gas at Holy Name Catholic Church, Central High School, and Lincoln High School.[316] Harold Holiday, a Missouri state representative, claimed that the riot solidified the belief among Blacks that there was "one standard of conduct permissible for Whites and another one for Blacks."[317] The riots had an enduring impact on the east side neighborhoods and the schools.

The lack of job opportunities, longstanding problems with the police, and frustrations in housing contributed to the "volatile emotional state of tension and frustration." So too did glaring problems of educational inequality. In 1969, a report by the Missouri School District Reorganization Commission suggested a radical new approach to public education: "While a sensible school district pattern alone will not cure all of the afflictions of the educational system, little progress can be expected without it."[318] A "tempting solution" was the creation of one school district in metropolitan Kansas City and another in metropolitan St. Louis, encompassing in each location the city and surrounding areas. This might more readily address problems of inequality of education and the complexity of racial integration. Interestingly, Superintendent Hazlett had been championing such an approach since the early 1960s and specifically highlighted a similar approach in "Concepts for Changing Times," in which he wrote:

> Any master plan for integration depends on geographic and population characteristics of the community to be served, and the plan must be adapted to those characteristics. The Kansas City School District is 80 square miles in area—only one-fourth the size of the city and a much smaller part of the metropolitan area. It is one of 17 public school districts that furnish educational services to the city. Yet it is the only district in the Missouri part of the metropolitan area that has important problems in integration.[319]

Superintendent Hazlett correctly asserted that the problems of integration and geography were, in the Kansas City metropolitan area, unique to the district. Still, it is also true that the district's track record throughout the 1960s revealed a certain reluctance to embrace meaningful desegregation. Among the most prominent examples of the district's lukewarm approach to desegregation included a lenient transfer policy, reluctance to hire Black administrators and teachers, and a stringent reliance on a neighborhood concept in the face of hardening residential segregation. Superintendent Hazlett eventually succumbed to the pressures of civil rights groups calling for his resignation. He announced his departure on June 5, 1969.[320]

6 | A School in Transition

A 1970 report, *Public Schools of the Southeast Side*, was released to allay fears that the southeast corridor schools were diminishing in quality. The report provided cautious optimism that the district's reading clinics, vocational and technical education, and school facilities would maintain the high standards established in southeast schools in previous years:

> With both increases and changes in population, parents often become concerned about a possible "watering-down" of their children's education. But parents are not alone in this concern. The new programs and technical equipment described earlier in this booklet are but a few of the attempts made by school personnel in the public schools of the Southeast side to maintain the high quality of education which has been characteristic of these schools.[321]

Nonetheless, by 1970, it was apparent that little could be done to keep Whites in the southeast area, regardless of the success of its schools. The southeast part of the city had already undergone a significant demographic shift, and the collective efforts of the real estate industry, the banking industry, and local, state, and federal housing policies were contributing to greater flight.

Central High School and Southeast High School serve as a lens through which neighborhood transformation in Kansas City can be viewed. By the end of the 1960s, Central's student population had been nearly all Black for years, going from all White to all Black between 1955 and 1962. Moreover, the neighborhoods around Central High School had undergone a rapid demographic shift in the second half of the 1950s. Southeast High School, located at Indiana Avenue and East Meyer Boulevard (Sixty-Fourth Street), conversely, was just shy of 3 percent Black during the 1961–1962 school year, the same year that Central High School was over 97 percent Black.[322] By the 1968–1969 school year, Southeast High School was nearly 43 percent Black, and by 1972–1973, it was almost 97 percent Black.[323] The trend of White flight was in a southeasterly pattern, which began in and around Twenty-Seventh Street and the Central High School attendance area, advancing southeast from there. When the report on the southeast side schools was released in 1970, the area was at a critical juncture. Based on the demographic data, Southeast High School continued to lose White students very quickly.

Year	Total # White Students	Total # of Students
1969-1970	819	1403
1970-1971	307	1463
1971-1972	132	1647
1972-1973	57	1894
1973-1974	46	2291

Table 4: Total White Students at Southeast High School between 1969–1974[324]

As the Kansas City, Missouri School District continued to rely on a neighborhood attendance policy into the 1970s, schools served as a microcosm of the neighborhoods in which they resided.

Proponents of the 1968 Fair Housing Act, which extended protections of the Civil Rights Act of 1964 that outlawed discrimination in employment and public education to the sale and rental of housing, hoped that it would create opportunities for people of color.[325] Thus, the Fair Housing Act attempted to respond directly to the harms caused by racial and social isolation upon individuals and communities.[326] Federal policies had historically impaired the ability of Black and

Brown people to acquire land and generate wealth.[327] Policies of the United States government, including housing subsidy and financing programs, promoted home ownership, land acquisition, and wealth accumulation for Whites but not for Blacks.[328] The significance of the 1968 Fair Housing Act was that it shifted the risk of financing inner-city housing to the Federal Housing Administration (FHA). Still, the vast majority of new construction, as a result of the Fair Housing Act, occurred in the suburbs and benefited Whites, not Blacks.[329] Almost 73 percent of the new construction financed through the Fair Housing Act occurred in the suburbs, and 80 percent of those participating were young White couples with children. On the contrary, over 90 percent of those who purchased existing homes due to the subsidy provided by the act were Blacks who were buying homes in all-Black census tracts.[330] As such, the risk-free environment resulting from relaxed mortgage lending standards ushered in a second wave of realtors exploiting Black residents. Consequently, census data for urban and suburban neighborhoods of Kansas City, Missouri, reflected the changing residential patterns of the late 1960s and 1970s. Despite the efforts of east side coalition groups such as Forty Nine-Sixty Three Neighborhood Coalition and the Marlborough Heights Neighborhood Association, which promoted multiracial neighborhoods, Whites continued to make use of FHA loans to resettle in the suburbs, and Blacks continued to secure housing in the urban core, thus reinforcing residential segregation.[331]

The growth of Kansas City's metropolitan suburbs during the late 1960s and 1970s is evident on both the Kansas and Missouri sides of the state line and is reflected in the 1970 census data. Raytown, Missouri, for example, a suburb located just south of the city in Jackson County, almost doubled in size between 1960 and 1970: it grew from 17,083 residents to 33,306.[332] Of the 33,306 residents of Raytown in 1970, 99 percent were White. In Kansas, a similar trend can be seen in population and demographic data for Overland Park, a suburb just southwest of Kansas City, Missouri, in Johnson County. With a population of 28,085 in 1960, Overland Park's population grew by almost 50,000 to 77,934 by 1970. Like Raytown, Missouri, roughly 99 percent of Overland Park, Kansas, residents were White.[333] The census tract around Central High School, by 1970, was 96.8 percent Black, an increase of nearly 15 percent compared to census data from 1960. Additionally, vacant houses in this area jumped to over 14 percent in 1970, up from 4 percent in 1960. Such data supports the idea that the Fair Housing Act of 1968 significantly affected neighborhoods like those surrounding Central High School, as the population was by 1970 almost entirely Black and, based on the unemployment rate and number of vacant houses, less financially stable. As the Central High School attendance area's neighborhood dynamics changed, so did the school's reputation. The dominant White view of the Black inner-city schools was being advanced in local Kansas City newspapers, especially in the *Kansas City Star* and *Kansas City Times*.

Falling Out of Favor

Central High School's reputation began to decline in the late 1960s. By 1970, public perception of Central grew increasingly unfavorable. The first mention of Central's decline occurred in the November 27, 1967, issue of a student publication, when two teachers addressed the Central student body and suggested that the image of Central was "slowly coming to a downfall."[334] A student editorial by Joyce Eddy corroborated what her teachers were saying:

> Dear old Central, far famed Central, two weeks ago, we, as students of Central, went through one of the worst ordeals Central has ever been forced to tolerate. The great name of Central was brought down to a point that it was disgraceful.[335]

The concern for Central's reputation corresponds with incidents that occurred on November 10 and November 11, 1967, outside of Central High School and resulted in the arrest of twelve.[336] Based on the report, those who were arrested were charged with creating a public disturbance; they were accused of throwing bottles and stones at police officers and equipment.[337] Following the November incident and in response to claims that Central High School's reputation was eroding, senior class president Mae Thompson suggested that the media was exaggerating the issue: "I truly believe that Central has become a victim of news sensationalism. The news media is so anxious to get a story that they'll blow up anything and Central just provided the happenings."[338] Few at the time, in 1967, could have predicted the accuracy of such a statement, but Thompson's comments can be viewed in hindsight as a precise premonition.

After the November 1967 incident, Centralites seemed to situate themselves on the defensive, which is understandable considering that nearly all media reports coming out of Central were negative. There was a fight between two female students in 1968, which was followed by an altercation at a basketball game between Central and Southeast High Schools, where one of Central's star players, W. D. Roby, was arrested for felonious assault of two referees.[339] Following the two incidents, Deffanie Harris wrote a student editorial claiming, "Central has a harder time upholding a good image than any other school in the city. . . . Many schools are jealous, jealous of our achievements. . . . Let's stand tall and show them that Central is as great as we think it is."[340] Then, in the spring of 1969, two Central students broke through a window and caused an estimated $10,000 in damage as they "tore through offices and classrooms on three floors, scattering and destroying records and materials."[341] Subsequently, in May of 1969, the *Kansas City Times* ran an article, "New Breed of Student at Central Aims to Change School's Image" and reported, "[T]here is a new breed of student at Central High School whose aim is to improve the school's image and create better student-teacher relationships."[342] Yet, Central High School mathematics teacher Charles Williams claimed, "[T]his isn't a bad school, although Central has apparently picked up a bad reputation."[343] Indeed, local newspapers were littered with negative articles about Central, and the damaging media reports seemed to be taking a toll, as one student noted:

Central has a bad name in the surrounding community. Through the aid of the news media, sporadic incidents that occur at Central or involve Centralites are blown out of proportion and give our school a bad reputation. Those who do not attend Central or are not associated with it in any way readily accept these news items as fact and believe that the majority of those who attend Central are not assets to the community. Is this true? Well of course not![344]

However, the bad press intensified and grew even more widespread throughout the 1970s, which ultimately led to the decision by the district to place armed guards within Central High School:

Authorization by the Board of Education for security guards at Central High School to carry guns is a festering symptom of deep trouble in the schools and the society in which the schools—and all of us—exist . . . when the Board of Education believes firearms are a necessary adjunct to routine discipline, then something is terribly wrong.[345]

Students were troubled by the increased security. Security guards carrying revolvers particularly disturbed them: "I don't think they need guns. All they are going to do is start more trouble."[346] Central students were fed up. One such student, Janell Walden, wrote an insightful editorial in which she stated:

Prejudiced people who are seeking to justify their beliefs and those who are ignorant to the happenings and students in a Black high school—Central High School—would believe that most, if not all, of the students are hall-birds and frustrated English students. Such people would believe that Central high school is a hopeless Blackboard jungle where learning and productivity run a poor second to discipline. . . . Were it such, I would not charge the illustrious *Kansas City Star* with manifesting itself as definitely bigoted toward Central high school—a Black school. . . . It is my estimation that the

Star's article has dealt Central a severe blow, but I am hoping that my out-cry, and all others like it, can help encourage publication of more truthful and consequently inclusive views of the interior of the building at 3221 Indiana Avenue.[347]

Like Walden, Marion Halim and Arthur Jackson, both students at Central in the early 1970s, did not remember Central as a bad place. However, they were aware of Central's slipping reputation. Halim explained:

Well you know what, we had that reputation, but I can't say that I remember that being a reality. I mean, of course there were fights. There were fights at every school, you know. . . . In the neighborhood, there was, you know, violence around there, but I just can't remember that there was a threatening or harmful environment inside of the school.[348]

Jackson affirmed Halim's recollection. "Violent? No. Central was not violent."[349]

Yet the barrage of public negativity and portrayal of Central as the most dangerous and violent school in Kansas City was having an adverse affect on the Central community. "We are tired of being portrayed as underdogs and outcasts by the news media," one Central student said, ". . . but as long as the news media has justification for its stories, it will continue to paint a derogatory tableau of our school."[350] Some of Central's students were so concerned that they took their grievances to the school board, claiming that "the vast majority of students . . . were good students, went to school to learn, did not believe in carrying weapons, and do not engage in fights."[351] Central parents, too, were fed up. In January of 1971 a group of parents who were part of the Community Involvement Committee of Central High School toured the school. One of the parents on the committee, a Mrs. Edward C. Warren, recorded her thoughts in an editorial in the *Kansas City Call*. "That 2,300 children in America in

1971 are allowed to attend a facility that is so inadequately equipped and insufficiently maintained in the riches of the most affluent society in the world," she wrote, "any student who succeeds in an environment such as this could excel any place."[352] The editorial went on to criticize various aspects of the school, from physical deterioration to curricular shortcomings.[353] Morale at Central High School in the early 1970s was low, very low.

Ultimately, this led to the ouster of its principal, David W. Porter, in February of 1972.[354] The bad press did not relent, and the loss of Porter to controversy only contributed to the onslaught. After just a year at the helm, Porter was officially removed from the principalship and reassigned to a temporary administrative capacity. Having previously served as a principal in Dallas, Texas, Porter was pressured out of his leadership position at Central due to demands from parents who alleged that he was "weak" and allowed students to roam the halls and gamble on school grounds.[355] Many students and parents were displeased with the district's decision, though it did not seem to matter much. Upon Porter's dismissal, Daniel Britton stepped into the head spot.[356] In a parting shot to the district administration, Porter, when asked about his removal, said, "I couldn't care less"; he immediately followed the comment with a very different tone and one that speaks to the racial tension at play within the district at the time. He stated: "I'm Black, and I've spent half of a century working with Black people. Those kids have been real nice to me."[357] Central supporters were growing increasingly resentful and indignant about the lack of regard for Central. Such frustration was revealed in the most unlikely of places—a basketball game held in 1972 in Maryville, Missouri.

Riot in Maryville, Missouri

Maryville was the location of the March 1972 district quarterfinal basketball game between suburban and all-White Raytown South High School and Central High School. The fact that the game was being played in Maryville and not Kansas City was largely due to

Central's reputation and the fear among White schools that playing in the inner city would result in conflict. Thus, state officials decided that Maryville, a city with a deeply racist history, was a better location for the basketball game than Kansas City, a decision that Dr. Edward Fields, the school district's head of the Division of Urban Education, said in hindsight was "foolhardy."[358] The decision proved disastrous. A riot broke out between Central spectators and Raytown South spectators following the overtime thriller. Jackson, a team manager for Central's basketball team, recalled the game and the chaos that unfolded in its aftermath:

> The game was close; matter fact Raytown was leading by one. There might have been about 15 or 20 seconds left in the game. Raytown had the ball. Raytown came down, guy drives to the bucket for a shot. He shoots the shot up, Lyonell Harden . . . goes up, blocks his shot, wipes the shot off. Central gets the rebound, the ball's passed out. We were getting ready to run our fast break and this referee that was past half court, blonde haired referee, blows his whistle. [He] comes running down the court and calls goaltending. They already had an official already down there that didn't even call the play and he's right there. Raytown goes to the line and hits two free throws, and now they lead by one. Jack Bush calls a timeout. The scorekeeper didn't stop the clock. . . . we called a timeout with maybe 8 or 10 seconds. . . . they didn't stop the clock . . . [it] ran down to three seconds. . . . Now the only thing you could really do is do the hail Mary. . . . We throw it in. Tim Abney catches it— almost makes a spectacular shot . . . it hits the rim . . . the clock hit zero and it was a stampede. The fight was on.[359]

According to Jackson, the fight lasted a full twenty minutes. "You could hear bottles breaking. . . . I remember seeing the ref that made that call. He had just blood. . . . he was full of blood. You just see chairs flying, people hollering."[360] In the end, fourteen persons were injured, none seriously. The damage was more emotional than physical. Jackson explained: "They cheated us. And they [were] always cheating us."[361]

Immediately following the riot, Central was blamed for the incident and placed on probation, even though the players on both teams had little, if any, involvement in the melee. Bud Lathrop, Raytown South's coach, commented that many of the Central players came to the aid of Raytown South players. Eyewitnesses suggested that, if anything, Raytown South fans provoked the Central crowd with racial epithets and taunts. However, the most harmful aspect of the riot was the media storm that followed the incident. Central was assailed in the local media with more than twenty articles written in the *Kansas City Star* and *Kansas City Times*, and nearly all of them assumed Central's responsibility and guilt in the conflict. Just two days after the game, the nineteen members of the Northwest Missouri School Administrators Association recommended that Central High School be suspended from the Missouri State High School Activities Association, a blow that would affect not only athletics but music, speech, drama, and debate.[362] The decision, officially handed down on March 23, 1972, placed Central on probation for the 1973–1974 school year and banned the team from the 1973 regional basketball tournament, a ban that was eventually lifted in January 1973 with assistance from the NAACP.[363]

The very public and widely circulated Maryville incident served as a culminating event. It affirmed a reputation that all-Black Central High School was a dangerous place, and it was widely believed to be true, especially among Kansas City's Whites. "Central, the school located on Linwood and Indiana, is not as bad as the news media proclaims it to be," wrote Nancy Heydon, a student at all-White Southwest High School who spent the day at Central in March of 1973 as part of a school exchange; she continued:

I have read many times of the prejudice that seemingly existed at Central and, truthfully, was apprehensive of attending the exchange. But, going to Central was a rewarding experience, and I found that the school life at Central is much like my own. But importantly, the people were friendly and congenial. . . . I believe that we need many more school exchanges for we all need to be opened to the lives of each other.[364]

By 1973, White and Black students were attending separate schools and thus were relegated to being in each other's company only during "school exchanges." Whites were not interested in attending "dangerous" all-Black Central High School, nor were they keen on attending district schools with Black students. With Blacks comprising nearly 60 percent of its student population in 1973, the Kansas City, Missouri School District was resegregated, and there was little evidence to suggest that the trend would reverse.

A District in Crisis

As of 1973, nearly all of the school district's high schools were racially segregated. Blacks and Whites lived in different neighborhoods and attended different neighborhood schools.

School	% Black Enrollment	% White Enrollment
Central High School	100%	0%
Lincoln High School	99.7%	.03%
Manual High School	99.9%	.01%
Paseo High School	99.8%	.02%
Southeast High School	97.9%	2.1%
Van Horn High School	.01%	99.9%
Northeast High School	3.1%	96.9%
Southwest High School	6.6%	93.4%
East High School	23%	77%

Table 5: Kansas City, Missouri School District High School Enrollment Data by Race, 1973[365]

Twenty years after the school district had initiated its desegregation plan, its schools were firmly divided by race. This did not go unnoticed by federal investigators, who had been concerned with Kansas City's segregated schools since their first site visit in 1967.

The Kansas City, Missouri School District received its first note of noncompliance from the Department of Health, Education, and Welfare (HEW) in 1971. Still, HEW granted the district a one-year grace period to address deficiencies. The primary areas of concern were not new. They were the same issues that had long caught the ire of Kansas City's civil rights groups: a lack of staff integration, problematic and inequitable administrative assignments, a student transfer policy that too liberally granted White transfers, and an academically talented program that favored Whites.[366] The year 1971 was also the year that the Kansas City, Missouri Human Relations Commission released its report, *Quality of Urban Life*, urging integration of Kansas City, Missouri, students and faculty:

> No progress has been made in integration of the student bodies; on the contrary, the pattern is very distinctly one of re-segregation. Progress on integration of faculties is not uniform throughout the school district. Emphasis should be placed on developing techniques for accomplishing integration—both to assure quality education for all students and to avoid federal intervention.[367]

The report criticized the neighborhood school concept, but it offered a conciliatory tone in stating that "Laying sole blame on the real estate industry for this condition constitutes an easy excuse."[368] The school board, the report determined, "has permitted the student body and faculty of many of its schools to remain predominantly White or to become predominantly Black."[369] The report also outlined specific recommendations, including extending school boundaries to encompass all of Jackson County and considering the implementation of the 1967 Havighurst Plan and 1968 cluster plan, which were controversially never utilized.[370]

Kansas City was not the only Midwestern city confronting educational inequality and segregation; many of America's northern and western states faced similar situations, especially in the Border States. The percentage of Black students in the North and West attending 80 percent to 100 percent "minority" schools in 1970 was 57 percent, more than 13 percent higher than in the South. In the Border States, it was over 60 percent, nearly 20 percent higher than in the South.[371] Comparatively, the percentage of Black students in White schools in the South rose from 18.4 percent in 1968 to 38.1 percent in 1970.[372] Democratic Senator Abraham Ribicoff (who had been Secretary of HEW from 1949 to 1953) explained the discrepancy between desegregation in the North and South in a 1972 congressional address:

> For years we have fought the battle of integration primarily in the South where the problem was severe. It was a long, arduous fight that deserved to be fought and needed to be won. Unfortunately, as the problem of racial isolation has moved north of the Mason-Dixon Line, many northerners have bid an evasive farewell to the 100-year struggle for racial equality. Our motto seems to have been "Do to southerners what you do not want to do to yourself." Good reasons have always been offered, of course, for not moving vigorously ahead in the North as well as the South.[373]

HEW's focus, therefore, had shifted by the early 1970s from the South to the North, and in 1972, HEW subsequently listed Kansas City as one of twelve major Northern cities of concern.[374]

Congress enacted the Emergency School Aid Act (ESAA) in June of 1972 to allow school districts like Kansas City to compete for federal financial assistance to "reduce minority group isolation and to upgrade the quality of education for all students."[375] The ESAA was designed to accomplish three purposes. It was to meet the unique needs arising from school desegregation in elementary and secondary schools, to encourage the voluntary reduction of group isolation in schools with substantial proportions of "minority group students," and to aid school children in overcoming the educational disadvantages of their group isolation.[376]

Falling Short

Beginning with Superintendent James Hazlett, who served from 1955 to 1969, district officials had been bemoaning the effects of residential segregation on efforts toward desegregation, claiming that the district was powerless to effect meaningful change in segregated schooling as a result of segregation in housing and residential neighborhoods. A 1973 article in the *Kansas City Star* addressed the dilemma, defending the school district:

> There can be no question that the Kansas City Schools indeed are disproportionate in racial balance. As examples, consider Central and Lincoln High Schools are all Black and that Paseo has one white student. . . . An urban district such as Kansas City is helpless with its fixed boundaries and pattern of de facto real estate segregation that has existed for many years. . . . It is not fair, and it is wrong but the fact remains that strenuous efforts to desegregate schools within a district quite often will only speed the white migration to the suburbs and other districts.[377]

The district had long argued that any attempt to integrate its schools would result in greater White flight, but HEW was not satisfied with this rationale, and their investigation was lengthy and thorough.

District Judge John A. Pratt's decision in the 1972 case *Adams v. Richardson* established that HEW had failed to enforce compliance with Title VI in numerous states and schools where noncompliance had been determined in 1969 and 1970.[378] Title VI prohibits discrimination on the basis of race, color, and national origin in programs and activities receiving federal financial assistance. The NAACP had taken on the case, and the Secretary of HEW, Elliot Richardson, was the listed defendant. Judge Pratt, in finding that HEW had neglected its responsibilities to enforce desegregation under

Title VI, also ruled that HEW had failed to enforce the *Swann v. Charlotte-Mecklenburg Board of Education* ruling that described as its objective the elimination from public schools "all vestiges of state-imposed segregation."[379] If school districts maintained segregated schools that departed by more than 20 percent from the racial composition of the district as a whole, they were required to provide adequate documentation and justification for doing so.[380]

The *Swann* case, then, established that it was HEW's responsibility to evaluate districts that were out of compliance and withhold funding. The *Adams* case determined HEW was failing to do its job effectively.[381] The Kansas City, Missouri School District was one of the districts out of compliance with the parameters established in *Swann*.

During the 1971–1972 academic year, the district was just over 57 percent Black, but most schools remained highly segregated.[382] Because of this, a lawsuit was filed by the Southern Christian Leadership Conference (SCLC) in Federal District Court in 1973, alleging unlawful racial segregation.[383] The case was dropped in 1974, largely due to SCLC's inability to fund a legal defense team. However, the Kansas City, Missouri School District's legal troubles were far from over, as the *Adams* ruling empowered HEW aggressively to pursue districts out of compliance. In 1973, HEW began its court-ordered enforcement proceedings against eighty-five school districts nationwide that were "substantially disproportionate" in racial composition. Kansas City, Missouri, found itself among the listed districts and was notified on April 17, 1973.

On February 16, 1973, the United States District Court, in the case of *Adams v. Richardson*, entered an order placing Kansas City "on notice" to "rebut or explain the substantial racial disproportion in one or more of the district's schools."[384] Upon receiving Holmes's letter, acting superintendent Glenn Travis responded in a letter of his own dated April 30, 1973, in which he sent OCR statistical data that documented the racial makeup of the district, defended the district's neighborhood school approach, and suggested that residential segregation was to blame for the racial makeup of the school district and not the district itself.[385]

In Kansas City, district officials began preparing an application for ESAA grant money in January of 1973. On January 22, 1973, the Commission on Human Relations commended the Kansas City School Board for taking steps to qualify for the ESAA and urged it to develop and submit an application to the United States Office of Education for funds pursuant to racial isolation.[386] The Office of Education defined racial isolation as a condition in which the enrollment at a school was greater than 50 percent minority.[387]

Despite the public note of encouragement from the Commission on Human Relations and the formation of a Citizens' Advisory Committee consisting of eighty-four members comprised of an equal number of Whites, Blacks, and Hispanics to assist in the ESAA grant application, the district adopted only narrow measures to relieve racial isolation.[388] Busing, in particular, elicited deep emotions, especially among those in opposition to it.

Clustering or pairing of schools was a tactic that HEW and the federal government supported to integrate segregated neighborhood schools. Still, it often involved large-scale busing, and "forced busing" had long been widely opposed by the Kansas City, Missouri School District's White parents. Many White parents did not want their children bused to schools with Black children, nor did they want Black children bused to their White schools. The Van Horn attendance area, which was 99.9 percent White in 1973, was particularly vocal about preserving their all-White schools. Robert Lund of the Van Horn High School's Patrons Association provided insight into the parents' opposition to busing when he stated the following at a public meeting: "I suppose we White people might consider it flattery that some Black people think that just mixing children will give Black children a better education. This is ridiculous."[389]

At the same meeting, an unidentified man in the audience stood up and professed, "We don't want colored out here and they don't want to come."[390]

Ultimately, the Van Horn High School Patrons Association voted unanimously to oppose all desegregation options proposed by the school district. The community hostility toward a plan that included busing options led Bob MacNeven, assistant superintendent, to conclude that the board would not accept a far-reaching desegregation plan. MacNeven went so far as to ask the chief education branch officer for the Office for Civil Rights (OCR) to advise him on the minimum amount of student desegregation the district could undertake that would render them eligible for ESAA funds.[391] Consequently, unsatisfied with the district's grant proposal, HEW initiated a lengthy probe of the Kansas City, Missouri School District in 1973, marking the beginning of a contentious and difficult period for district officials.

Flat Broke and Federal Scrutiny

Between 1969 and 1987, district voters rejected nineteen consecutive bond issue and tax levy initiatives. In 1973, Kansas City constituents had not passed a bond issue or tax levy in four years, a distinct reversal from previous decades in which the school district enjoyed widespread support. Of the seventeen bond issues offered to voters between the district's inception in 1867 and 1956, only one had failed.[392] But the district had changed considerably between 1956 and 1973.

Year	Black Students	White Students	Total Student Population
1956	13,944	49,440	63,384
1973	30,086	26,639	53,725

Table 6: Kansas City, Missouri School District Enrollment by Race[393]

The last year that the district secured a tax levy, 1969, was also the last year the district was majority White, pointing to racial hostility in Kansas City, Missouri.[394] Many middle-class Whites had, by 1969, left for the suburbs. Those who remained were starting to send their White children to parochial schools and seemingly saw little reason or value in supporting a majority Black school district, a district that their children were no longer attending. The district's inability to find money through conventional means meant a growing reliance on federal grants. As early as 1966, the district had applied for and received over $2 million in Title I funding.[395] But as financial constraints grew tighter throughout the 1970s and federal grants more difficult to secure, especially for school districts like Kansas City's that were out of compliance with Title VI of the 1964 Civil Rights Act, the financial hardship fell heavily on the district's teachers.

The teacher strike of 1974, an indication of the growing frustration of district teachers, displaced students for six weeks. The strike incentivized parents, teetering on the edge of pulling their students out of the district, to act. Between the 1974–1975 school year and the 1975–1976 school year, the district lost nearly six thousand students. Those who left either enrolled in private schools or moved to suburban public schools.[396] In only one other two-year time frame, between 1976 and 1978, did the district lose roughly as many students as it did between 1974 and 1976.[397] Many of the district's White parents viewed the teacher strike as the final straw, but the strike was an indication of deeper issues.

In light of the district's financial situation, federal grant acquisition through OCR and ESAA funding became critical. The Kansas City, Missouri School District, as of 1968, received 10 percent of its budget from the federal government. The increase in federal funding was accompanied by greater federal oversight. In a memo to a colleague, the regional representative to the director of OCR noted five "problems" with the district's application for eligibility under ESAA. The five areas included: faculty assignment supporting racially identifiable schools; basic organizational structure of the district, which included an urban education division that oversaw most of the district's Black, inner-city schools; racial composition of classes for the "mentally retarded" that consisted of 78 percent minority students; lack of a bilingual education program; and ability grouping and tracking methods that produced racial segregation of students within "desegregated schools."[398] But OCR was "specifically concerned" with Kansas City's "inter-attendance zone transfer of students" that allowed students to transfer from schools where their race was below 50 percent to a school where their race was above 50 percent.[399] OCR notified the school district on April 3, 1974, that the processing of their ESAA application for 1974 funds had been temporarily suspended.[400]

When they learned of the suspension, the school district scrambled to appease OCR. Still, they continued to advance the argument they had long relied upon: a change in the transfer policy would result in White resentment and, thus, greater flight.[401] By January 1975, the district decided to take a stand against OCR and its claims of noncompliance. Superintendent Medcalf publicly declared that he believed the district had complied with federal demands to carry out civil rights assurances in integration of administrators, discrimination in the Academically Talented Program, and student transfers.[402] HEW did not agree and, in February 1975, it suspended payments to the school district.[403] HEW's approach with the Kansas City, Missouri School District grew bolder. In May, HEW asked a federal judge to force the district to repay all their ESAA funds already spent for the 1974–1975 school year. The prospect of repaying federal funds was alarming for a financially-strapped district.[404]

Meanwhile, the district hurried to devise a plan to satisfy OCR, though the superintendent and school board feared losing White students. For this reason, the school board conceived a plan to integrate some of its schools by busing 2,600 Black students.[405] The plan was almost immediately criticized by parents of Black students, who began an organized effort in opposition to a busing scheme that bused Black students but not White students. Part of the concern lay in the fact that Black parents worried about sending their children to Independence, an area of town that had long exhibited racist tendencies toward Black students. One parent suggested that Independence was "George Wallace country."[406] The Kansas City Chapter of the Southern Christian Leadership Conference (SCLC) was particularly vocal about their displeasure with the district's plan. "The board's desegregation plan is unfair and inequitable. . . . Black parents are just not going to send their kids to Independence."[407] Emmanuel Cleaver, SCLC executive director, was especially determined in his disapproval of busing Black children out of the central city and into nineteen district schools in the northeast part of the district's attendance area: "Only at gunpoint would I put my twins on a bus out to Independence."[408]

The SCLC admonished the district for its desegregation efforts and told the board of education that they could not accept the desegregation plan as proposed. Instead, the SCLC offered a plan calling for a merger of the Kansas City, Missouri School District, and Center School District, a small independent district on the southern edge of Kansas City, which was at the time overwhelmingly majority White. The plan also recommended that the merger include clusters of elementary schools and a consolidated high school.[409] Consistent with its pattern of neglecting the demands of Kansas City's Black community, the district rejected the SCLC's plan, suggesting that the district's desegregation plan that would bus Black students to White schools was "the only way to achieve some measure of desegregation while preventing a massive flight of White parents to the suburbs and private schools."[410] The school district submitted its controversial plan to OCR, which became known as Plan E, and awaited a decision on funding.

It took OCR only four weeks to conclude that Plan E was unacceptable because it preserved segregation at a level of 90 percent or higher in as many as twenty district schools and additionally placed the burden of busing almost solely on Black students.[411] The district responded by scrapping Plan E just over a week after receiving OCR's decision. Subsequently, it opened the 1975–1976 school year without a comprehensive desegregation plan and instead relied on the neighborhood system, in which students attended schools closest to their residence.[412] Given that residential segregation was high in Kansas City, Missouri, the reliance on a neighborhood school attendance policy meant that schools remained highly segregated.

In the wake of the Plan E fiasco, the district formed a community task force, and two separate plans were developed: Plan A and Plan 6. Plan A was described as "total desegregation," so thorough that students of color would comprise two-thirds of every school within the school district through busing, clustering, pairing, and student exchanges.[413] Plan 6 consisted of three options, the most popular of which was Plan 6C, which proposed enrollment of 50 percent Black and White in most schools, though it established 30 percent "minority" enrollment as a minimum. Additionally, the plan provided for a shifting of attendance zones and, like Plan E before it, the busing of over two thousand Black students to White schools on the urban fringe.[414] Predictably, the board voted in favor of Plan 6C despite the opposition of many in the Black community, including the NAACP.

7 | The Ongoing Struggle for Meaningful Desegregation

Following the board's approval of Plan 6C in December of 1976, serious concerns surfaced. The chairman of the community task force, Isaac Gardner, Jr., suggested that the proposal would disrupt the Black community and impose one-way busing, stating that it was "abundantly clear that while this plan conveniently stabilizes several White communities, it totally disrupts the Black community."[415] Likewise, Dr. Cameron, former teacher at Central High School turned NAACP activist, expressed his concerns regarding the fact that Plan 6C left Central, Lincoln, Paseo, and Southeast High Schools and their feeders all Black. He also expressed alarm that Black students would bear the brunt of busing:

> There are still things in it that give me a great deal of concern—like how many Black children are going to be bused. . . . The Black community will not tolerate the wholesale bussing of Black children and negligible busing of white children.[416]

Busing was not just controversial in Kansas City; by 1976, forced busing had garnered national criticism. In the aftermath of Boston's violent opposition to busing in 1974, in which Black children were pelted with eggs, bricks, and bottles, leading to the involvement of the National Guard, Congress in 1975, approved the Byrd Amendment, which prohibited HEW from using funds to require transportation of any student to a school other than the one nearest their home.[417] This proved a problem in Kansas City because Plan 6C relied heavily on busing. In July 1977, Director of OCR David Tatel informed newly appointed superintendent Robert Wheeler that Plan 6C did not "achieve the level of desegregation required by prevailing constitutional and statutory standards."[418] In his letter to Wheeler, Tatel alleged that the plan perpetuated discriminatory attendance zone lines, transported "minority" students away from their neighborhood schools, and limited desegregation at the secondary level, reducing the number of all-Black secondary schools from nine to eight.[419]

OCR recommended modifications, which included implementing a magnet school at Lincoln High School, educational programming at the elementary level to promote desegregation, discontinuing the high school transfer policy, and promoting greater faculty integration.[420] OCR and the school district settled their differences with regard to Plan 6C, as the district agreed to the modifications and subsequently voted them into policy in February of 1978, making them effective in September 1978.

Despite the district's willingness to appease OCR and secure federal funding through the modifications to Plan 6C, their focus had shifted from efforts of intradistrict desegregation to interdistrict. Intradistrict desegregation meant the Kansas City, Missouri School District would have to find a way to integrate its schools within its own district boundaries, whereas an interdistrict remedy would allow the district to integrate by pulling in neighboring school districts, all of which were majority White.

The shift to an interdistrict approach was not new. Superintendent Hazlett publicly recognized the importance of considering metropolitan residential patterns in district policy with his 1968 release of "Concepts for Changing Times," in which he stated:

> Master plans must recognize social, political, and economic realities and the attitudes of people. New patterns of school reorganization and pupil assignment to make schools integrated must be studied in their relationships to the enlargement of de facto residential patterns, the out-migration of white residents.[421]

By 1975, the district was ready to consider a desegregation plan that was metropolitan in scope, and the district's legal team began investigating the possibility of the school district filing a metropolitan desegregation lawsuit. A metropolitan plan, however, was not going to be easily achieved. When the district began entertaining the idea of a metropolitan plan, it was already embroiled in a struggle with HEW for federal funding, and the *Milliken v. Bradley* case had set a legal precedent that made city-suburban desegregation less likely.

In 1970, the NAACP filed a suit against Michigan state officials, including William Milliken, the state's governor, alleging a relationship between housing and education. After a roughly month-long trial, a district court judge ruled in favor of the plaintiffs and provided for creating a massive metropolitan district in Detroit, Michigan, whereby the Detroit public schools would be involved in a cross-busing plan with fifty-three surrounding suburban school districts.[422] The Detroit public schools were majority Black, and the surrounding suburban districts were majority White. Thus, the district court ruling meant that both districts would be required to participate in the desegregation plan. The case, however, eventually reached the Supreme Court on appeal, which overturned the district court's ruling. The Supreme Court ruled that any city-suburban desegregation plan had to demonstrate that the suburbs or the state took actions that contributed to segregation in the city.[423] The decision represented a significant blow to cities such as Kansas City, where the city schools were majority Black and suburban schools were majority White. *Milliken* protected the suburbs, affirming the notion that the suburbs were off-limits with regard to efforts of desegregation within the city. So when the Kansas City, Missouri School District announced its decision to seek city-suburban desegregation, an announcement coincidentally that was made on March 20, 1977, the same day on which the school board approved Plan 6C, it was obvious that the road to metropolitan desegregation would be difficult.

The Suburban Dilemma

The Kansas City, Missouri School District leadership desired to include the suburban school districts in a desegregation remedy, and it began to take shape in 1977 when the district's student population was 63.9 percent Black. This percentage would only increase in subsequent years.[424] Moreover, while the overall percentage of Black students was increasing, the district's total student population was decreasing at an alarming rate.

Year	Total District Student Population	Total White Student Population	Total Black Student Population
1967	74,997	41,399	33,598
1968	74,477	39,630	34,847
1969	72,674	37,332	35,342
1970	70,756	35,252	35,504
1971	68,606	32,986	35,620
1972	64,481	27,183	35,034
1973	62,685	25,455	34,920
1974	56,700	21,405	33,001
1975	53,725	19,090	32,454
1976	51,047	17,560	31,208
1977	45,726	14,378	29,233

Table 7: Total Kansas City, Missouri School District Enrollment, 1967–1977[425]

Between 1967 and 1977, the district's overall student population fell by nearly thirty thousand; the majority went from White to Black.

Those leaving the Kansas City, Missouri School District were relocating to the surrounding metropolitan suburbs. Johnson County, Kansas, and Clay County, Missouri, experienced impressive growth between 1960 and 1980. Johnson County, home to Overland Park, Olathe, Shawnee, and Prairie Village, grew from 217,662 residents in 1960 to 270,269 residents in 1980, and the population remained overwhelmingly White.[426] Likewise, Clay County, Missouri, underwent a similarly noteworthy population growth. Consisting of predominantly White northern suburban towns such as Liberty, Parkville, Gladstone, and North Kansas City, Clay County grew from 87,474 in 1960 to 136,488 in 1980.[427]

The suburban school districts residing within each suburban town on both sides of the state line were also large and mostly all White. Thus, it was not altogether surprising that in 1977, the Missouri Advisory Committee, also known as the Bi-State Committee on Education, suggested a metropolitan desegregation plan was the only way to integrate the Kansas City, Missouri School District meaningfully.

The Bi-State Committee independently assessed over twenty school districts in metropolitan Kansas City.[428] The report, released in January of 1977, was designed to advise the Commission on Civil Rights regarding the "current status of educational activities and problems" in the Metropolitan Kansas City area, as well as the significance of segregated housing patterns and activities of civic and political leadership.[429] The committee called for school districts in Missouri and Kansas to work cooperatively with each other to develop a program of voluntary student transfers and regional magnet schools:

> A well designed voluntary program, with strong community support, could improve significantly the quality of public education throughout the area. At the same time, it would have an important impact in reducing the racial and economic isolation that pervades the school districts in the area.[430]

The committee provided a disclaimer:

> If suburban districts manifested no cooperative interest within two months after the report was released, a suit should be brought seeking a compulsory remedy.[431]

Roughly two months after the report was released in January of 1977, KCMSD did just as the committee suggested and decided to seek a mandatory desegregation plan involving the surrounding suburban school districts.

The work of Daniel Levine and Robert Freilich, both University of Missouri-Kansas City professors, provided the impetus for the lawsuit.[432] Levine and Freilich's study concluded that Kansas City had promising prospects for a metropolitan desegregation plan, mainly based on two prior Supreme Court rulings, *Green v. New Kent County School Board* and *Keyes v. Denver School District*.[433] *Green* established that school districts had to dismantle segregated systems, but it was the *Keyes* case that, according to Levine and Freilich, represented reason for optimism in Kansas City. *Keyes* was the first ruling on school segregation in the North and West, in which the school district was considered responsible for policies that resulted in racial segregation in the school system. This included constructing schools in segregated neighborhoods and gerrymandering attendance zones.[434] Moreover, *Keyes* affirmed that if there was segregation in one part of the district, the entire district was also presumed to be illegally segregated.[435] This reasoning led Freilich to conclude that "if area school districts fostered segregation in the 1950s . . . there could be a 'presumption' that they continued to do so in later years."[436] The challenge was finding a way to include the suburban districts in the remedy. A lawsuit in Kansas City would have to overcome *Milliken* and show that the suburban school district and the state had fostered segregation.

The district's initial lawsuit was huge. Several plaintiff groups were listed, including the Kansas City, Missouri School District and the children of school board members Joyce Stark and Edward Skaggs, and the complaint listed sixty-seven defendants; among them were school districts in both Missouri and Kansas, as well as the federal agencies of Health, Education, and Welfare (HEW), Housing and Urban Development (HUD), and the Department of Transportation (DOT).[437] The core of the complaint was that governmental action, even if it did not have the intent to segregate but did have the effect of segregation, was a Constitutional violation.[438] The plaintiffs argued that the actions of the defendants had resulted in a demographic shift that left the public schools in Kansas City, Missouri, racially isolated and that obligated the state to stop desegregation. In positioning the argument in this way, the district believed that the limitations of *Milliken* could be avoided, thereby opening up the possibility of a mandatory metropolitan remedy. It ultimately hinged on the judicial interpretation.

Judge Russell Clark, a conservative Democrat and a native Missourian who grew up in a small rural area of southern Missouri, presided over the case. Clark had been appointed by President Jimmy Carter in 1977 to the District Court for the Western District of Missouri. Clark believed strongly in public education and supported local school district control and the importance of school boards and school districts having autonomy.[439]

Civil rights lawyer Arthur Benson, only thirty-five years old, was approached in 1979 to represent the school children of the Kansas City, Missouri School District in this case. Benson obliged. Benson was a known civil rights attorney in Kansas City who began his career with the Legal Aid Society before embarking on a legal career in private practice. It took Benson only a short time to establish a reputation as a guardian of the poor. He was known for taking on corrupt car dealers, landlords, and anyone who targeted and exploited the impoverished.[440] With Benson's knowledge of Kansas City, his liberal agenda, and his strong reputation as a civil rights lawyer, he was well-suited to represent the children of the Kansas City, Missouri School District. Benson recalled meeting with Jim Borthwick of Blackwell-Sanders, an attorney who represented the school district, in 1979:

> I can remember Jim Borthwick sitting right across from me and saying, "Here's the deal. The school children have no plaintiff so they need a lawyer. We, Blackwell-Sanders and the school board, really

. . . would like you . . . . We support you if that's your decision."
And they said, "To allay your concerns; the way I see it," and this
is Borthwick speaking. He said, "You'll be sitting in the front of the
boat with the plaintiffs, and we'll be in the center, or we'll be doing
the rowing for the school board."[441]

With such support, Benson took the opportunity to represent the
school children, though soon after he did, the school district, as he
explained, was no longer willing to "sit in the middle and pull the
oars."[442] The district had decided that they could not afford to support
Benson and his case, so Benson looked elsewhere, sending letters to
elicit support, and the NAACP Legal Defense Fund (LDF) agreed to
send two lawyers, Jim Liebman and Teddy Shaw, as well as "a ton of
resources."[443] The NAACP, in the aftermath of the *Milliken* case, was
eager to find a place to seek a viable interdistrict metropolitan plan:
Kansas City, they decided, was the place to do it.

Benson knew that the fight for a metropolitan desegregation
remedy was fraught with obstacles, specifically a conservative
democrat as a judge and a precedent established in *Milliken* that
made interdistrict desegregation challenging. Benson was consumed
with trial preparation materials, conducting nearly three hundred
depositions and hiring twenty-five law students, paid by the LDF, to
conduct extensive research about housing and education.[444] Benson's
intuition, however, proved correct; a metropolitan remedy would be
a struggle. What Judge Clark was seeking was hard evidence, specific
acts of discrimination against Blacks by the suburban school districts
or public officials in the suburbs, and he seemed dissatisfied with the
plaintiff's ability to deliver direct evidence.[445] In Clark's view, there
was no justification for holding the suburbs accountable, thereby
shutting the door to a metropolitan remedial order.

Benson, though, remained hopeful that Clark's willingness
to continue to consider the state's role in segregation meant an
interdistrict plan was still viable. Benson was convinced that the
eleven area suburban school districts and the Kansas City, Missouri

School District could be consolidated into one large district in which students would be mandated to participate in a low-cost metropolitan plan. Benson reasoned that such a plan would mitigate White flight because all schools in the greater metropolitan area would have been involved. Whites would have to participate unless they were willing to move beyond Kansas City's suburbs.[446] Additionally, while Benson's efforts were being poured into proving an interdistrict case against the State, a backup plan was in the works. The backup plan was a remedy that would shift focus from a mandatory desegregation plan to a voluntary one through the use of magnet schools. All the while, Central struggled and revealed how dire the situation had become.

Central and Socioeconomic Decline

In 1976, the Reverend Jesse Jackson visited Kansas City to promote his "Push for Excellence" program (People United to Save Humanity). Rev. Jackson was the president of the organization.[447] The Rainbow PUSH Coalition was a social justice movement that grew out of the Southern Christian Leadership Conference's Operation Breadbasket, which was founded by Rev. Dr. Martin Luther King, Jr. and sought to combine theology and social justice.[448] PUSH Excel was the education arm of the organization that was created to work with Black youth within schools and to encourage school attendance, learning, and instructional competence.[449] At the beginning of the 1977–1978 school year, the program was rolled out in Kansas City at Central High School. Dr. Will McCarther took over leadership of the program at Central, where it would represent one of the first Excel programs in the country. In October of 1977, Jackson was in Kansas City to initiate the program and to personally address Central's students and faculty.[450]

Quite a bit of optimism accompanied Jackson's Project Excel, and for the first time in years, the Central community seemed to revel in a bit of hope. A Central Alumni Association, one of the strongest in the city, had been created in the mid-1970s, and Central's principal, Daniel Britton, by 1977 when Project Excel commenced, had been the leader of the school for six years. This might not seem like long, but given that his two predecessors each lasted fewer than two years, this was indeed progress. Project Excel was garnering widespread publicity, and this time—the first time in a long while—the news coming out of Central was not all negative. Unfortunately, the good vibes were short-lived. Project Excel, which had expanded to another district high school in 1978, East High School, was terminated at Central in 1979.[451] This was followed two years later by the departure of beloved Central principal, Daniel Britton.[452] Just as things were looking up, Central once again was confronted with new challenges.

The early 1980s was a time when Central High School and the neighborhoods around the school were undergoing further transition. Central had already been labeled one of Kansas City's worst and most dangerous inner-city Black schools.[453] Because the area around Central High School had gotten poorer, that perception only strengthened. While the causes of socioeconomic decline in the Central High School attendance area were many and varied, several stand out: disinvestment in the urban core, greater housing opportunities for middle-class Black families in suburban areas, and the financial struggles and declining reputation of the Kansas City, Missouri School District.

With the enactment of fair housing laws, the Community Reinvestment Act of 1977, and the Home Mortgage Disclosure Act of 1975, along with changes to the Act in the 1980s, housing opportunities improved for Black middle-class families who could afford to move out of the central city.[454] Before 1970 and middle-class outmigration, middle-class Black families in inner-city neighborhoods maintained a viable community where these families and their resources were community assets.[455] The outmigration affected the spatial element of the urban neighborhood. The White middle class had long before abandoned Black urban neighborhoods. As opportunities improved for the Black middle class, many took advantage of the chance for bigger and newer houses in the fringe suburbs and fled the inner city. However, by the early 1980s, such movement left urban neighborhoods with higher percentages of people living in poverty than ever before.

Kansas City's urban neighborhoods followed this trend. The historic census data between 1940 and 1980 shows how significantly the area around Central High School changed. Not only did the area transform from almost entirely White to nearly all Black, but it also became less socioeconomically diverse, with the percentage of poor residents growing in number and the middle class declining. The unemployment rate provides a picture of the socioeconomic viability of a neighborhood, and between 1940 and 1970, the unemployment rate in the Central High School attendance area was relatively low. However, the unemployment rate shot up dramatically between 1970 and 1990. The Central High School census tract enjoyed a consistently low unemployment rate through 1970: 4 percent in 1940, 1 percent in 1950, 4 percent again in 1960, and 5 percent in 1970.[456]

Year	National Unemployment Rate	Central High School Attendance Area Unemployment Rate
1980	7.2%	11.6%
1990	6.3%	24.1%

Table 8: Central High Attendance Area Unemployment Rate, 1980 and 1990[457]

Certainly, the socioeconomic makeup of the neighborhood affected Central High School and the other inner-city district schools that served a student population that, by the late 1980s, had become much poorer, while the schools had fewer and fewer resources.

Terry Godard, the seventh of nine children, graduated from Central in 1980. He and all his siblings (except for one of his older brothers) attended Central. Lee Barnes, Jr. and Connie Wright graduated from Central High School in 1982. Their memories provide an informative view of Central in the early 1980s. All three grew up attending Kansas City's public schools and graduated from four-year universities. Godard and Barnes, Jr. received their degrees in engineering. Wright earned her bachelor's degree before getting her master's degree. Each attributed their success in college to their preparation at Central High School in the early 1980s. Wright explained how she was surprised when she got to college, as her preparation seemed superior to that of her college classmates despite the reputation of Central as an inferior all-Black urban high school. Wright described an ever-present bias among her college professors and classmates. When talking about how she felt about her classmates from local suburban schools, she claimed, "They [didn't] know anything; I was totally prepared."[458] Wright described how she was "an inner-city Black girl" but had experienced committed teachers at Central who had prepared her well.[459] At the time, roughly 70 percent of Central's teachers were Black. The Central teachers that Wright recalled most affectionately were almost exclusively Black. Godard and Barnes, Jr. remembered those same Black teachers. They also mentioned that the teachers shouldered a particular burden to ensure their students did not give in to the stereotypes and biases surrounding them. To Wright, it felt as though her Black teachers were still teaching Central students like they were teaching in a segregated school. "They [The teachers] were," she explained, "preparing us to compete with the White man."[460]

Godard, Wright, and Barnes, Jr. spent their childhoods in the neighborhoods around Central High School. Barnes, Jr. explained that his experience growing up in the same house throughout his elementary, junior high, and high school years was beneficial: "That was one of the key elements of the neighborhood. There was some stability."[461] Godard was one of eight in his family to attend Central, and Wright one of ten. They both spoke of a tangible sense of community within the neighborhood and the school. Still, Wright noticed a change in the neighborhood and the school in the late 1970s and early 1980s that she attributed to the busing of neighborhood Central students, her peers, out of Central and into surrounding district high schools that were predominantly White, such as Van Horn and East.

Busing did indeed lower the overall number of students attending Central, as Black students were pulled from their neighborhood schools and bused out into White schools as part of an effort to diversify the district. "We still tease people who went to Van Horn and East," Barnes, Jr. stated, whose wife was among the students who lived in the Central attendance area but spent most of her high school years at East High School.[462] Between the 1975–1976 academic year and the 1983–1984 academic year, Central's total annual enrollment decreased from 2,025 to 682.[463]

The burden of busing had always been one for Black families and Black students to bear; never White students. So it is unsurprising that the technique, once again deployed in the early 1980s, drew the ire of the Black community. "Why does Van Horn have a priority on students living at 29th and Indiana or 34th and Bales? So that white students will not have to be bussed," asked president of the NAACP, Dr. Jeremiah Cameron, whose "N.A.A.C.P. in Action" was a weekly staple in the *Kansas City Call*.[464] Cameron, you might recall from Chapter 5, taught at Central in the 1960s where he claimed to have worked with "the finest and brightest children, black and white." He was a champion of Central High School, which is why he was disgusted with the school district's decision to, once again, appease White interests and undertake a one-way busing program sending Black students away from Central. This time it especially soured Cameron, as it did many in the Black community, because it was being done by the district's first Black superintendent, Robert Wheeler. Wheeler's strategy was no doubt harming Central, a school where he once served as vice principal, and it was resulting in rumors that the school might not survive. As the school lost students, the neighborhoods surrounding it experienced population loss as well.

Neighborhood census data show that the census tract around Central High School significantly decreased in both population and population density between 1970 and 1990, though the size of the tract remained constant at one-half square mile.

Year	Total Population	Population Density Per Sq. Mile
1970	8,260	16,918
1980	6,112	12,524
1990	4,768	9,566

Table 9: Central High School Attendance Area Total Population and Population Density, 1970–1990[465]

Both Godard's and Barnes, Jr.'s families were among those who left the Central attendance area during the 1980s. Godard's parents moved shortly after he graduated in the early 1980s, and Lee Barnes's parents followed in the mid-1980s, both families relocating to the southern portion of Kansas City, Missouri—still in Kansas City but on the southern edge near the suburbs of Raytown, Lee's Summit, and Grandview. "My parents left," Barnes, Jr. explained, "for a nicer, bigger house."[466] Indeed, many Black families left the Central attendance area in the 1980s, a large number of whom headed to the southern part of the city. Census tracts in south Jackson County reveal a noticeable change in the area beginning in the late 1960s and continuing in a southern pattern throughout the 1970s, 1980s, and 1990s, whereby Black families began moving south in the late 1960s and by the 1980s and 1990s were landing in and around southern Jackson County inner suburban communities of Raytown and Grandview. Kansas City, Missouri School District leadership was losing patience. Something had to be done to salvage the district, and that "something" needed to be grand in scale. By 1982, the district had lost over thirty thousand students in the previous fifteen years.[467] The looming question, of course, remained—how could the district be revived?

Voluntary Desegregation

Incorporating magnet schools into the Kansas City, Missouri School District had been suggested by both the Bi-State Committee and the OCR. In their 1977 report, the Bi-State Committee recommended the following with regard to magnet schools:

A stable, quality educational system is the goal of the Bi-State Committee. To achieve this it will be necessary to upgrade education in the entire area. . . . This will require cooperative efforts by all school districts in the area as well as substantial State and Federal financial assistance. Assistance for a magnet school program is needed from local colleges and universities and from the business and civic communities. These magnet schools should be designed in cooperation with the suburban districts to minimize duplication of services and offer the widest possible range of educational opportunities for students in the region.[468]

In 1978, after the district's submission of Plan 6C, OCR Director David Tatel reasoned that turning Lincoln High School into a magnet school might accomplish an increase in White enrollment from 15 percent to 30 percent.[469] The district worked to convert Lincoln High School into a magnet school in September 1978 and renamed it the Lincoln Academy for Accelerated Study.[470] The conversion of Lincoln from a traditional to a magnet school came with $4.2 million in federal funding, and Thomas Eagleton, a Democratic senator from Missouri, proclaimed the district would need "every penny" for the conversion.[471] Lincoln, Eagleton explained, had crumbling plaster, peeling paint, broken light fixtures, and science labs that had been burned in a fire just several weeks before Eagleton's visit. "Why," Eagleton asked, "would a student from Van Horn High School decide to go to Lincoln Academy?"[472] Eagleton's question was valid. The Kansas City, Missouri School District's White students historically showed little interest in attending school with Black students. Given the state of Lincoln's facilities, a new magnet theme was unlikely to attract many White students. However, the district secured funding for updates to Lincoln High School in May 1978, though the budget was tight. Still, Lincoln's transition to a magnet school left district officials hopeful and resulted in the identification of four elementary schools as potential sites for all-day magnet kindergarten programs and a business management philosophy magnet for West High School.[473]

Magnet schools originated in the late 1970s when urban districts, such as the Kansas City, Missouri School District, began seeking alternatives to court-ordered desegregation mandates.[474] Following the United States Court of Appeals ruling in *Morgan v. Kerrigan*, magnet schools became a viable option for desegregation and to make schools attractive to parents, students, and educators.[475] The concept of a magnet school was to offer specialized, unique programs to attract a diverse student body.[476] Magnet schools became popular during the early 1980s as a strategy toward school improvement and desegregation. Their growing attractiveness can be seen in their widespread implementation nationwide from 1980 onward. Part of the appeal of the magnet philosophy in Kansas City was the promising outcomes of magnet implementation in places such as Dallas, Chicago, Los Angeles, New York, and San Diego, as well as Missouri's own St. Louis. Dallas and Chicago, in particular, Thomas Eagleton noted in a letter to Hale Champion of HEW, attracted students with their "brand-spanking new facilities" and "truly challenging and innovative curricula."[477]

By the 1983–1984 school year, Los Angeles had magnet programs at the elementary, junior high, and senior high levels, and evaluations showed students in nearly all the magnet programs scoring at or above both district and national levels.[478] Results in New York were equally impressive. A 1985 study of forty-one of the one hundred magnet schools across eight New York districts provided extensive evidence that magnet schools could improve educational quality, suggesting that choice was a powerful incentive in improving New York schools.[479] By 1984, the magnet schools of Milwaukee had grown to include twenty elementary and middle schools and five senior high schools. Black students were attending suburban schools, and White students were attending city schools.[480] San Diego Public Schools had implemented a voluntary desegregation plan and used magnet schools, which proved popular and successful.[481] In St. Louis, Missouri, a magnet plan was initiated in 1981, which resulted in an interdistrict desegregation plan that brought Whites to the city's magnet schools.[482] Despite the optimism surrounding magnet schools in the early 1980s, they were not a panacea; magnet schools were not trouble-free.

Magnet schools were intended to entice parents to remove their children from their home schools and place them in specialty schools possibly outside of their neighborhood school.[483] While magnet schools provided an alternative to forced busing and mandatory desegregation, there was danger in the magnet theme that stemmed from their selectivity and elitism. Thus, there was a risk of establishing a two-tiered system within urban school districts whereby low-achieving students would attend poorly functioning traditional schools, and academically oriented magnet schools would house the highest-performing students. Often, this two-tiered system had racial implications:

> Lots of places were doing magnet schools. So what they do is they take an all-Black school and the first thing they do is throw out half of the Blacks. Well, that's not good. And then they spend more money on that school to attract Whites in. So it's doubly discriminatory. Half the Blacks become victims of the remedy and then you have the perception that a school's only worth spending more money on if you're going to try to get Whites to come.[484]

To avoid such a system in Kansas City, Daniel Levine and Eugene Eubanks, both of whom were professors in the Department of Education at the University of Missouri-Kansas City and had significant involvement in desegregation efforts in Kansas City, suggested three key guidelines: "Magnetize" as many schools as possible to provide maximum opportunity, take steps to improve the effectiveness of education in schools that are left as traditional, and minimize the use of academic criteria in magnet admissions.[485]

Employing a comprehensive magnet concept would, it was thought, avoid detracting from the quality of instruction in inner-city schools that resulted from the draining off of the best students and teachers and thereby leaving them even more devoid of positive academic leadership than they were in the first place.[486] The vision that was being championed by Levine and Eubanks was both systematic and transformative. Houston, Cincinnati, and Chicago were looked to as examples of how magnet schools could attract young middle-class families back into the city. By the early 1980s, big urban school districts, including the Kansas City, Missouri School District, were at a critical juncture. While most White families had already left the cities for the suburbs, many middle-class Black families remained, yet this began to change throughout the decade. As housing opportunities opened for Blacks in the fringe suburbs, middle-class Black families began to leave the central city. Thus, the early 1980s signify a time when urban schools, already strapped for cash, faced a declining tax base, old and decrepit buildings, and an increasingly impoverished population of students. Central High School provides a particularly compelling example of this phenomenon.

Moving Forward with Magnets

"Grown men would cry," explained attorney Arthur Benson, referring to the physical deterioration of the Kansas City, Missouri School District, which by the mid-1980s was in bad shape.[487] He continued:

> I mean, the school district had no financing. The buildings were just so dilapidated. . . . I mean they were foul and stinky and oppressively hot in the winter and people would come out almost gagging. And the president of the Kansas City Southern Railroad was crying when he came out of one of these schools. He said, "I cannot believe that there are children in our community that I am responsible for that we are educating in conditions like this." Fire code violations, I mean, just horrible.[488]

A board-commissioned study in 1980 found that just bringing the district buildings into compliance with code and safety regulations and meeting minimal educational standards would cost more than

$36 million.[489] At the same time, the district's financial situation was dire. By 1984, it had been fifteen years since voters had passed a tax levy.[490] In 1969, when the last tax levy had been passed, the Kansas City, Missouri School District consisted of 72,674 students; that number dwindled to 36,650 in 1984.[491]

The Plaintiff's counsel, Arthur Benson, was optimistic that Judge Clark would rule in their favor and against the state, ordering an interdistrict remedy at the state's expense. This stemmed from the September 1984 ruling in which Judge Clark ruled in favor of the district children, the plaintiffs, and against the school district and the state. Thus, Clark found that the Kansas City, Missouri School District had suffered continuous effects of pre-1954 segregation and that the State of Missouri had failed to correct the problem:

> Since the State under its Constitution has the duty to establish and maintain free public schools, it has the primary responsibility for insuring that the public education systems in the State comport with the United States Constitution. The State Board of Education and the Kansas City, Missouri School District Board of Education have much more expertise than this Court in the operation and management of public schools within this State . . . the State Board of Education and the Kansas City, Missouri School District Board of Education are hereby directed to prepare a plan which would establish a unitary school system within the Kansas City, Missouri School District.[492]

Working alongside the district, Arthur Benson and his team of litigators focused on convincing Clark to accept a two-way busing plan that involved sending urban students to suburban schools and suburban students to urban schools—a true metropolitan-wide plan.

For district supporters, Judge Clark's ruling could not come too soon. As mentioned, the district's financial problems were mounting, which was exacerbating the steady yet alarming decline in enrollment and departure of both affluent businesses and middle-class and upper-class residents from the district's attendance area. This, accompanied by the district's failure to secure consistent federal assistance, made it clear that something needed to be done. For Arthur Benson and the Kansas City, Missouri School District, it was hoped that it would be an interdistrict, metropolitan desegregation remedy, but it ultimately hinged on Judge Clark's judgment. And while the metropolitan plan was a laborious undertaking that required years of forethought, it took Clark no more than a week to dismiss it.[493] Clark referred to the metropolitan plan as "thorough" and "thoughtful," but offered the opinion that the proposal went beyond the nature and extent of the constitutional violation.[494] Instead, Clark ordered that a plan be developed that only involved schools within the Kansas City, Missouri School District.

With the possibility of an interdistrict desegregation policy officially off the table, Benson and his team of litigators and educational experts reluctantly turned to magnet schools as a remedy:

> We recognized there were a lot of problems with magnet . . . and we didn't want to do it. Because they would not be fully effective the way that they had traditionally been done. Plus, they were expensive and we thought they were discriminatory.[495]

Many magnet schools had been designed as selective schools with certain admission requirements—an exam, portfolio, or audition determining one's acceptance. In this way, magnet schools seemed to privilege certain students over others, resulting in inequitable access to resources and opportunities.[496] Benson recognized the discriminatory process by which magnets had historically functioned and pledged to avoid replicating such a system in Kansas City. The new magnet plan, as imagined by Benson's team, required massive educational improvements available to all students. The vision, therefore, for the voluntary interdistrict remedy included, as Benson explained, a plan to "magnetize the entire district."[497] Transforming most of the district's schools into magnet schools solved the problem of access, but the critical issue that remained uncertain was how such a plan would be paid for.

The financing of a remedial plan proved to be a divisive issue from the beginning, and when Judge Clark adopted a magnet remedy in June of 1986, it was clear that costs would be high. Conservative Missouri Attorney General William Webster and conservative Governor John Ashcroft were determined to safeguard the state and limit its fiscal responsibility. Already involved in a costly desegregation settlement in St. Louis, the State of Missouri was motivated to push back another expensive desegregation plan in Kansas City. Thus, the State opposed nearly every recommendation advanced by Dr. Eugene Eubanks and the Desegregation Monitoring Committee (DMC), a committee established by Clark to oversee the implementation and effectiveness of Kansas City, Missouri School District's desegregation efforts. Consequently, the more than 30-year *Jenkins* court case developed into a collection of appeals, whereby the DMC would make a suggestion to the court, and the State of Missouri would appeal the measure.[498] But by July 1986, the district had a clear vision, and Clark appeared fully supportive despite the State's defiance.

The Long Range Magnet Plan was principally devised by two educational consultants, Daniel Levine and Phale Hale, but also involved the expertise and support of school district officials and plaintiff's attorneys. It was a comprehensive plan that detailed the conversion of all of the district high schools and middle schools and approximately half of the elementary schools to magnet schools.[499] Only eighteen elementary schools were not part of the magnet plan. Instead, they were involved in the district's Effective Schools program, which left the school in its traditional format but emphasized a uniform Effective Schools framework, emphasizing a philosophical approach that all students can learn and embodying the notion that schools must be held accountable. The Effective Schools movement was built upon principles that included active parental participation, a clear and focused mission, and frequent monitoring of student progress.[500] The eighteen Effective Schools in Kansas City were dubbed the

"Black corridor schools" and were referred to as such because they consisted of a student body that was all Black and resided deep within neighborhoods that were also all Black.[501] District administrators did not foresee a magnet theme attracting White students to these particular elementary schools and thus decided on an Effective Schools program instead.[502] The State, however, argued that the proposed magnet plan, despite leaving eighteen elementary schools in a traditional format, was hastily drafted and converted too many of the district's schools into magnet schools.[503] The court acknowledged the State's position but affirmed the plan with convincing language:

> The Court finds that the proposed plan would serve the objectives of its overall desegregation program. First, the carefully chosen magnet themes would provide a greater educational opportunity to all Kansas City, Missouri School District students. The plan magnetizes such a large number of schools that every high school and middle school student will attend a magnet school. At the elementary level, there would be a sufficient number of magnets to permit every student desiring to attend a magnet school to do so.[504]

The design of the magnet plan in Kansas City was unique in its all-inclusive nature, done to avoid issues of inequity and the formation of a two-tier educational system. The Long Range Magnet Plan, as it was called, identified the 1991–1992 academic year as the target date for completion. Considering the scope of the project, the five- to six-year window seemed reasonable, as the district faced a considerable amount of building renovation and new construction to implement the far-ranging magnet themes, which included foreign languages, computers, performing arts, agribusiness, environmental science, engineering and technology, health professions, and classical Greek.[505] Indeed, the plan was costly, with a projected six-year implementation phase of $143 million and an additional $53 million in capital improvements.[506]

The capital improvements were slotted for eleven district schools that required work to ready them for the new magnet theme. Additionally, some of the $53 million accounted for four new schools. Despite the State's insistence that the condition of the district's schools was a result of lack of maintenance on the part of the Kansas City, Missouri School District, the court did not agree:

> The Court finds that even if the State by its constitutional violations and subsequent failure to affirmatively act to remove the vestiges of the dual school system did not directly cause the deterioration of the school facilities it certainly contributed to, if not precipitated, an atmosphere which prevented the Kansas City, Missouri School District from raising the necessary funds to maintain its schools. Furthermore, the capital facilities program requested by the Kansas City, Missouri School District is a proper remedy through which to remove the vestiges of racial segregation, and is needed to attract non-minority students back to Kansas City, Missouri School District.[507]

The district, it appears, was benefiting from a court that had bought into the notion that the substantial resources requested were reasonable, considering that the "constitutional violations committed were also substantial."[508] Although the State of Missouri appealed the court's order, its appeals failed; neither the Eighth Circuit Court of Appeals nor the Supreme Court were willing to oppose Clark's support of The Long Range Plan. With the district's magnet plan firmly in place, work began toward implementation.

Educational consultant Richard C. Hunter, a professor from the University of North Carolina and former superintendent of the Richmond, Virginia, and Dayton, Ohio, public schools, was commissioned by the district to evaluate the extent of capital improvement needs. His evaluation involved a school-by-school assessment of all the district's schools and some of the surrounding suburban schools. Dr. Hunter's 1987 report was thorough and troubling:

> The school buildings are generally very old and in poor condition. The Kansas City, Missouri School District has failed to obtain necessary financial resources from the community and the state for proper maintenance, substantial renovation, or replacement of the school buildings. Thus, some have become unserviceable. Over the years, several unsuccessful attempts have been made to pass capital improvements bond issues.[509]

At the time of the report, in January of 1987, the Kansas City, Missouri School District consisted of eighty-one buildings: fifty elementary schools, eight junior high schools, nine high schools, and fourteen special or closed schools. The average age of the buildings was 53.8 years, with eleven buildings having been built seventy-five or more years before.[510] Moreover, Hunter concluded that the district's schools adversely affected education and discouraged parents from enrolling their children in the district and that the buildings represented safety and health hazards.[511] The report concluded that seventeen schools should be demolished, twenty-one should be constructed anew, and all of the buildings should be renovated for a projected cost of $265 million.[512]

Hunter's assessment of Central High School represented how decrepit the district schools had become and how massive Kansas City, Missouri's magnet-themed project would be. He described Central High School as being in the worst condition of any of the district secondary schools, noting it was "deplorable."[513] In his deposition, Hunter explained that Central required work on both the inside and outside. He suggested the outside of the building needed "a lot of work," but the inside was the most distressing. Hunter suggested that Central was "just a depressing facility to walk in." In several parts of the building, paint was peeling from the walls, and the ceiling was collapsing due to severe water damage. In the auditorium, Hunter claimed that the daylight peered through a hole in the roof.[514] Arthur Rainwater, principal at Central High School from 1989 to 1990 and later an assistant to the superintendent, remembered Central to be in terrible condition when he assumed his position as principal: "My office was on the top floor of the building and we had buckets out on the floor when it would rain. I mean it was really in bad shape."[515]

Central, however, represented only one of many buildings that Hunter determined needed to be rebuilt or renovated. Upon receipt of Hunter's report, the school board, the DMC, and Judge Clark approved it. In a show of support for upgrading the district's facilities, Clark, in a September 1987 ruling, exercised the court's "broad equitable power to remedy the evils of segregation" by ordering a tax increase on the residents of Kansas City, Missouri.[516] Clark's reasoning was based on the notion that the majority had no right to deny others their constitutional rights:

> This Court, having found that vestiges of unconstitutional discrimination still exist in the Kansas City, Missouri School District, is not so callous as to accept the proposition that it is helpless to enforce a remedy to correct past violations. Failure of the Kansas City, Missouri School District to come forward with its share of funds to implement the remedial plan would certainly operate to hinder vindication of federal constitutional guarantees to which the school children in the Kansas City, Missouri School District are entitled. This Court cannot shrink its sworn duty to uphold the Constitution of the United States. . . . The Court is of the firm conclusion that it has no alternative but to impose tax measures which will enable the Kansas City, Missouri School District to meet its share of the cost.[517]

Thus, Clark imposed a 1.5 percent increase on the Missouri State Income Tax, which raised the tax to 7.5 percent on residents and non-residents of the Kansas City, Missouri School District alike, as well as business associations, partnerships, and corporations who earned salaries, wages, commissions and all other compensation subject to the Missouri State Income Tax. Additionally, Clark raised the property tax of Kansas City, Missouri School District residents by $1.95 per $100 assessed valuation, which amounted to over $27 million annually.[518]

Clark's decision resulted in an almost immediate backlash and cries of an imperial judiciary. The income tax surcharge was appealed and overturned just a year after Clark's decision, but the increase in property tax withstood an appeal to the Supreme Court. By 1987, the district's magnet plan was unfolding as well as could have been hoped by its supporters. Judge Clark fully supported the district's Long Range Magnet Plan, and the State of Missouri was held responsible for much of the financial burden. But 1987 was just the beginning, and there is perhaps no better demonstration of how the magnet concept materialized than the example of Central High School.

8 | Central Computers Unlimited/Classical Greek High School

In 1987, a district task force was established with the intended purpose of transitioning Central High School from a traditional high school to a magnet school, focusing on computer technology and classical Greek and Olympic athletic competition. The unique curricula of Central's magnet theme required a unique building.[519] The Long Range Magnet Plan had established overall standards for magnet program development, including guidelines for a new Central High School, which was to provide exceptional features that would attract White parents and students from surrounding private schools and suburban schools to choose to attend Central voluntarily. To obtain the court-ordered 40 percent White enrollment, the scope of the programs was considered essential, as Central would be a challenge to desegregate:

> Central High School promises to be the most difficult school to desegregate, both because of its location in the highly segregated central corridor of the city and because of its reputation as a problem school with a history of academic failure. . . . In order to attract white students, Central must offer an exceptional program in an exceptional facility.[520]

Accordingly, the new Central High School was to be spacious and robustly equipped with the latest computer technology, sports, and physical education equipment and facilities.

The new building's design was impressive, especially the natatorium, which was planned to house all the aquatic sports.

The pool included a six-foot-by-six-foot underwater window with observation space, underwater speakers for synchronized swimming, two one-meter diving boards, two three-meter diving boards, a platform diving tower, a gutter system for overflow and circulation, a hydrostatic relief system for stabilization, and an automatic timing system with scoreboard.[521] The aquatic facility was intended for school and community use in recreational and competitive swimming and diving, as well as water polo and synchronized swimming.

In addition to the natatorium, the new Central would have a state-of-the-art field house to accommodate gymnastics, basketball, and indoor track and field, among other sports. The overall concept of the athletic facilities was to create an environment conducive to attracting and developing young people for world-class competition.[522]

On the computer side, the new building was to have roughly one thousand computers in total, with fifteen computer-equipped classrooms, each having twenty-five computers in a perimeter arrangement, as well as six computer-equipped science labs; several specialized computer labs, including a graphic arts lab, robotics lab, electronics lab, drafting design lab, and two business labs; four computer programming classrooms; and a computer mainframe or resource room for Central students to use during extended-day opportunities.[523] While this might not seem impressive by today's standards, at the time, it was. After all, computers were not even found in classrooms until the early 1980s.

With the new building planned to open during the 1991–1992 academic year, Central Computers Unlimited/Classical Greek Magnet High School was going to be, its supporters proclaimed, one of the best and most unique secondary schools in the nation. The new building's design was remarkable, but it was also expensive. The site location had been decided in 1987, which was the least disruptive of the three sites considered, as it required little additional land acquisition.[524] The new building wrapped around the old building and was built within a few feet of it. Initially, in 1986, the district estimated the new Central would cost $15,243,050, and the court agreed. By 1988, however, the district began considering an increase in the construction budget, which was approved by the court's DMC and eventually by Judge Clark. Thus, construction costs were raised, increasing the overall cost of Central from just over $15 million to $23,474,615.[525] The State of Missouri vehemently opposed the measure:

> One is left with the conclusion that the Kansas City, Missouri School District's motion to modify the construction budget regarding Central is the result of educators creating a wish list. One can imagine the district educators reviewing the Court's approved programs and insisting on the inclusion of frill after frill, like sharks in a feeding frenzy. . . . It is an outrage that the district has chosen to make a sham of the desegregation process, converting it into something resembling a money grab.[526]

Despite the State's opposition, the Kansas City, Missouri School District insisted that the new Central High School was within the parameters outlined by the Long Range Magnet Plan, and Judge Clark supported the assertion. Construction of the new Central High School moved forward as planned, with a completion date of fall 1991.

The Kansas City, Missouri School District hired Arthur Rainwater as Central's principal in 1989. Before assuming the principalship at Central, Rainwater had spent his career in Catholic education. He was hired chiefly for his expertise in athletics and technology:

> My background was certainly in athletics, and I also had spent a lot of time working with technology in schools. I was, at that time, very technology proficient, and so that particular job appealed to me because of the dual magnet themes.[527]

Rainwater, who led the planning task force, remembered Central Magnet's planning phase as "fun," though the job was a big one considering the project's scope.[528] As noted, Central's magnet theme was conceptualized with two academic tracks; one was constructed around computers and technology, and the other in classical Greek and athletics. The computer side emphasized the growing interest in computer technology: "Computers unlimited magnet schools will provide students with educational opportunities specifically in computer technology and information technology to a greater extent than they are presently offered in the Kansas City metropolitan area."[529] Computers, Rainwater noted, were the "vehicle for communication, computation, and management."[530] The feeder schools for the computers unlimited magnet program were Richardson Elementary and Central Middle School, just next door to Central High School. Access was of critical importance for the computer magnet schools. The availability of appropriate computer hardware and software was essential for proper implementation.

All classrooms at Central Magnet were designed to be equipped with twenty-five computers, and the computers would be used in three ways: through academic core classes, computer-themed classes, and direct instruction.[531] Computers would serve as an instructional tool in all traditional academic courses so that students would use computers as everyday learning tools. In computer-themed classes, computers would provide a broad base of computer knowledge and taught in "specially equipped laboratories," thus qualifying students for college, training programs, and job entry.[532] The management of instruction, it was suggested, would revolve around computers and technology, in which classrooms, teacher preparation spaces, laboratories, administrative offices, and secretarial stations would all employ computers and promote a paperless environment.[533] Central Computers Unlimited High School would also cooperate with the city's leading businesses and universities to prepare graduates for entry into college or directly into the workforce.[534]

The classical Greek side of the curriculum was based on the principle of "a sound mind in a sound body" and was designed to provide students with a strong liberal arts education featuring philosophy, debate, forensics, and "pursuit of Greek culture" in addition to a unique and comprehensive athletic program that would be built around the ideals of the Olympiad.[535] It was hoped that the classical Greek program would attract students, particularly suburban students, interested in Olympic sports, such as aquatics, fencing, or martial arts. While it was thought Central would attract serious athletes, the school was open to students of all athletic ability levels. The state-of-the-art facilities and top-notch coaches would allow all students to reach their fullest potential and allow many to develop to a nationally competitive level.[536]

The athletic program was to be demanding. Students would be required to participate in one individual sport and one team sport, which would be part of the student's personal development plan utilized to maximize physical development throughout the student's four years in high school.[537] By providing unique Olympic athletic programs, Central would offer "tremendous opportunities for inner-city kids" while also attracting suburban students and parents seeking to replace expensive and inconvenient out-of-school athletic programs, such as swimming or gymnastics.[538] The athletics program was split between two paths, one consisting of "interscholastic athletics" and the other, Olympic development.[539] The interscholastic pathway was designed for students wanting to compete in traditional high school sports, such as basketball, baseball, or football. However, students participating in interscholastic sports were required to partake in two different sports, one of which would be individual and the other team. The Olympic program was to include a rigorous twelve-month training program in one sport, with the training designed to assist students in reaching a high skill level in their sport of choice.[540] But the classical Greek magnet would not focus on only athletics, as the academic programming was to be attractive as well.

Central was the only school in the Kansas City, Missouri School District that would offer a classical education. Rainwater suggested that the academics on the Greek side would be particularly challenging:

> I think you will find that the Greek program has probably the most rigorous academic programs in the whole city. . . . The academic

program, on the Greek side particularly, is so demanding and so structured that it is every bit a co-equal part.[541]

The emphasis on a robust academic curriculum was partly motivated by fear that if a solid academic program were not exceptional at a magnet school promoting athletics, it would turn into a place to "dump" athletes.[542] Therefore, the site task force designed the classical Greek curriculum to include a required classical studies component. As part of the classical studies, Central students would have to complete a sports biology class, as well as classical Greek, Greek art and archeology, Greek literature and philosophy, and Greek drama.[543] The task force was careful to ensure that the public perception of Central's dual tracks—computers and classical Greek— not be one of computers versus athletics but a dual curriculum school designed for students interested in computers and athletics with a common aim of academic excellence.

While the new Central would not be ready until 1991, in the fall of 1988, the old Central was equipped with technology upgrades to incorporate the initial phase of computer magnet programming. In August of 1988, Central High School opened its doors as a computer magnet high school; the classical Greek and Olympic athletic magnet would not be implemented until 1991. Central students like Crystal Shakur and Daryl Norton were eager to get started. A new era had begun.

The First Magnet Students

When Shakur entered Central High School for her senior year in 1988, the Central Computers Unlimited Magnet, as it was renamed, still occupied the old 1915 building. However, it had received a facelift and had been rewired to accommodate computer technology. The comprehensive magnet plan was underway, but would it work—would it lead to greater integration and improved academic performance?

Shakur recalled a thrust to incorporate computers into the curriculum in her senior year, 1988–1989, the first year of the magnet program. District administrators understood that implementing a new computer-themed magnet would take time to effect a shift in the demographic makeup of the school. Arthur Rainwater explained the district's cautious optimism: "people expect an immediate turnaround, and that just isn't going to happen. It is going to take a long time to remedy the vestiges of desegregation that were here."[544] Thus, during the first year of implementation, seniors like Shakur would not benefit as greatly as students who entered Central Computers Unlimited as freshmen in 1988 and spent four full years in the program. The implementation phase, monitored by annual formative evaluations, was viewed as a three-year process, and success was to be reported in a summative assessment relying on achievement test results, interviews, and observations.[545] The 1988–1989 formative report revealed how slowly change might unfold. Enrollment increased from 809 to 967. The number of "non-minority" students increased from one out of thirty-seven or under 1 percent to 4 percent. Student achievement continued to lag well behind both district and state averages.[546] The Long Range Magnet School Plan emphasized the need for "major" improvements in the mathematics curriculum and instruction.[547] Central's tenth-grade students' scores, for example, in the math portion of the Missouri Mastery and Achievement Tests (MMAT)—given at the third, sixth, eighth, and tenth grades and based on core competencies and critical skills—jumped from 249 to 282 between 1987 and 1989. Still, it was ten points behind the district-wide average and nearly fifty points behind the statewide average.[548] Moreover, mean math and science scores across all grade levels on the Tests of Academic Proficiency (TAP) measuring basic skills in reading, math, written expression, science, and social studies were lower at Central than the district-wide mean scores.[549]

Shakur, though recognizing the push to incorporate computers in the classroom and acknowledging the availability of computer technology, did not notice a significant difference in her education or in the facility after the initiation of the magnet program in 1988, despite the roughly $37 million in capital improvements under the court's 1985 order and over $8 million annual budget increase for magnet implementation:[550] "The only thing was," Shakur explained, "the programs just were different. That's the only thing I noticed . . . I didn't really notice how the money may have come in."[551] The reality was that most high school students were not tuned in to the details of the magnet program, and why would they be? As adolescents, most only had a cursory understanding of the why behind the magnet philosophy. This was true of Shakur, who was not particularly interested in computers. A self-described "people-person," Shakur claimed to have had some knowledge of the magnet plan from her service on the student council and participation in a 1988 marketing campaign for the new magnet school. And though Shakur never felt a passion for computers, her allegiance to Central, her neighborhood school, was strong enough that she was not tempted to attend a different school. She stayed with Central for her final year of high school.

Like Shakur, Daryl Norton, a junior at Central in 1988, had little awareness of the magnet plan or impending court case. However, Norton was intrigued by computers and welcomed the new emphasis on computer technology.[552] Norton recalled, specifically, a meeting with then principal Arthur Rainwater, in which Rainwater described Norton and his classmates as the "stepping stone" to the future. Norton was energized by the conversation and noted that students at Central had been routinely left wanting and, finally, due to the new magnet theme, were seeing what he described as new "stuff." Indeed, building upgrades were underway, and new computers and technology were in classrooms. Experiential learning opportunities were becoming more widespread as well. There was a commitment under the Long Range Magnet Plan to provide Central Computers Unlimited students and all district students with an opportunity for practical application and field experiences.[553]

Norton, for example, was involved in a group known as the Central Lanterns, which was comprised of high-performing students interested in computer-related careers. The Lanterns served as technical support within the school building. If a computer problem arose, the Lanterns would identify the problem and fix it. In essence, the Lanterns served as network administrators, an experience Norton described as "fulfilling."[554] Norton felt satisfied outside of the classroom, particularly through the Lantern program and outreach programs with local businesses in the community. However, he also felt challenged in the classroom, something he attributed to Central's teachers.[555]

Despite Norton's fondness for his teachers, there was little change in the achievement test data between the 1988–1989 and 1989–1990 school years. In year two of the magnet program, tenth-grade students had tested below both district and state mean scores on the MMAT. Central students performed slightly worse in math and science in 1990 than in 1989. TAP scores, however, revealed progress. Central students across all grade levels showed improvement in reading. Ninth graders, in particular, experienced substantial gains. Thus, based on TAP scores, Central students' achievement and proficiency in all tested areas were catching up with district-wide mean scores, but they were still performing well below national norms.[556] Like student achievement data, integration data revealed little in the way of meaningful progress. The total number of students fell from 967 in 1988–1989 to 885 in 1989–1990. The number of "non-minority" students increased, though only modestly, from 4 percent to 6 percent.[557] The magnet plan was only in its second year of implementation, but the data was less than impressive. Yet those involved in the planning warned that it was too early to determine success or failure.

Meanwhile, students like Shakur and Norton graduated with one and two years of magnet programming, respectively. It is unfair to presume too much from the student experience when Central's magnet transformation was still in its infancy and was being implemented in a limited way. Central, in 1989 and 1990, still resided in the original building. The new building would not be completed until the 1991–1992 school year. Moreover, only one-half of the magnet theme was operational—the computer magnet side—and even that was in a limited manner. The classical Greek and Olympic athletic side would not be rolled out until the new building was complete.

Most students at Central between 1988 and 1990 were residing in the surrounding neighborhoods. While the magnet program's intent was multidimensional, one of the most important purposes was to integrate the school by attracting White students back to the district. This would require students to come from neighborhoods outside of Central's neighborhood attendance area, which was over 96 percent Black at the time.[558] Central's innovative academic and athletic programming, along with a brand new state-of-the-art building, it was hoped, would lead to significant integration.

The highly anticipated and routinely criticized new Central High School building opened its doors in the fall of 1991. Now came the hard part—the quest for success.

A New Era Begins

Central Computers Unlimited/Classical Greek Magnet School was the most expensive school in the nation.[559] At a price tag of $32 million, Central was said to rival many colleges: "It's like a mansion," proclaimed one Central student upon entering the new Central building; "it's about time they did something like this," exclaimed another student.[560] Lead attorney for the plaintiffs, Arthur Benson, described Central as the "most phenomenal high school building in the nation" and "[he] speculated that it would be the most sought-after high school in the district."[561] Central's gleaming new facilities included the nation's first fifty-meter indoor Olympic-sized pool located within a high school, three full basketball courts, handball courts, an indoor track, and robustly equipped classrooms with twenty-five computers per room.[562] Yet not everyone was happy with the new $32 million Central High School.[563]

A 1992 *Kansas City Star* article labeled the new Central the school that Missouri taxpayers "love to hate," suggesting that it epitomized excess and was a "prime example of everything frivolous and wasteful in a desegregation plan."[564] Just prior to the opening of the new Central building, the superintendent, George Garcia, the eighth Kansas City, Missouri School District Superintendent in eighteen years and fifth within the decade, resigned. His resignation was allegedly a result of a divided school board, which reflected a citizenry skeptical of district capital improvements, financed in part through an increase in property taxes.[565] Judge Clark's decision to mandate a tax increase for anyone living within the Kansas City, Missouri School District was unusual and unpopular. Clark argued that paying for the district's upgrades and improvements was necessary. Nevertheless, it conflicted with a basic premise of American identity, "no taxation without representation." Yet, given that it had been roughly twenty years since district constituents approved a tax levy, Clark may have believed it was the only way forward. The issue was described as a "lightning rod" at the time, with taxpayers, particularly a White constituency, angered by financing expensive educational improvements within a district that their children were not attending.[566] District taxpayers had long been unwilling to support public schools within Kansas City, Missouri. The year 1969 marked the last time district constituents passed a tax levy, and at that point, the district was majority White and more than twice the size that it was in 1991.[567]

It was not just district taxpayers who were dissatisfied with the magnet plan. Per Clark's ruling, the State of Missouri was also responsible for footing much of Kansas City's total magnet cost, impacting all Missouri taxpayers. White rural taxpayers were voicing frustration. "People are angry at the way they feel Kansas City is wasting the money," stated North Daviess, Superintendent in rural Coffey, Missouri, "and at Judge Clark for giving it to them." However dissatisfied, they were powerless to resist the price tag of district capital improvements as approved by the courts. Throughout the 1980s and early 1990s, Judge Clark's decisions were routinely supported by the

Eighth Circuit Court of Appeals, which was aggressively pro-deseg-regation. The typical pattern in the early years of *Jenkins v. Missouri* was of Benson and his litigating team advocating school district pro-gramming proposals, tax increases, and building upgrades to Judge Clark. Clark would approve the motion. The State of Missouri would appeal. Then, the Eighth Circuit would uphold Clark's ruling. While arguments played out in the courts, students were just beginning to enjoy the new district facilities.

Fencing and More

Jeremy Summers, a student in Central's 1991 inaugural Classical Greek freshman class, was just the type of student the district hoped the voluntary magnet approach would lure. Summers, a White sub-urbanite from neighboring Independence, Missouri, convinced his parents that he should take advantage of the district-provided taxi service and shuttle into the city and the halls of the brand-new Cen-tral Computers Unlimited/Classical Greek Magnet. The Magnet's ultimate goal was a 40-to-60 ratio by 1998—40 percent White and 60 percent students of color. This was the reason for door-to-door taxi service for suburban students who decided to leave their neigh-borhood schools behind and attend a Kansas City, Missouri School District magnet school. This aspect of the magnet remedy drew the ire of the state government, which considered such measures extravagant and unnecessary, especially since the state was responsible for pay-ing the bill. Nonetheless, taxi service remained an important aspect of magnet programming in the early stages. Since Central's student body was over 99 percent Black prior to magnet implementation, convenient transportation might make the difference between success or failure.

As early as 1986, district leaders were being told that recruiting White students would be challenging and that magnet themes should be targeted toward White families and White students. Central's highly segregated student body resulted in favoritism and racial quotas. Even as the new Central was being conceived, it was obvious that the magnet theme of Olympic athletics was done with an eye toward the suburbs. The classical Greek program allowed suburban parents to replace expensive and inconvenient out-of-school athletic programs with in-school opportunities, such as gymnastics, swimming, diving, fencing, synchronized swimming, wrestling, etc., which were free to students.[568] Central needed White students to meet the established 40 percent White student quota by 1998. It was no secret that most of those White students resided in the surrounding suburbs. Christopher Slaughter, a Black student who arrived in Kansas City from St. Louis in 1991 and eagerly anticipated his admission into Central's Classical Greek program, became one of the early victims of White favoritism when his initial application was rejected. "They would only take so many Black kids," asserted Slaughter, "if you're a White kid—go ahead. Go to Central."[569] Slaughter was correct. The school district prioritized White enrollment despite the public façade of Kansas City's magnet program advantaging Black and White students equally. While champions of the magnetization of Kansas City's schools celebrated the district's approach as equitable, the reality was that for the magnet plan to work, the district needed White students. "We didn't want to call it that [Whites only transfer policy]," stated Arthur Benson, one of the principal architects of the plan, "but in effect, it was Whites only [who] could transfer into the school district for the purposes of integration."[570] The district was 75 percent "minority" during the 1990–1991 school year; Central was 92 percent "minority" that same year.[571]

Whites spent the post-*Brown* decades fleeing the neighborhoods around Central, and given the media's portrayal of Central as a dangerous all-Black urban school throughout the 1970s and 1980s, it was clear that a counter-narrative would take time. Still, time was not on the district's side.

Meanwhile, Jeremy Summers headed into the city to attend Central, uncertain what to expect. He hoped Central's commitment to athletics would ultimately lead to a collegiate soccer scholarship. That was, after all, what convinced him to take a chance on Central in the first place. Summers was the exception. He was one of one hundred and eighty-eight additional White students at Central during the 1991–1992 school year, up from seventy-three White students a year before.[572] Still less than 17 percent of the total population of students, but a sizeable jump from a mere 7 percent the year before. This was, at least, progress.

The soccer program, which lured Summers to Central, crumbled almost immediately. Before the season was even underway, Central's soccer coach had resigned. Uncertain what to do, Summers made a decision that would change his life. He joined the fencing team.

Central's commitment to Olympic sports resulted in a rare collection of athletic opportunities for students enrolled in classical Greek programming. In addition to fencing, Central offered Olympic weightlifting, water polo, kayaking, synchronized swimming, and gymnastics, among other individual and team sports.[573] This required hiring specialized coaches who could prepare Central athletes for Olympic competition.

Longtime administrator Willie Mahone assumed oversight of Classical Greek programming at Central in 1991, and he managed to assemble an impressive lineup of coaches. There was swim coach Bill Shalley, who had won multiple championships in suburban Blue Springs; diving coach Tom Garabedian; handball coach and Olympian Mary Phyl Dwight; weightlifting coach Ed Bielik from the University of Kansas; legendary tennis coach Fred Johnson; and of course, the headliner, three-time Olympic gold medalist, ten-time world champion, and one of the best fencers the sport has ever seen, Vladimir Nazlymov.[574]

Nazlymov's path to Central was anything but routine. Named the world's best sabre fencer in 1975 and 1977 by the International Fencing Federation, Nazlymov took up coaching in the 1980s. He rapidly developed into one of the world's best fencing coaches. He worked his way up the Soviet coaching ranks, eventually serving as coach of the Soviet National Team, a position he held until the disbanding of the Soviet Sports Commission just before the collapse of the Soviet Union.[575] With his impressive fencing pedigree as both athlete and coach, Nazlymov was highly regarded within the fencing community. Thus, upon his dismissal from the Soviet Sports Commission, Nazlymov became a hot coaching commodity and found many Western countries among his suitors, each hoping to land him as part of their national team. Indeed, Nazlymov welcomed the opportunity to leave his Soviet roots behind and pursue an opportunity in the West.[576]

In 1990, Nazlymov packed his bags and boarded a plane bound for his new home in the United States. Nazlymov began searching for a new job doing what he loved most: he wanted to coach. He found such an opportunity in the most unlikely of places, the new Central High Computers Unlimited/Classical Greek Magnet High School in Kansas City, Missouri. While Nazlymov had a few connections in Kansas City, Central was an unusual decision for one of the top coaching prospects in the world, but Nazlymov wanted a challenge. He knew that he would have access to top-notch facilities and what seemed, at the time, an endless budget.

Like all aspects of the school district's magnet programming, Central's fencing program did not spare any cost. In marketing the fencing program, Central students were promised extensive travel, and travel they did—all over the world. Central's top fencers took trips to France, Italy, Spain, Germany, and Hungary, and they did so all at the district's expense. A 1993 district memo suggested that four members of the fencing program's trip to Germany cost the district $7000.[577] While the fencing team's travel was most impressive, other teams were also traveling. Program administrator Willie Mahone recalled, "[w]e traveled everywhere; I mean, in style too . . . we traveled first class." It could be argued that the travel was beneficial despite its costly nature, especially in fencing and weightlifting. Both sports exceeded even the most optimistic expectations after just two short years of implementation. Terrence Lasker, a Black student who lived south of Central's attendance area but within the school district's boundaries, transferred to Central in

1991 as a freshman. Lasker was particularly interested in Central's computer program, but the promise of extensive travel led him, on a whim, to Nazlymov's fencing program. He fell in love with it, and by 1993, Lasker had developed into the top-ranked fencer in the under-seventeen sabre division, won the gold medal in the February 1993 Junior Olympics, and finished sixth in the world in under-twenty sabre.[578] Fencing had changed Lasker's life and had him eyeing the 1996 Olympics.

The men's and women's weightlifting teams were also championship-level. The women's team placed third at the United States Junior Weightlifting Championships and the AAU National Junior Olympic Championships; the men finished second at the AAU National Junior Olympic Championships and the Canadian Interprovincial Championships.[579] These were impressive feats. However, for all of the magnet successes, there were ongoing challenges, not least the issue of White favoritism. Certainly, one of the major criticisms of Kansas City's magnet plan, especially among many in the Black community, was the prioritization shown to White suburban students.

The issue of racial quotas remained a source of friction. As early as 1989, parents of Black students sued the Kansas City, Missouri School District, alleging that the desegregation plan was denying Black students access to the best public schools.[580] Yet, supporters of the magnet plan, including Arthur Benson, continued to champion the magnet approach, reasoning that magnetizing the entire district afforded all Black and White students the greatest opportunity for educational equity. By the 1991–1992 school year, Central Computers Unlimited/Classical Greek Magnet housed 862 students in computers and 240 in classical Greek. Thirteen percent of those enrolled in computers unlimted were "non-minority," whereas thirty-one percent in classical Greek were "non-minority."[581] Thus, of 1,102 students, Central was roughly 17 percent "non-minority" during the 1991–1992 school year—an impressive statistic considering that Central had only one White student in the 1986 graduating class. That number rose to three in 1988.[582] Though the 1991–1992 numbers were well short of the larger 40 percent goal, it revealed tangible progress, especially considering that this occurred within year one of the implementation of the new Central building. It was not just Central either; the number of White students district-wide grew by more than three hundred and fifty students between the 1989–1990 and 1990–1991 school years.[583] Since the number of White students had fallen by more than seven hundred in the five years previous, there was at last movement in the right direction.

Desegregation was one major goal; the other was academic achievement. The dual programming of computers and classical Greek within Central's magnet theme was carefully planned to incorporate academic rigor and college readiness. As conceived and outlined in the Long Range Magnet Plan, the computer program would "provide students with educational opportunities specifically in computer technology and generally in information technology to a greater extent than they were offered in the Kansas City metropolitan area." It would create "exceptional educational opportunities" that would "prepare students for university level."[584] Similarly, the classical Greek program, in addition to emphasizing Olympic sports, was designed for students who wanted "a strong liberal arts education," and for whom a "rigorous academic program" would "prepare students for college work in language, art, music, architecture, literature, science, physical education, physical therapy, biology, archeology, and education."[585]

Determining Academic Success

It was hoped that Central's innovative magnet themes, revised curricular focus, and facility upgrades would improve student academic achievement, measured almost exclusively through standardized testing. The modern era of standardized testing found its footing in 1965 with the passage of the Elementary and Secondary Education Act. In the state of Missouri, however, the National Defense Education Act of 1958 ushered in voluntary standardized testing, a Cold War relic motivated by fear that the Soviets were making gains against American students, particularly in the area of science.[586] This was followed by mandatory testing for all eighth-grade students as part of the Basic Essential Skills Test (BEST), implemented in 1978 and mandated by 1979.[587] With the 1985 Excellence in Education Act, a major education reform bill in Missouri, statewide standardized testing became more widespread and more routinely used, as the act mandated the development of criterion-referenced tests in core content.[588]

By the early 1990s, large-scale standardized norm-referenced and criterion-referenced tests were widely applied in Missouri and nationwide to measure student achievement. Given the context, Central's success and the success of the magnet program as a whole hinged on student performance on standardized tests. Fairness aside, standardized testing was the primary way schools and students were categorized as successes or failures. This trend became more significant with the No Child Left Behind Act of 2001, a bipartisan federal act signed into law by George W. Bush, which held schools accountable for student outcomes based on standardized test scores. By the early 1990s, large-scale standardized testing was perceived to be the defining feature of school success. Thus, Kansas City's magnet schools had to show student achievement and progress using standardized tests.

The DMC had, in 1989, described middle school and high school standardized test scores as "abysmal." As measured by normed tests, the struggles in academic performance regressed between 1989 and 1992, despite the DMC's proclamation in 1991 that the combination of programming, instruction, and facilities in the district's schools made them better than any other in the metropolitan area. This same statement, however, was counter-intuitively followed by a cautionary statement that students' academic performance suggested that the district offered the "worst of education in the Kansas City area."[589] Though the DMC was purposed as the primary advocate and overseer of the district's magnet overhaul, it was often the district's toughest critic, creating a tenuous and often contentious relationship between the DMC and district administration. However, the DMC was positioned as the enforcer of magnet programming by the court. The court, specifically Judge Clark, reasoned that large-scale standardized test scores should measure the district's academic progress and magnet success. This coincided with a national push to emphasize the importance of such data as an accurate measurement of a student's academic progress.

The district's test scores in the early grades—kindergarten through grade four—were promising. For example, during the 1991–1992 school year, students in the early grades scored above national averages in most subjects.[590] Scores dropped off after that, however, revealing that district high school students were more than eighteen months below national norms and sixth graders were roughly a year behind.[591] District consultant and former superintendent John Murphy began questioning the heavy emphasis on testing, openly wondering if testing was resulting in teachers focusing almost entirely on the drilling of facts that would lead to better test scores and thus limiting the scope of the student experience.[592] Murphy was hired for his ability as a district leader to improve academic performance, particularly for students of color, and he was not the only one to conclude that students were being harmed by an acute emphasis on teaching basic facts for success on standardized tests. As was often the case with this approach, test scores showed promise in the early grades only to reveal deficiencies in later grades. This notion of "teaching to the test" grew in popularity with high-stakes testing since districts, schools, and sometimes even teachers were evaluated based on student performance. Such was the case in Kansas City when students' test scores came to represent the success or failure of the entire magnet program.

Though routinely used as the only measurement of student success, test scores represent merely one dimension, and a flawed one at that, especially for students of color. The gap between the performance of White students and students of color on standardized tests still persists, as does the gap between students of high and low socioeconomic status. The student experience is multi-dimensional, complex, and far too varied to rely on standardized test scores alone as a single measurement of success or failure. What about students like Kyle Sheumaker, Syed Rahman, and Jayson Vantuyl who placed first in the 1996 Computer Science Olympiad Competition at Northwest Missouri State University, or Albert Lowe, who participated in the 1997 Missouri Valley Division 2 Championship Swim Meet, or Andre Haynes, Shaunteh Elliott, Chad Johnson, Dion Maltbia, Valerie Nevels, Stephen Pointer, Michael Robinson, Darren Smith, Greg Strong, Tony Whitney, and Angelic Williams, who traveled to Blaine, Minnesota, in April of 1993 for the Junior National Weightlifting Championships?[593] How might these experiences be quantified? Such a line of inquiry holds particular relevance within Central's fencing program. Between 1991 and 1995, fencing at Central changed lives.

As Christopher Slaughter, class of 1992, reflects on his time at Central, he confidently states: "I got more education from Vladimir Nazlymov than all those classes I took."[594] Central's influential fencing program led by Nazlymov was indeed an impressive feature of Central's magnet program and was living up to the hype. As noted earlier, Slaughter was initially a victim of the magnet racial quotas as a Black student trying to transfer into Central. Still, he described how his father was persistent and found a way to get him enrolled at Central despite racial quotas. Slaughter moved to Central from Ladue High School, an inner-ring suburb of St. Louis, and having had some exposure to fencing in St. Louis, was intrigued by the fencing program at Central. Central's fencing program would change everything. Slaughter described how Nazlymov treated members of his fencing team like his own children. He made such an impression on Central's young fencing students that Slaughter is one of three former Central fencers who made careers for themselves in fencing. The life trajectories of Slaughter's good friends Terrence Lasker and Jeremy Summers were changed by Nazlymov's fencing program as well.

Upon graduating from Central in 1992, Slaughter attempted to make the Olympic fencing team and achieved a national ranking as high as sixteenth. However, the training and travel were too costly. He ran out of money and was forced to abandon his Olympic dream. Nevertheless, fencing had become his passion, and he founded several youth fencing programs in St. Louis, Kansas City, and Frisco, Texas, where he is still coaching.

Like Slaughter, Lasker and Summers, class of 1995, developed into nationally ranked fencers, and both were eyeing the 1996 and 2000 Olympic teams. Lasker, like Slaughter, was a Black student who had to navigate his way through racial quotas at Central just to be admitted, and Summers, a White student, was transported into the city from the neighboring suburb of Independence. Upon graduating from Central, both spurned impressive college scholarship offers and instead chose to train with their beloved Coach Nazlymov. And while Nazlymov allowed them to train for free, they had to finance extensive international travel to compete at an elite level. These were competitions and travel that the school district had financed while they were students. Without that support, both struggled financially. Nevertheless, Lasker qualified as the first alternate for the 1996 Olympic team, and Summers was the first alternate for the 2000 Olympic team, and both fencers were members of the United States National team. By the early 2000s, however, Lasker and Summers were finished with competitive fencing, but like Slaughter before them, they have remained in fencing beyond their days of elite competition. Lasker is currently the head sabre coach at an elite private fencing club in Atlanta, Georgia, Nellya Fencing, and was named the 2017 Developmental Coach of the Year by the United States Olympic Committee.[595] Summers received his Doctor of Chiropractic and Diplomate as a Chiropractic Sports Physician and served as the USA Fencing Director of Sports Medicine for twelve years and became the organization's first-ever full-time sports medicine staff member in 2015.

Central's magnet programming undeniably changed the lives of Slaughter, Lasker, and Summers. It is not a stretch to presume that had it not been for Central's fencing program, magnet theme, and the tutelage of their world-renowned coach, Vladimir Nazlymov, life would have looked different for these three individuals. They all credit Central's fencing program and, specifically, Nazlymov for their professional successes. So what about Nazlymov—what happened to this legendary coach who shocked the fencing world by taking a job at Kansas City's Central High School?

Nazlymov served as Central's fencing coach from 1991 to 1996, when he moved from Central to an affluent suburb of Kansas City, Overland Park, Kansas, and opened a private fencing club. He remained in Overland Park until 1999, until he accepted the position as head fencing coach at The Ohio State University. While at Ohio State, Nazlymov flourished. His teams finished in the top five in the nation for seventeen years in a row, Nazlymov, in nineteen seasons, won three national championships, nine individual NCAA titles, and eleven Midwest Conference crowns.[596] He is among the best fencing trainers ever to coach the sport. Yet, despite all of his accolades and accomplishments, Nazlymov will tell you that among his greatest achievements was the fencing program he established at Central in 1991.[597]

Nazlymov was not likely to stay in Kansas City for the duration of his career. He left Central in 1996 at a point when Central's fencing program was perhaps at its strongest position, having just produced three of the country's best young fencers. It was not Central per se that caused Nazlymov to flee to the suburbs and eventually leave Kansas City altogether; it was the jurisprudential environment surrounding the district's magnet system. In 1995, the Supreme Court agreed to hear the Kansas City legal case once again on appeal from the State of Missouri. The State had argued unsuccessfully on appeal to the Supreme Court in 1990, *Jenkins II*. In 1995, however, *Jenkins III* put Kansas City's magnet program in real jeopardy just four years after full implementation.

Central High School Senior Class of 1899

Central High School at 11th and Locust in 1890 where the school resided until it was moved in 1915.

1916 photo of the original high school building at 3221 Linwood Avenue.

Central's longest-serving principal, Otto Dubach, 1929. Dubach served as principal between 1920 and 1946.

An undated photo of the original Central building at 3221 Linwood Ave.

James Boyd, 1962. Boyd served as Central's principal between 1960 and 1969.

**PRINCIPAL
C.S. SETTLES**

101

Central High School's first Black principal, C.S. Settles, 1970. Settles served as principal between 1969 and 1971.

A Visit From Rev. Jesse Jackson!

Jesse Jackson posing with Central Students during his visit to Central in 1976.

The brand-new Central Computers Unlimited/Classical Greek Magnet High School shortly after its completion, 1991.

Central's legendary fencing coach, Vladimir Nazlymov, and his fencing team, 1993.

Computers Unlimited

Central High School is the leader in the country in utilizing computers to augment education. The school uses a variety of methods to expose students to many fields computers are used in, such as: robotics, CADD, computer programming, and computer repair.

The use of computers at Central is one of a kind in the sense that every class uses computers. Some teachers use them to help give a better understanding of a subject, and others use them as their primary teaching tool.

Central is preparing students for the highly computerized world of tomorrow. The motto "Computers Unlimited" tells you Central's students will lead everyone in computer applications for years to come.

To the Central Eagles,

Central is reaching its potential in education and athletics this year. The faculty and administration are doing all they can to ensure that we, the students, are doing our best. The teachers are here everyday giving us the finest education possible. The students do all they can so the effort is not wasted, so they can apply this new found knowledge in the classroom and beyond.

The Seniors are making the big push to graduate. The Juniors are waiting in the wings to make their debut in "94" as the center of attention. The

Central's Computer Unlimited program on display, 1997.

9 | Magnets No More

On January 11, 1995, the Supreme Court heard oral arguments in *Missouri v. Jenkins*. This was a different Court than 1990, when the State of Missouri had last argued their case.[598] Clarence Thomas replaced Thurgood Marshall in 1991, thus securing a conservative majority. In 1995, and due to its more conservative makeup, the Supreme Court, in a five-to-four decision, ruled in favor of the State of Missouri. The decision signaled to all parties that the end of the magnet remedy in Kansas City, Missouri, was near.[599] The Court's majority ruling was on a technicality. The Court sided with the State and reasoned that district salary increases violated the intradistrict remedy of the magnet plan by introducing an interdistrict element and thus luring teachers and students from neighboring suburban schools. The more significant implication, however, was that the Court called into question the broader magnet remedy altogether and specifically took issue with capital improvements and the suburban transfer program. The decision is one that still haunts Arthur Benson:

> The Supreme Court really cut us off at the knees. You know, we won in the Supreme Court the time before on the really contentious issue about whether a federal judge can cause taxes to be raised without a vote of the people. We won that five-to-four, and then [Thurgood] Marshall retires. He's replaced with [Clarence] Thomas, and we lose five-to-four. Because of that vote. I mean it's clearly, I mean if Marshall had not retired, or, you know . . . who knows?[600]

In the years leading up to the summer of 1995, the district's magnet schools had attracted roughly two thousand suburban White students. By the end of the summer of 1995, hundreds of those same suburban Whites had been lost.[601] The uncertainty about tuition waivers[602] seemed to be the most significant factor in persuading suburban students to look elsewhere, despite the Kansas City, Missouri School District's guarantee that they could attend district schools for free during the 1995–1996 school year. The unpredictability surrounding the future of magnet schools resulted in many suburban families looking for more stable options outside the district. By August 1995, just a month after the district and State agreed that desegregation funding would end by 1999, nearly 40 percent of suburban students who planned to attend district schools had pulled out.[603] "A lot of people are angry," suggested Al Winder, the district transportation director at the time. "A one year deal is not good enough . . . they [parents] have to make plans."[604] Whereas the State had been picking up the $6.4 million annual transportation cost for suburban students to ride taxis from their suburban residences, the Supreme Court's 1995 decision terminated the transportation budget. Beginning in the fall of 1995, while suburban students could attend the Kansas City, Missouri School District for free, no transportation outside district boundaries was provided.[605]

The chaotic nature of the district leadership, which by 1995 had garnered a reputation as dysfunctional, was a further complication. A revolving door of superintendents became the norm. No superintendent lasted more than three years after 1977, and superintendent-school board relationships were consistently problematic. In February of 1995, for example, the Kansas City, Missouri School District School Board relieved Superintendent Marks of his duties just a week after a television report questioned Marks's medical leave, which Marks claimed was caused by stress sustained on the job.[606]

With six new school board members having been elected in April of 1994 and many of them critical of the magnet approach, the board, once again, began searching for a new superintendent. One newly appointed Black board member, Edward Newsome, revealed the district's changing attitude and direction. A 1995 *Wall Street Journal* article described Newsome as "controversial" and "outspoken" and stated that his rhetoric sounded more like Clarence Thomas than Martin Luther King, Jr.[607] Newsome was an active member of the Coalition for Education and Economic Justice (CEEJ), an organization whose explicit purpose was to end the magnet remedy and return the district to neighborhood schools, an effort the CEEJ called "the movement."[608] The movement's philosophical approach in opposition to the magnet plan and emphasis on education rather than integration was reminiscent of Booker T. Washington, who more than seventy years prior, prioritized elevation and racial solidarity over desegregation. By the early 1990s, the CEEJ was making noise in Kansas City and winning school board seats.

With new faces and many board members looking for a way out of the magnet plan, a bitterly divided board attempted to hire a superintendent. The school board offered the job to John Murphy, superintendent in Charlotte, North Carolina, in September 1995 amid considerable controversy. Murphy, a White man, had been superintendent of the nearly all-Black Prince George County Public Schools in Maryland from 1984 to 1990 when he left for North Carolina. At Prince George County, Murphy spearheaded an effort, much like that in Kansas City, to create magnet schools to attract White students. Still, by 1990, he suggested abandoning the effort, claiming that magnet schools were not the best approach and that "the problems of the '90s" needed "different solutions."[609] Despite Murphy's theoretical alignment with many board members in moving away from magnets, he never landed in Kansas City. He declined the $250,000 package, citing fears of poor support among the school board, and instead remained in Charlotte.[610]

Meanwhile, the acting superintendent through the transitional period, Willie Giles, faced complaints of sexual harassment and having hired a relative who had been convicted of stealing from his former job. Giles was eventually suspended by the board and replaced by Associate Superintendent Larry Ramsey in October of 1995.[611] Ramsey was gone by June of 1996 after calling out the school board and alleging that their actions were worse than those of "the school children they are supposed to lead."[612] Henry Williams followed Ramsey. Williams, the former superintendent of Little Rock, Arkansas, was a proponent of neighborhood schools, but like his predecessors, Williams's tenure was short-lived—just two years.[613] Eight superintendents came and went between 1991 and 2000.

During this time, the district's school board was undergoing a significant philosophical change in board priorities, as well. This, coupled with the Supreme Court's 1995 decision, made it clear: the school board was ready to move in a new direction, and the courts were beginning to follow suit. In January 1997, Judge Clark, who had presided over the *Jenkins* case for roughly two decades and endured death threats and routine public criticism, announced that he was recusing himself, but not before one final ruling.[614] Clark gave the district three years to achieve unitary status, a legal term used to describe that the court no longer oversees a school district after eliminating the effects of past segregation to the extent practicable. This ruling included a phase-out of the State's financial obligation. By March 1997, Judge Clark had stepped down, and he was replaced in a random drawing, as was the process, by Judge Dean Whipple, a conservative Reagan appointee.[615] Whipple moved quickly to bring *Jenkins* to a close.

Central was among the first schools to experience the district's movement away from magnets. The classical Greek magnet theme was eliminated before the beginning of the 1997 academic year due to alleged "low academic success, low attractiveness, low school climate, and fairly high per pupil cost."[616] This was a mere five years after the classical Greek magnet was fully operational and six years after the new Central High School was constructed with intentional upgrades specific to the Classical Greek theme. Along with Central, the classical Greek programs at Roberson Middle School and Pitcher, Woodland, and Paige Elementary schools were also eliminated.[617]

While the termination of the classical Greek magnet theme was the first, it was not the last—by the 2000–2001 academic year, 71 percent of district schools had been converted back to neighborhood schools, and only two of ten high schools remained magnet-themed.[618] The prevailing and consistent narrative of magnet failure guided the return to neighborhood schools.

Measuring Magnets

Jenkins had four primary remedial tasks, which the magnet plan was intended to address: integration, capital improvements, funding, and academic achievement.[619] Good progress was made in integration, capital improvements, and funding during the magnet years. However, academic achievement was a different story.

By the early 1990s, district-wide White enrollment had increased, arresting a consistent trend of White enrollment decline that began during the 1958–1959 academic year when the district was home to 53,743 White students. That number dropped to 8,785 during the 1989–1990 academic year. By 1990–1991, White enrollment inched up to 8,891. Through 1994, White enrollment was consistently over 9,000.[620] The index of dissimilarity and interracial exposure analyses also showed progress. The index of dissimilarity is a statistical measure used to quantify the level of segregation between two groups within a geographic area, in which one represents full segregation and one zero segregation. The index was at its lowest in Kansas City, Missouri School District between 1992 and 1995.[621] Similarly, measurements of interracial exposure, which refers to the interaction between individuals from different racial or ethnic backgrounds, were believed to have reached the maximum level possible within the district by 1996.[622]

In all, about fifty Kansas City, Missouri School District schools were transitioned to magnet schools. This included all the high schools, middle schools, and roughly half of the elementary schools. Hundreds of millions of dollars were spent on capital improvements. Buildings were torn down and rebuilt, and by the mid-1990s, the district had effectively been reconstructed. In addition, the magnet school transition inspired increased per-pupil funding and more than tripled the district's budget. In contrast to the traditional practice, much of the increase resulted from state funding, not local funding. Nevertheless, local taxes increased during the magnet years, including a levy set by the state constitution, which was amended and remains in place today.

As previously discussed, academic achievement was exclusively measured through building-level and district-level performance on statewide standardized achievement tests. The results of these tests for the Kansas City, Missouri School District were always low, but with the initiation of the Show Me Standards and Missouri Assessment Program (MAP) in 1997, test scores were abysmal of which became a real problem for magnet supporters.

District MAP testing commenced in the spring of 1997 in certain tested areas and in 1998 in others, and levels of proficiency ranged from zero to seven percent. The Desegregation Monitoring Committee noted results across grade levels to be of "critical concern."[623] For instance, test results revealed that only 3 percent of tenth graders scored "proficient" in math and 1 percent in science; 8 percent of eleventh graders scored "proficient" in communication arts.[624] Scores, though better at the elementary and middle level, were still disappointingly low. Eleven percent of fourth graders were proficient in math, eleven percent of third graders were proficient in communication arts, and sixteen percent were proficient in science.[625] Such performance led the State in 1998 to downgrade the district to a provisional accreditation status.

Stakes were high for the district. A 1999 *Kansas City Star* article stated, "The results of this year's MAP tests will be used to determine whether the district regains full accreditation."[626] Student scores in 1999 remained low, and, in many cases, even dropped. On October 21, 1999, the Missouri Board of Education voted unanimously to strip the Kansas City, Missouri School District of accreditation. It marked the first time in the nation's history a school district lost accreditation. The State gave the district until June 30, 2002 to regain accreditation or face State takeover.[627] Further complicating the issue, less than a month after the State's decision, Judge Whipple dismissed the *Jenkins* case in a surprise ruling without a hearing, suggesting that the district had done all it could to eliminate segregation.[628] The decision was appealed and overturned. Following Whipple's move to dismiss, in February 2000, a three-member panel of federal appeals court removed Judge Whipple from the case, suggesting that he had erred in dismissing the case without a hearing.[629] By June 2000, however, a twelve-judge appeals court returned the case to Whipple.

By 1999, Central existed as a magnet school in name only. The classical Greek magnet theme and offerings were already gone by 1997, and eliminating the transportation budget after the Court's 1995 ruling hobbled Central's ability to attract students from across the city. Thus, Central began pulling most of its students from surrounding neighborhoods. Central effectively operated as a neighborhood school, though it was not officially such until 2000.

Between 1991 and 1995, Central, during its time as a comprehensive magnet school, proved that magnet programs could drive and sustain integration. Before magnet implementation, Central had only one White student during the 1985–1986 academic year. In contrast, between 1993 and 1995, Central had risen to over two hundred White students—that is, 99.8 percent Black to 78.9 percent Black.[630] However, when the magnet program was threatened, the trend reversed in 1995–1996. Between 1996 and 2000, Central's White student population fell from one hundred and eighty-one to forty-four, and the school went from just over 80 percent Black to over 95 percent Black.[631]

Central's changing demographics correspond with the 1995 Court order and the district's subsequent move away from magnet schools, effectively resegregating the district. Arthur Rainwater, one of the architects of Central's magnet themes, wondered what might have been—"there just wasn't that much time."[632] Just before the Court's ruling, Superintendent Walter Marks agreed with Rainwater, saying in 1995, "We need to give the effort here a few more years. This desegregation plan wasn't fully implemented until two or three years ago, and that isn't enough time."[633] Critics have argued that in 1995, when the Supreme Court shut down aspects of the district's magnet approach, *Jenkins* was eighteen years in. That is indeed true, but Central, for example, operated as a computer magnet in limited form only from 1988 to 1991. It was not until the 1992–1993 academic year that Central Computers Unlimited/Classical Greek Magnet School was fully operational, which means Central was given only three years to succeed.

"What most people forget," suggested Dr. Stuart McAninch, associate professor in Education History at the University of Missouri-Kansas City, "is that the magnet themes worked."[634] Maybe Rainwater and Marks were right; there wasn't enough time for substantive change. Regardless, the prevailing storyline remains that the Kansas City, Missouri School District spent over $2 billion on their magnet remedy and had little to show for it. Consequently, Central stands as the foremost example of magnet excess and failure.

It's Officially Over

In March 2002, Judge Whipple significantly narrowed the scope of *Jenkins*, releasing the Kansas City, Missouri School District from federal oversight in areas of racial balance, facilities, budgeting, and transportation.[635] One issue remained—narrowing the achievement gap between Black and White students. Less than a year later, in January of 2003, the district requested that Judge Whipple end the case.[636]

On August 13, 2003, Judge Whipple released the district from the case and brought the twenty-six-year *Jenkins* odyssey to a formal close, leaving many pondering what lay ahead.

By 2003, the educational landscape in Kansas City looked dramatically different than it did in 1977 when the case began. District enrollment in 1977 was 45,726; it had dropped to 28,721 in 2003. This was in part due to the growth of charter schools, particularly within Jackson County and the central city. "Charter schools could rejuvenate public school in Kansas City," suggested Barbara Shelly, a columnist for the *Kansas City Star*, "or they could become the refuge of parents seeking to band with their own kind." Shelly continued, "They hold great promise for city children," and "they hold the potential to dig the most disadvantaged students deeper into an educational pit."[637] Some twenty years later, we are grappling with the same scenarios that Shelly outlined. What is clear is that charter schools have experienced tremendous growth in Kansas City since their inception, and this growth has profoundly affected public education in Kansas City.

Albert Shanker, president of the American Federation of Teachers (AFT) teacher's union from 1974 to 1997, proposed the concept of charter schools in 1988. This is ironic given that the AFT is deeply critical of the current state of charter school education in the United States. Included within their organization's resolution is the following language:

> Whereas the proliferation of charter schools in the United States
> is sometimes driven not by children's educational needs but rather
> by corporate or political interests, which can create a competitive
> system of winners and losers that is damaging to public school
> districts and ultimately destructive to public education as a whole
> . . ."[638]

Shanker envisioned charter schools as small learning communities working in collaboration with traditional public schools and serving the neediest of students.[639] However, charter schools today often compete with traditional public schools for the same students. That competition plays out through standardized testing, whereby schools try to outperform one another.

Charter schools are public schools, meaning they are tuition-free and receive the same per-pupil state funding as traditional public schools. Still, charters operate with greater independence and flexibility than traditional public schools. This results from the charter school structure, which allows for greater autonomy at the school level. Charter schools are able to make decisions independent of large school districts about, for example, finance, personnel, scheduling, and curriculum and instruction. Charter schools work with a sponsoring body—the chartering body—which in Missouri consists of three possible types of sponsors: school boards of accredited school districts, qualifying universities, or the Missouri Charter Public School Commission. The school and their respective sponsor develop individual agreements and specific targets. If the charter school does not fulfill the agreed upon terms and conditions, they can face closure. As such, charter schools are incentivized to meet their expected outcomes.

When charter schools were opened in Kansas City, district leadership was immediately concerned about their impact on district schools. Their worry was warranted. Charter schools were approved by the State of Missouri General Assembly in 1999 and are operated under Missouri Charter School Law, but only for students attending school in the St. Louis, Missouri Public School District and the Kansas City, Missouri School District.[640] This remains true today, though the state statute has been revised to allow charter school creation within any unaccredited Missouri school district.[641] There are currently twenty operating charter schools in Kansas City, Missouri, and seventeen in St. Louis, Missouri.

A district executive summary from June 2002 noted, "The two major factors contributing to enrollment decline are the dismantling of the desegregation magnet program and charter schools."[642] In 1999, the first year charters were allowed in Kansas City, Missouri, fifteen charter schools opened with just shy of five thousand students. This represents roughly 14 percent of the public school students within the geographic boundary.[643] That same year, district enrollment dropped by 4,400 students.[644]

Just months after the General Assembly in Missouri approved charter schools, two for-profit school management companies took over former Kansas City, Missouri School District high schools: Southwest High School and Westport High School, respectively. The Kansas City, Missouri School District leased the Southwest High School building to Missouri State University, which chartered a grade six through twelve neighborhood school managed by Imagine Schools, Inc. By the spring of 2005, Missouri State had pulled their charter due to lack of academic progress.[645] Similarly, in 1999, the district's school board voted to sponsor a transition of Westport High School and Westport Middle School into charter schools managed by Edison Schools, Inc. Like Southwest High School, Westport's charter was revoked by the district in 2004.[646] With the closure of Southwest in 2005 and the uncertainty surrounding Westport, students began searching for other school options. Some ended up at Central High School, adding complexity to the school culture.

This was also a time when there was grave uncertainty surrounding the district. Not only was the magnet remedy ending, but the State of Missouri pulled the Kansas City, Missouri School District's accreditation in May of 2000. Superintendent Benjamin Demps, who had been recently appointed, assured students and their families that the district would not close.[647] Yet Demps was fired less than a year later and subsequently began claiming in the media that the State should consider a district takeover. Comments like this were not good for a district fighting for survival.[648] Despite Demps's media tour, the Kansas City, Missouri School District was not taken over by the State. Under the leadership of Demps's successor, Dr. Bernard Taylor, the district regained provisional accreditation in 2002 after meeting four of the State's eleven academic performance standards. This was a win for the district, but it was not the last time the district would confront accreditation issues.

10 | The Struggle Continues

By the 2000–2001 academic year, all magnet programming at Central had been officially discontinued. Central, in effect, was operating as a neighborhood school between 1995 and 2000, with the termination of the magnet transportation plan in 1995. This was followed by district approval of the 1997 transition plan, which began the elimination of magnet themes. Central was affected by the initial phase of the transition plan, with athletic magnet programming discontinued in 1997. Still, the computer magnet theme would remain until 1999, when all district high schools, except Lincoln College Preparatory Academy, were converted back to traditional neighborhood schools. However, students were still benefiting from the computer theme as late as 1997, despite the Kansas City, Missouri School District's decision in favor of magnet elimination. Jermaine Wilson, a 1997 graduate, described how he was involved in internships in wiring networks and computer programming throughout his senior year.[649] Such opportunities were scaled back after Wilson graduated, and by the end of the 1999–2000 school year, they no longer existed.

When William McClendon assumed Central High School's principalship in 2001, he inherited a school that was in transition from a magnet to a neighborhood school; it had also just been flagged by the State of Missouri as "Academically Deficient."[650] This decision by the State of Missouri was the first of its kind. Central became one of five district schools with the unenviable label placed upon them by the state board of education, sharing the distinction with Southeast

High School, Northeast High School, Central Middle School, and King Middle School.[651] However, the state's audit team was particularly concerned with Central High School, as they specifically highlighted "safety concerns" in their report and noted that discipline was receiving greater emphasis than instruction.[652]

McClendon was no stranger to Central; he graduated from Central and returned in the late 1960s as a student teacher.[653] When he took the job as principal, he prioritized student responsibility, community, and family involvement, aspects of his high school experience at Central that he felt had been lost by the time he became principal. Upon his arrival, McClendon worked to ensure students arrived on time and remained in their classes for the duration of the class period. He implemented a uniform policy and set up teaming among teachers.[654] McClendon initiated a "Raising the Bar" program to elicit more parental involvement and support, which included signed covenants that outlined parent responsibilities, such as school volunteer hours and weekly parent-student-teacher dialogues.[655] McClendon, however, would not see the program fully implemented. His five-year tenure as Central's principal ended in 2006 with his retirement. Deborah McGill succeeded him.

McGill, like McClendon, was a Central graduate. Appointed in 2008, McGill's time as Central's principal was marked by controversy, not least because she lacked experience and had only temporary administrative certification.[656] Her mother, Helen Ragsdale, was a longtime school board member, which also raised red flags and aroused rumors of nepotism. At the end of McGill's first year, the Raising the Bar program developed by her predecessor, which had generated widespread enthusiasm in McGill's first months, was effectively over. Parents who had assisted in its development lamented the program's failed implementation and alleged that McGill was to blame. Staff were frustrated, too, with some voicing concern about increased violence occurring within and around the school during McGill's administration.[657]

Just two years after her hire, McGill was out, and so was her mother. McGill was removed in early 2010, and Ragsdale stepped down from the school board two months later, in April of that year. McGill was replaced by assistant principal and acting principal Derek Jordan.[658] Once again, Central was searching for a principal. McClendon's and McGill's principalships mark a particularly turbulent time at Central High School.

The neighborhoods around Central have been over 95 percent Black since the 1960s. Central's demographics in 2005, just two years after the end of *Jenkins* and the formal reinstatement of neighborhood schools, again reflected that of the neighborhood.[659] Kansas City's history of residential segregation was unchanged. However, the most recent census data does indicate a growing Latinx population within the area—a 306 percent increase between 2010 and 2020.[660] School enrollment reflects this demographic shift as well, but 90 percent of Central's students today identify as Black. Eight percent identify as Hispanic.[661]

White residential patterns in the area have remained consistent, with 5 percent or fewer of the population identifying as White in the last fifty years.[662] The only time in the post-*Brown* period in which Central's school demographics did not mirror that of the census tract was during the height of the magnet years, 1991–1996, but especially between 1992–1995, when the school's White enrollment grew to almost 20 percent, though racial residential patterns remained steady.

Census data from 2010 also shows that the area around Central High School is among the poorest in the city, with median household incomes under $15,000.[663] Historic census data supports that by the 1960s, the neighborhoods around Central were becoming less affluent, and that trend has continued. The area's economic viability has been one contributing factor affecting school enrollment.

Central's total enrollment declined to under one thousand in 1989, just before the new Central magnet's grand opening. Enrollment exceeded one thousand students in 1991 and remained above this threshold until

2002, when enrollment again dipped below one thousand students. Central's total student enrollment hit an historic low in 2023—467.[664] Logic would suggest that the attendance area has undergone a significant trimming. Not so, at least not in the last decade. Between 2010 and 2020, Central's census tract experienced a total population growth of nearly 5 percent.[665] Despite this, Central has lost students at an alarming rate, an indication that students who live within the Central attendance area are not enrolling at Central and are most likely exercising choice and attending charter or private schools. The post-magnet years have been particularly challenging for the district as a whole, but especially for Central, a school that has gone from a premier magnet school to a target of school closure.

Central's Negative Reputation

There was little positive news coming out of Central High School in the post-magnet years, aside from the occasional sports accomplishment and the debate team, which was the subject of the 2006 book, *Cross-X*.[666] Still, even then, Central was portrayed as unsafe and its students self-destructive. While this perception was not entirely new, it was more intense. Beginning in the late 1960s, all-Black Central was portrayed as an inferior institution, but after the magnet years, Central was completely written off as a hopeless menace. The constant bombardment of negative news stories advanced a widespread, clear, and specific storyline: Central was a violent and dangerous place, a school to avoid. This view only hardened as a series of negative events at Central played out in the local media.

The closing of Westport and Southwest High Schools in 1998 led to the mixing of student populations. This created student conflict since students from different neighborhoods and, in some cases, with opposing gang affiliations, began attending the same school. One such conflict was particularly severe. Westport transfer student James Whitehead enrolled at Central in the fall of 2004. A year later, in 2005, Whitehead attacked fellow Central student Craig Dydell in the cafeteria, striking him from behind with a box-cutter, slicing his throat, and nearly killing him.[667] It was an unprovoked attack that left Dydell traumatized and unable and unwilling to return to Central.

During that same year—on Friday, November 18, 2005—only thirty-eight of Central's seventy teachers showed up for work. Teachers had staged a "sick-out" in response to the district's handling of another incident in which a Central student showed up to school with a taser and was suspended for three weeks.[668] Many of Central's teachers were unhappy with the administration's disciplinary action, believing three weeks was too lenient a response. Thus, nearly half of Central's teachers called in sick on that Friday in November when the suspended student was allowed back into the building. The district subsequently docked a day's pay for any teacher who skipped school on November 18. The teacher's union, the Kansas City Federation of Teachers, filed a grievance in response to the school district's decision to penalize teachers a day's pay for the sick-out, though no formal action was taken.[669] The teachers, however, perceived the measure as a worthwhile endeavor, despite the loss of pay. They praised the work of the majority of students and cautioned that "the good work of the majority" was threatened by a lax approach in enforcing the code of conduct.[670]

The situation was exacerbated when Superintendent Bernard Taylor determined that the perpetrator of the taser incident was to return to Central after a three-week suspension, stating his case to the board of directors: "[i]f we put them out, lock them up, refer to them as thugs, who will be in our schools?"[671] Superintendent Taylor was referring to the growing narrative that Central was a dangerous school of "thugs." The term "thug" is often a racially charged one that Jon McWhorter, Columbia University linguist, describes as a "nominally polite way of using the N-word."[672]

In addition to the taser incident and Dydell attack, media stories about violence in and around Central High School became more prevalent during the early 2000s: "Black on Black Crime is Still a

Plague," "Deadly Shooting Prompts Outrage," "Gangs' Reach Extends Clear into Eighth Grade," "Police Investigate Shooting that Killed Teen," "Mentors Needed at Central High School," "Shots Fired Near Kansas City's Central High School," "Student Arrested after Taking Gun to School," "Wounded Boy Dies at Help's Door."[673] As local media continued to report these stories, the school district's chief of staff, Jeffery McDaniels, publicly discussed the possibility of building a perimeter fence around the grounds of Central High School.[674] "We are looking at the entire school." McDaniels stated, "[p]arents and students need to have the assurance that we are serious, that we will do whatever is necessary to have a learning environment at Central High School."[675]

Kayla Neal was a student at Central High School between 2005 and 2009 at the height of the negative press. Neal's insight is valuable, as she returned to Central in adulthood and currently works there as the school's trauma sensitive clinician. While Neal's story is uniquely her own, it captures the essence of the individual and structural nature of a Central student's journey.

Kayla Neal

In September 1989, President George H.W. Bush sat in the Oval Office on national television and held in his hand a bag of crack cocaine, which had allegedly been confiscated near the White House. Bush declared crack cocaine the "gravest domestic threat" and he suggested that although "it's as innocent looking as candy," it is "turning our cities into battle zones."[676] The possession of crack, which garnered one hundred times the prison time of possession of cocaine (the powdered version of crack), was treated as criminal behavior rather than as a public health crisis.[677] Moreover, the crack epidemic and subsequent war on crime hit poor communities of color hard. Despite crack and cocaine being chemically similar, crack is cheaper, is typically smoked, and is often marketed to marginalized communities of color. Crack has been disproportionately policed, carrying much harsher penalties than cocaine. Legislation of the 1980s and 1990s resulted in tough-on-crime and racially biased anti-drug policies that ravaged many urban communities; the neighborhoods around Central High School were no exception.

Just a little over a year after his nationally televised declaration about the crack epidemic, Bush was in Kansas City, Missouri, to meet with the Ad Hoc Group Against Crime and its founder, Alvin Brooks. The private meeting, which featured Bush and his drug czar, William Bennett, was the result of Brooks's efforts to combat the crack epidemic gripping the neighborhoods around Central High School. Kansas City became a focal point, a result of Brooks's organization and its offshoot, "Black Men Together," which employed grassroots tactics to close drug houses. Recognized by Bennett as one of the nation's "front-line soldiers" in the nation's war on drugs, Brooks would eventually be named to President Bush's Drug Advisory Council.[678] Brooks's recognition was a result of the growing problem of crack within Kansas City's Black communities, in particular, east of Troost Avenue. Kayla Neal's parents became two of its victims.

Born to a mother addicted to crack and a father who was arrested and incarcerated for crack possession, the crack epidemic changed the trajectory of Neal's life. Neal was raised by her grandmother. She recalled how, when just a young child, her father was arrested, and her mother fled, leaving Neal and her two siblings alone in their apartment. Neal was five years old when her mother left and social workers arrived. Neal would not see her mother again until she was eighteen and her mother was on her deathbed. Neal's dad fell victim to the three-strikes law, an aspect of the Violent Crime Control and Law Enforcement Act of 1994 or "crime bill," which included mandatory life sentences for individuals with three or more felony convictions or "strikes."[679] This disproportionately affected communities of color, with nearly 80 percent of Americans serving life sentences identifying as people of color.[680] Neal's father became one of the statistics. He served ten years in prison before he was paroled, and he missed the formative years of Neal's adolescence. Neal, however, persisted despite her circumstances.

As the salutatorian of Central's class of 2009, one would assume that
school came naturally for Neal. Not exactly. While she described high
school as somewhat effortless, she attributes that partly to Central's
lack of rigor. The year Neal graduated, in 2009, only half of Central's
students graduated in four years.[681] Of those who graduated, roughly
29 percent went on to a four-year college or university. Compare
this to Lincoln College Preparatory Academy, one of the district's
remaining magnet holdovers with a deliberate and explicit college
preparatory curriculum. In 2009, Lincoln's four-year graduation
rate was 100 percent, and nearly 84 percent of Lincoln's students
went on to attend a two- or four-year college upon graduation.[682]
Though the district had firmly transitioned its high schools back to a
neighborhood attendance policy by 2000, one exception was Lincoln
College Preparatory Academy.

Lincoln's history is rooted in segregation, but today, it is the
most integrated of all district high schools, and is home to the highest proportion of White students of any district high school. Lincoln
is also the highest-performing high school in the district. In 2022,
nearly 98 percent of seniors graduated; of those graduates, over 83
percent continued to college. Comparatively, Central's graduation
rate in 2022 was 56 percent, and only 23 percent of its graduates
attended a college or university. Moreover, Lincoln's enrollment is
over one thousand students, more than double the enrollment at
Central.[683] Unlike Central and the other neighborhood district high
schools, Lincoln's admission policy requires students to maintain a
3.0 grade point average in core classes and 90 percent attendance;
its disciplinary policy restricts students to no more than two moderate school offenses. What happens if a student does not maintain
such a standard? They are removed from the school and must attend
their neighborhood high school instead. Thus, Lincoln has become
Kansas City, Missouri's leading district high school and home to the
school district's only International Baccalaureate program, a rigorous
and widely recognized honors program and an attractive option for

high-performing and academically driven students. Lincoln was and is the go-to option for students like Neal.[684] Neal, though, remained at Central despite knowing that her academic opportunities were not equivalent to those of her peers at Lincoln.

For Neal, Central was home, and that feeling of comfort and belonging is still with her today. Neal grew up in the neighborhoods around Central and had family members who had graduated from Central—she valued these connections. Now working at Central High School, Neal claims to have no interest in working at a school outside of Central. When asked whether she would work at another high school if Central were closed, she responded, "No, I have no interest; I would go work in a hospital setting or something like that, but Central is the only school job I'll ever do."[685] It was not as though Neal's journey had been easy, but her fondness for her alma mater was apparent. It is not, however, the kind of blind admiration that sometimes accompanies nostalgia. Neal acknowledges Central had issues, most notably its lack of academic opportunity and rigor.

Neal was not prepared for college-level work. She described how she had to take remedial coursework in her first year and felt overwhelmed and inadequate, especially after receiving her first F. She noted that although she was a straight-A student in high school, once in college, she quickly understood Central had not prepared or challenged her appropriately. Nevertheless, she not only graduated in four years with her bachelor's degree, but she went on to get her master's degree as well. Neal charted her own path, but she was one of just a handful of Central graduates whose post-high school journey from the class of 2009 included success in college. Neal was an exception.

The district was struggling when Neal graduated from Central in 2009. The Kansas City, Missouri School District was only provisionally accredited and had been for the previous seven years. Superintendents were coming and going at a rapid pace. With the threat of another State takeover—the second within ten years—something had to be done. Enter John Covington.

Right-Sizing

The Kansas City, Missouri School District's accreditation struggles began in 2000, when the district lost its accreditation before regaining it in 2002, but only on a provisional basis. When it was still only provisionally accredited in 2006, the State of Missouri revised its accreditation standards as part of the No Child Left Behind Act, and it did not look promising for the district. The 2006 annual performance review revealed that the school district met only three out of a possible fourteen standards, the lowest of any district in the metropolitan area by a considerable margin, and insufficient to keep its provisional accreditation, let alone gain full accreditation. Districts were required to meet nine of fourteen standards for full accreditation.[686] The Kansas City, Missouri School District did, in fact, do enough to keep provisional certification after its 2008 state review. As it had in the past, the district again was provided a two-year window to improve its status and achieve full accreditation or face State takeover. To compound issues, just before the State's review in 2007, Superintendent Anthony Amato was facing allegations and formal complaints of alleged race and gender slurs and was accused of referring to female members of the school board in derogatory ways.[687] A month later, less than two years into his post, Amato resigned. Once more, the district was led by an interim superintendent—John Martin—and the school board was searching for a new superintendent—its twenty-sixth in forty years.

In a rather unusual consensus, the Kansas City, Missouri School District school board unanimously supported the hire of John Covington as superintendent in 2009. Covington came to Kansas City with high praise: "It could well be the most fortunate day for Kansas City," suggested a former school board member with whom Covington worked in Alabama.[688] Covington, who served as superintendent in Pueblo, Colorado, for three years before coming to Kansas City, had a reputation for a no-nonsense approach to reform. The Kansas City, Missouri School District School Board was looking for a superintendent who could orchestrate a district turnaround in short order. Covington arrived in Kansas City in July of 2009. Six months later, he was proposing the school district close half of its schools.

Covington was not the first superintendent to suggest school closures and massive reorganization. School closings were floated in 2000, 2003, and 2005. The school closure plans routinely met firm community resistance. By 2006, it was estimated that the district's seventy school buildings were, on average, 65 percent full.[689] That number was cut to sixty-three schools in 2007, as the Kansas City, Missouri School District lost seven schools to the Independence School District in a contentious annexation struggle between the Independence School District and the Kansas City, Missouri School District. The predominant issue involved schools within Independence city limits that had long been a part of Kansas City, Missouri School District. The overwhelming majority of Independence residents supported the move and had been critical of the Kansas City, Missouri School District, blaming the district for the area's economic decline. Independence residents were keen to have schools within their community join the fully accredited Independence School District. This was a blow for the Kansas City, Missouri School District because it resulted in losing students, and the district had been hemorrhaging students for years. In 2007, total enrollment stood at 24,449, down 10,000 students from 2000 and down over 50,000 students from the height of district enrollment in 1964.[690] When Covington arrived, district enrollment had dropped to 17,677.

School superintendents typically do not survive school closures, and 80 percent list navigating school closures at the top when asked about the most difficult aspects of their job.[691] In Kansas City, Missouri, Covington's predecessors—Bernard Taylor and Anthony Amato—backed away from closing schools as the politically charged nature of the act resulted in community push-back that prohibited them from acting. By 2009, the Kansas City, Missouri School District high schools were only 39.7 percent full, and the district's schools were, on average, only at half capacity.[692] It was clear that something had to be done, especially with an accreditation decision looming. That "something" by March of 2010 became the closure of nearly half of the district's sixty-one schools.

In a 5-4 decision, the school board approved closing twenty-six public schools and educational facilities city-wide.[693] Moreover, all district secondary schools were to serve students in grades seven through twelve, expanding the high schools to include students from the middle schools phased out during Anthony Amato's superintendency. In a cost-saving measure, Amato in 2007 sent all sixth, seventh, and eighth graders (except those at Lincoln College Preparatory Academy and Paseo Academy) to elementary schools rather than closing schools. This was done even though the Kansas City, Missouri School District had commissioned a facilities study that resulted in three scenarios, all of which called for closing between seven and eleven schools. Amato decided to close only middle schools. Covington's right-sizing plan kept middle schools closed but shifted middle school-aged children from district elementary schools to district high schools, a decision that would prove problematic. Ultimately, Covington's plan had a projected savings of $50 million. Along with school closures, it reduced the number of staff by one thousand and implemented a standards-based educational approach that moved away from traditional grade levels and instead emphasized skills achievement.[694]

The "right-sizing Plan" and reorganization of the district saved the district close to $70 million, but just as Covington was implementing what he called phase two of the plan, it was over. Covington resigned in August of 2011, just two years after he had arrived. Superintendent-school board conflict resulted in another Kansas City, Missouri School District superintendent's resignation, and once again, it fell short of the average urban school superintendent's tenure of 2.8 years.[695] The reported conflict between board president Airick Leonard West and Superintendent Covington, which involved a power struggle over who—the board or superintendent—should enter into charter and contract partnerships, was apparently too much to overcome. Covington departed for the State of Michigan, taking a post as the chancellor of the state's Education Achievement Authority, which assumed control of the bottom five percent of Michigan's schools. Covington's position with the State of Michigan was somewhat ironic, as just after Covington left, the State of Missouri in September 2011 revoked Kansas City, Missouri School District's accreditation for a second time in nearly a decade. This was an embarrassing blow, as the district was one of eighteen school districts under review and the only district to lose accreditation.[696] Again, the decision by the state board of education gave the district two years to regain accreditation or face state takeover. Frank discussions unfolded thereafter, which considered several possible solutions. There was talk of an immediate dissolution of the district's school board and a mayoral takeover. One state senator, Jane Cunningham, even proposed legislation that called for dissolving the district altogether and allowing neighboring school districts to take it over. Despite all the noise and grandiose ideas around district dissolution, the Kansas City, Missouri School District remained intact under Covington's successor, Dr. Stephen Green.

The Kansas City, Missouri School District was renamed Kansas City Public Schools in 2013 and was granted provisional certification in 2014, roughly a year after Green signed a five-year contract extension to remain as superintendent, an agreement that would make him the longest-tenured district superintendent since Robert Wheeler, who lasted five years, 1977–1982. Three years into his superintendency, Green was awarded the 2015 Pearce Award as Missouri's Superintendent of the Year. He declared, "When I took this job, it was to stop the revolving door," and went on to say that he intended to stay with the district "as long as I am welcomed."[697] A month later, Superintendent Green announced his departure.

11 | Central and the Desire for Academic Excellence

In 2010, Superintendent Covington appointed Linda Collins to assume leadership at Central after the mid-year removal of Principal Deborah McGill. Collins had been principal at Northeast High School, where she had been successful. However, Collins and all district high school principals were informed that they would have to reapply for their jobs as part of a district initiative of contract non-renewal after the 2009–2010 school year.

Contract non-renewal is a legal tactic school districts use to release contracted employees, in this case principals, to hire different individuals. It is most often used during a period of leadership transition. In this case, Covington used this technique to hand-pick his building leadership team early in his tenure. It can be risky and disruptive. It angered Collins, pushing her to do something she did not honestly want—to leave the district. Collins was not interested in reapplying.[698]

Collins had spent her career moving from school to school. A self-described "clean-up" woman, Collins often transferred to schools to transform the school environment. She finally had landed at a school, Northeast High School, where she envisioned long-term stability and was having success—"I was a happy camper."[699] Then, rather suddenly, she was told she would have to reapply for her current position. Collins was hurt and frustrated—the thought of fighting for the position she already had did not interest her. So, Collins decided to move on. But then the phone rang; it was the district office. Collins recalls the conversation: "Ms. Collins, we noticed that you did not reapply [for a district position]," stated the woman on the line—"we would really like for you to do so."[700] After some reflection, Collins did indeed submit her application, though she had reservations. "Ms. Collins," Covington began after calling her in for a meeting, "we are going to renew you, but we're going to move you . . . "[701] "I knew! I knew!" affirmed Collins emphatically. "I knew they were going to send me to Central."[702] She was right. The "clean-up woman" was instructed to do at Central what she had done at Northeast, which was to improve Central's culture and academic performance. And though Collins did not say it, she was skeptical.

Collins brought with her to Central fifteen teachers and two assistant principals from Northeast High School. She was adamant that turning around Central would require the right people on her team. "The first thing we had to do was clean it up." Collins recalled how the building was in bad shape, with boxes of unopened textbooks filling classrooms piled from floor to ceiling—"it was a hot mess."[703]

The goal for the 2010–2011 school year, Collins explained, was to keep Central out of the news.[704] She was mostly successful in doing so. Collins's first year at Central was the most uneventful year the school had experienced in a decade: "The first thing to do was get order in the building. Now, the boundaries are in place. The expectations are in place."[705] It was not easy, however, and the work was taking its toll on her. Within her first year at Central, Collins was hospitalized with health issues. She attributes her multiple hospitalizations throughout her tenure at Central—between 2010 and 2013—to stress incurred while on the job. In part, the struggle at Central was particularly challenging during Collins's tenure due to the federal government's focus on low-performing schools like Central. Collins was faced with the demands of ensuring academic progress, and it was leading to chronic high blood pressure.

By 2011, the Obama administration had set aside $3.5 billion in federal aid to fund school improvement grants to turn around the nation's worst-performing schools. This was not a new concept since, between 1998 and 2006, No Child Left Behind had previously dispersed $1 billion through a competitive grants process aimed at high-poverty schools. Success was limited. This time, however, states used academic performance indicators to identify the bottom five percent of schools within their states. Missouri identified thirty-one schools statewide; Central High School was among the schools on the list. Collins accepted the challenge, suggesting it was time for a "no-excuses" mantra: "I believe in these kids. Forget the other stuff."[706] Nonetheless, Collins knew it was a lot to ask. What the federal government hoped for—a turnaround story—would require drastic measures. For Collins, one aspect of creating a culture of belief involved changing the school's name.

"It's part of a national trend," suggested Doug Thelman, executive director of the Missouri Charter Public School Association, when asked about Central's proposal to change its name from Central High School to Central Academy of Excellence.[707] "Schools want to distinguish themselves."[708] Indeed, within urban centers and with the growth of charter schools, traditional public schools faced greater student competition. This was most certainly true in Kansas City, where by 2012 when Collins proposed the name change, total enrollment within the city's charter schools was closing in on total district enrollment.[709]

Academy of Excellence

In her own words, Linda Collins described the environment at Central during her tenure as "tough."[710] She reasoned that a name change was a needed reset. "This year will be different," Collins claimed in the summer of 2012 as she prepared to open Central in the fall as the Central Academy of Excellence.[711] While Central struggled to keep its student enrollment up, it also attempted to find teachers. Changing the school's name might change the culture and lure teachers interested in an academically rigorous school environment. In Jared Kastelein's case, it worked.

Urban schools have long struggled to recruit and retain teachers. A 2017 study involving sixteen urban school districts across seven states determined the five-year turnover rate was 55 percent.[712] Within these sixteen urban districts, more than half the teachers left the profession within five years of accepting a job. Often, staffing an urban school, especially with highly qualified teachers, can be challenging. Considering the common perception of urban schools—violent and chaotic, under-resourced with ill-prepared and apathetic Black and Brown students and little parental and community support—it is no wonder teachers have avoided them. Urban schools face systemic challenges not typical in affluent suburban communities, and the media's sensationalism around urban schools advances stereotypes and a negative narrative. The vast majority of teachers are White— roughly 80 percent nationwide—and have few, if any, experiences within an urban school, and it is easy for them to believe the stereotypes.[713] In Kansas City, Central High School long ago became the school to avoid for both students and teachers alike, which makes it even more surprising that Kastelein, a White rural Illinoisan, applied for and accepted a teaching position at Kansas City's Central Academy of Excellence. The school's new name drew him in—"It got me in the door."[714] Kastelein knew nothing of Central when he interviewed for the open science position, but he remained at Central for six years and became an award-winning teacher. Kastelein's story is unusual; there are not many other Kasteleins. However, by the time Kastelein arrived in 2016, Central had been the Central Academy of Excellence for four years. The renaming process, which predated his arrival, was anything but easy and seamless.

The school board gave its stamp of approval in a unanimous vote in July of 2012 and left Superintendent Stephen Green optimistic as he assured the community, "this is not just a cosmetic change."[715] Collins, too, proclaimed that the Central Academy of Excellence would be different than Central High School: "The school will feature more technology in the classroom, stronger discipline, and the benefits of a new alternative school, among other changes."[716] The doors opened at Central Academy of Excellence in August of 2012, but not everyone was pleased.

The Central community, especially alumni, asked why the school's name was changed without a public meeting. Despite participating in the name change, Superintendent Green admitted that board policy was not followed.[717] Subsequently, in November 2012, a public forum was scheduled after the school had officially changed its name. The district was said to be reconsidering its decision. The Tuesday, November 13, 2012, meeting was well-attended and contentious.[718] Central alumni argued that the school's name was an important element of its historic legacy, while school and district representatives, including principal Linda Collins, reaffirmed their support for the change. Collins claimed that once alumni understood that she, too, had family who had graduated from Central and understood the importance of the new name, the community got behind it. Consequently, Central was renamed the Central Academy of Excellence for the 2012–2013 academic year; it would remain the school's official title through the 2018–2019 school year. It was quietly changed back to Central High School in 2019 following board approval, with no mention of the switch in the local media.

Dr. Lynne Shipley was teaching at Central during the name-change saga. She supported it. Shipley was the individual responsible for the presentation to the board, and it was her view that changing an institution's trajectory sometimes required rebranding to show the community that Central was "striving for excellence in a different way."[719] Principal Collins agreed. "Across the U.S.," she explained, "schools with the name of Central are viewed as urban, low-achieving, poverty-stricken schoolhouses."[720] Collins explained her point further:

When the name Central High School in Kansas City is mentioned today, most people raise their eyebrows and give a matter-of-fact look as though they can't say anything positive about the school. This negative image of Central seems to have a negative impact on the students currently enrolled at Central. In fact, many students act out as though they are fulfilling some notion of how they perceive they are supposed to misbehave.[721]

It was Collins's vision that Central Academy of Excellence would instill a sense of pride in its students and subsequently lead to greater opportunity and preparation for post-secondary success. Shipley describes Collins as a fair and equitable administrator unwilling to accept mediocrity. However, the Central Academy of Excellence outlived the administrator responsible for its creation. Though Central would remain the Central Academy of Excellence until 2019, Collins was out after the 2012–2013 school year. In the spring of 2013, she was informed that she would be moved out of Central and into another administrative position within the district. But Collins was done. She said, "I resigned; I got a lawyer; and I made them pay me."[722]

While it was hoped that "excellence" would follow the name change, the rebranding could not by itself achieve that goal. Central Academy of Excellence continued to confront the same problems that Central High School faced in the preceding years, and Central was consistently featured in the media for all the wrong reasons. "The good things we did [at Central]," suggested Shipley, "were never publicized." She would know. Teaching at Central in 2011, Shipley's nationally recognized project, "Segregation Denied," in which her Central students digitally recorded interviews with the first integrated class of Central High School, the class of 1959, earned an ING Unsung Heroes award. Shipley and her students received a $7,000 grant and earned third place in a field of over 1,400.[723] There was no widespread fanfare. The good happening within and around Central High School was almost always overshadowed by the bad. This was at least in part because the bad was indeed really bad. By 2011, homicides within the Central attendance area were among the highest in the city. The neighborhoods around Central High School became known as the "murder factory."[724]

Murder Factory

The number of homicides in 2023 in Kansas City, Missouri, was at its highest ever: 182. This exceeded the all-time high of 179 in 2020 and surpassed the 2022 total of 170.[725] This is not a new problem. The homicide rate in Kansas City, Missouri, has been, on average, three to four times that of the state of Missouri and five to six times that of the nation over the last twenty-five years.[726] It [violent crime] has been particularly acute east of Troost and, more specifically, within zip code 64130, an eight-square-mile area that borders Central High School to the north. The area has been the subject of a 2009 newspaper series and 2011 documentary that notoriously referenced the Central attendance area as the "murder factory."[727]

The economic viability and investment west of Troost, as previously noted, became the priority of city planners, developers, bankers, and real estate agents who saw profitability in racialized spaces and thus used Whiteness to represent safe investments and economic opportunity. Troost remains the division between the haves and have-nots, and race is still foremost. Communities east of Troost are highly segregated and produce social isolation, grinding poverty, and disadvantage. The neighborhoods and zip codes around Central High School, for example, have much higher incarceration rates, higher unemployment rates, higher levels of crime, lower earning potential, and based on the Opportunity Atlas, which traces the roots of affluence and poverty back to neighborhoods, some of the lowest opportunity rates in the city.[728] This includes zip codes 64127, 64128, 64129, and 64130; portions of each are within the attendance boundaries for Central High School.

On Tuesday, February 12, 2019, the violence that for years had been documented within the zip codes and neighborhoods around Central High School landed on its doorstep, literally. Fifteen-year-old Angenique Wright was murdered in the parking lot of Central High School.[729] At the time Wright was killed, the murder of Central students was not an anomaly but had become a tragic reality. Just four months before Wright was murdered, Antonio Jones, a Central honors student, was murdered at a nearby gas station.[730] On this evening in February 2019, however, it happened on the school grounds of Central just after an argument between her and a twenty-one-year-old woman, Jamya Norfleet. The incident started inside the school during a basketball game.[731] Norfleet and Wright were escorted out of the building and into the parking lot. Minutes later, Norfleet shot and killed Wright. Norfleet was arrested.[732]

Central's principal, Anthony Madry, arrived three years before the murder of Wright. He was there the night she was murdered. It is something that still haunts him today. Madry reflected on his time at Central and expressing outrage and astonishment at the trauma he and the entire Central community confronted in dealing with the murder of a student at Central.[733] "Eight kids killed," Madry exclaimed, "tell me a school where eight kids get killed."[734] Madry brought an unconventional leadership style that he described as "love"; it was a student-first approach rooted in his background in special education, resulting in sometimes nontraditional and unpredictable methods. For instance, Madry brought faith-based organizations and leaders into the school, and he also allowed students to determine cafeteria food options. It resulted in a rather tenuous relationship between him and district leadership. Madry's building-level approach sometimes conflicted with the desire of district-level administrators who favored predictable, consistent, and uniform leadership patterns across multiple schools.[735] Madry was not predictable.

To Madry's credit, he was committed to Central and its community. He served from 2016 to 2022—an unusually long time for a Central principal. He was instrumental in bringing back extracurricular activities that had been removed from Central due to falling enrollment and budgetary constraints, most notably the marching band, which Central had not had for a decade when Madry arrived. It was during his administration, as well, that choir, dance, and cheer were reintroduced.[736] Madry prioritized community involvement and extracurricular participation, but the graduation and attendance rates and academic performance were troubling, as was the case with the previous administrations. Madry felt hamstrung by a district that was disconnected and out of tune with the realities of what Central's students and staff were facing every day. It was the bureaucratic structure of the school district that drove Madry out. Moreover, the 2019 murder of Angenique Wright deeply troubled him. As principal during that time, Madry faced criticism and blame; he was even listed among several defendants in a lawsuit filed by Wright's mother, accusing Madry and others within KCPS of negligence. Madry had reached his limit. He was ready to move on, done with serving as the principal of a high school within the so-called murder factory.

The reference to the murder factory originated with a 2009 article in the *Kansas City Star* by Tim Rizzo entitled "Murder Factory: 64130, The Zip Code of Notoriety."[737] This was followed up by a 2011 documentary film, *Kansas City Murder Factory*.[738] Rizzo's piece was a three-part series that detailed the eight-square-mile area—zip code 64130—in Kansas City, Missouri, which he explained was home to 101 murderers incarcerated in Missouri: "No other zip code in Kansas City or St. Louis or any other part of the state comes close. . . . If society set out to produce an assembly line of killers, it's hard to imagine a model any more efficient than what exists within its boundaries. . . ."[739] In part three, Rizzo addressed how the murder factory could theoretically be dismantled. Of the six listed problems, "[l]ack of education" is one of them.[740] He goes on to consider "[w]hat Kansas City can do."[741] Rizzo's answer? Hire the right superintendent. In January 2009, when Rizzo wrote this article, the district was in the midst of one of its many superintendent searches. John Covington was hired. Still, by 2015, two superintendents had come and gone—Covington and his successor, Green—and the district was once again under the leadership of an interim, Al Tunis.

A Changing Educational Landscape

As Al Tunis's interim superintendency commenced in June 2015, he faced the same issues confronting his predecessors: low academic performance, falling enrollment, lack of community confidence, and accreditation concerns. District administrative consistency was another concern, given that the school board was filling a superintendent vacancy for the sixth time in a decade. Tunis was serving as the district's chief financial officer when he was called upon to fill Green's unexpected vacancy. He had served in his interim role for just over a year when the school board unanimously voted to hire Baltimore educator Mark Bedell as the district's forty-first superintendent. Like his predecessors, Bedell said the right things. He spoke of gaining full accreditation and ending the revolving door of superintendents, but this was Bedell's first time in the role. It was quite a project for an inexperienced superintendent.

Bedell arrived in Kansas City in time to assume leadership before the 2016–2017 school year. That year, Kansas City was home to twenty-two charter schools and had been fighting for accreditation for nearly two decades. Over that time, the district had been consistently losing students. Many of them left KCPS for charter schools. When Bedell arrived, the district was down to fewer than fifteen thousand students. When charters were initiated in 1998, the district's enrollment was over thirty-five thousand.[742] Bedell, however, did not view charter schools as adversaries:

> I've said this to everyone: I'm a pro-choice individual. I've been dealing with charter schools ever since I became an administrator in Houston. Houston, Texas is huge on charter schools. Parents deserve to have their kids in a school where they're going to be educated appropriately. I believe that charters are important, because you want to give people choices. We all should have one vision, and that vision is to make Kansas City the finest city in this country from an educational standpoint. This opportunity we have with the Kansas City Neighborhood Academy is a great opportunity for us to show that we are willing to participate in this charter school movement. Let's see how successful this is.[743]

The Kansas City Neighborhood Academy (KCNA), which Bedell referenced, was one of three new charter schools in 2016, but it was the first to be sponsored by the school district. The school was modeled after the Drew Charter School in Atlanta, Georgia, and was part of Kansas City's Urban Neighborhood Initiative. It was hoped that the school could boost the district's educational image and attract new residents.[744] In a somewhat controversial move, KCNA was moved into the high-performing Wendell Phillips Elementary School for the 2016–2017 school year, and children from Wendell Phillips were moved to Crispus Attucks Elementary School. By the spring of 2019, KCNA was one of two Kansas City charter schools closing, just three years after it had been opened. KCNA struggled to meet its enrollment goals and financial responsibilities. There is a harsh reality with charter schools: they can be closed if they do not fulfill their financial responsibilities and performance or enrollment goals. This most certainly complicates an educational landscape that has become increasingly challenging to navigate.

Upon his arrival in Kansas City, when Bedell affirmed the notion of choice in schooling, choice and competition had been securely established as core elements of the modern public school system in most US cities, including Kansas City. When Bedell took over KCPS, the district was already among the top five districts in the country by percentage of charter school enrollment, and this has remained consistent. A report published in 2022 by the *National Alliance for Public Charter Schools* ranked Kansas City and KCPS third among all cities and school districts in the United States—meaning that charter school enrollment is the third highest in the country, with 49 percent of KCPS school-aged children attending charter schools.[745] It should be noted that an educational choice market is complex and inequitable. This became the focus of a 2023 quantitative study in which the authors, Saatcioglu and Snethen, explored parent satisfaction and what they called "preference compromise" within school choice "markets" in Kansas City, Missouri.[746]

Preference compromise gets at the compromises parents make regarding school attendance. In essence, school choice introduces market influences and positions parents as consumers who, like all consumers, must make choices based on their priorities. According to the authors, many parents within Kansas City, Missouri, exercise choice and, therefore, make compromises about their child's or children's education and schooling. Of the roughly thirty thousand school-attending children in Kansas City, Missouri, as of 2023, only 25 percent attend their neighborhood-zoned public school.[747] This means that parents of 75 percent of Kansas City, Missouri, students are typically selecting charter schools, private schools, or KCPS thematic signature schools. There are nine KCPS signature schools, which operate like magnet schools and are open to all KCPS students but often include selective admission criteria, such as language proficiency, behavioral expectations, and grade point average requirements.[748]

Ultimately, the study affirms that preference compromise inequity exists within the choice market, that "low-income and less educated parents and those from historically marginalized racial/ethnic backgrounds engage in a greater degree of preference compromise" and are thus less satisfied with their respective school choices.[749] Parents' highest-ranked preferences are teacher quality, academic performance, curriculum, and safety.[750] While the unit of analysis of a choice system is at the individual level, it is also important to recognize the systemic issues that affect how individuals experience the act of choice. Said differently, choosing a school is not equitable or fair; it is not experienced the same by all—and there is a definitive socioeconomic and racial element in this process.

In a 2021 interview, author Jon Hale, whose book, *The Choice We Face*, which focuses on the issue of race within the school choice debate, suggested that race is "baked into" the notion of school choice.[751] Hale asserts that while school choice has been framed in a way that emphasizes freedom and individualism, it has been used to preserve segregation and maintain racist and classist inequalities.[752]

Often, charter schools, particularly in marginalized communities, are promoted as vanguards of equality and empowerment. Nationally, the numbers do not support such an assertion, nor do they in Kansas City, Missouri.

School Choice in Kansas City, Missouri

The new educational landscape in Kansas City, Missouri, is often referred to as "The Kansas City Public Education System (KCPES)," which encompasses KCPS and charter schools as one "system."[753] This results from the fact that KCPS and Kansas City, Missouri, charter schools serve the same students and community. The importance of this new school order, especially regarding student enrollment, demographics, and student performance, cannot be overstated. The system of district and charter schools—KCPES—results in school system fragmentation, posing challenges for families who struggle to navigate the twenty-three separate public school systems within the KCPS geographic area, which operate under different rules of governance and educational models.[754]

A recent systems analysis by the University of Missouri-Kansas City's Urban Education Research Center explored this new educational landscape in Kansas City, and the investigation yielded some interesting data. With the creation of charters within Kansas City in 1998, charter enrollment quickly expanded, and KCPS and charter enrollment is roughly a 50/50 split. The demographics are almost identical, as well.[755]

Race	KCPS	Charter	KCPES
Black	54%	54%	54%
Latinx	28%	29%	28%
White	10%	12%	11%
Multiracial	2%	4%	4%
Other	6%	1%	3%

Table 10: Comparison of KCPS, Charter School, and KCPES Enrollment by Race, 2023

It should be noted that KCPS has a higher population of students with disabilities and students who have limited English proficiency than charters schools, at 3 percent and 4 percent, respectively.[756] Regarding race, the difference between KCPS and charter schools is almost indistinguishable.

Perhaps the most alarming finding from the demographic study is related to mobility and homelessness. Within KCPES—district and charter schools—nearly 25 percent of all students changed schools at least once in 2022, and almost 10 percent of all KCPES students were homeless in the same year.[757] The Missouri Department of Elementary and Secondary Education (DESE) calculates that the mobility rates system-wide are well above state averages. Within KCPS neighborhood schools, however, mobility rates have been consistently high for the last decade, reaching nearly 50 percent between 2016 and 2018, meaning almost half of KCPS students enrolled in a neighborhood school changed schools at least once within a school year.[758] It is not as if this was occurring under the radar. In 2015, Turn the Page KC, a local nonprofit organization, hosted a summit on student mobility. This was followed up by initiatives through the Kansas City Eviction Project and The Family Stability Initiative of the United Way of Kansas City, which both focused on the student mobility problem in Kansas City.[759] These efforts led to a rather unusual data-sharing agreement between Kansas City nonprofits and KCPS. Yet, issues of student mobility and retention persist.

At the individual level, student mobility leads to lower individual test scores, a higher rate of grade retention (having to repeat a grade level), and an increased risk of dropping out of school.[760] Even one move can lead to a greater risk of not graduating or delaying graduation, let alone multiple moves, which Chester Hartman of the Poverty and Race Research Action Council suggests lead to "chaos" and makes reforms such as better trained teachers, smaller class sizes, and better facilities "irrelevant."[761] Student mobility often has implications for schools as well, reducing performance and accountability measures.[762] Performance and accountability serve as the primary measures of accreditation. Schools need students, not only to meet minimum attendance requirements, but also to be prepared for state testing.

Of particular concern within KCPES is the retention of high school students, who are leaving at an unusually high rate. KCPES serves 47 percent fewer students in twelfth grade than in kindergarten, which naturally leads to enrollment issues at the high school level.[763] A KCPS Systems Analysis publicized in 2019 suggested that 57 percent of all KCPS schools are below the district's desired school size range and well below national standards. The 2016 KCPS Master Plan determined the desired school enrollment range for high schools at between 700 and 1,200 students. As of 2019, twelve of fifteen KCPES high schools were below 700 students; one high school was approaching the target, and two were within the desired range.[764] KCPES does not keep its high school students through matriculation, as system-wide enrollment decreases of 20 percent or more over the last five years have been common between ninth and tenth grade.[765] Within KCPS, many ninth-grade students have to repeat ninth grade from the previous year—for example, 22 percent in 2019.[766] A snapshot from 2017 suggests that 74 percent of the students who left a KCPS school that year left the district altogether. All of this harms student performance.

KCPS, compared to the state of Missouri overall, has underperformed for over two decades on every macro-level measurement of academic performance—state assessments, graduation rates, ACT, etc., and the district's performance is lower than that of the state. Over the last five years, district performance on state assessments in English language arts (ELA) and math has been, on average, 20 percent or more below that of the state.[767] When it comes to district schools and charter schools, however, the difference is minimal. The gap between district and charter ELA performance has narrowed in the last two years, with charters outperforming district schools by 4 percent in 2022; the same is true in Math at 4 percent. Both district and charter schools remain well below the state average and significantly behind Missouri suburban districts, such as Lee's Summit and Blue Springs, whose combined ELA and math proficiency scores are roughly 30 percent higher.[768] Lee's Summit and Blue Springs are school districts where 70 percent of all students are White.[769] There is an unmistakable racial component at play here, whereby White students are outperforming both Black and Latinx students. The Black-White gap within KCPES alone in combined ELA and math proficiency in 2022 was 37 percent; the Latinx-White gap was 31 percent.[770] Moreover, within KCPS, there is a clear distinction in academic performance between district neighborhood schools and district signature schools. Among district high schools, Central has one of the lowest academic performances.

Central, Lincoln, and the Two-Tiered System

An essential feature of The Long Range Magnet Plan orchestrated in Kansas City, Missouri, throughout the 1980s and 1990s, was a comprehensive, district-wide magnet approach. This resulted in all district high schools and middle schools (and half of its elementary schools) being reconceptualized as themed magnet schools. The comprehensive aspect of the magnet approach was intentional insofar as the objective was to avoid a two-tiered system whereby one school could be advantaged over another. The fear at the time was that an educational choice system featuring only a handful of magnet schools would generate widespread inequity. As the district deconstructed its magnet plan and converted many of its magnet schools to neighborhood schools in the late 1990s and early 2000s, including Central High School, there were exceptions.

Some of the district's magnet schools were left intact. The magnet schools, now called "signature" schools, include three high school options—African-Centered College Preparatory Academy, Lincoln College Preparatory Academy, and Paseo Academy of Fine and Performing Arts. The Early College Academy (ECA) can also be included on the list. The ECA is a dual-credit partnership program between the school district and the local community college, Penn Valley Community College. Participating high school students who qualify leave their home high school during their final two years of high school to attend community college and simultaneously earn their Associate of Arts degree and high school diploma.[771] Lincoln and Paseo are the two stand-alone themed high school options; Central, East, Northeast, and Southeast are the district's current neighborhood schools. Among the district high schools, Central and Lincoln, the district's two most historic high schools, provide a rather interesting juxtaposition.

School	Central High School	East High School	Lincoln College Preparatory Academy	Paseo Academy of Fine and Performing Arts	Northeast High School	Southeast High School
Type	Neighborhood	Neighborhood	Signature	Signature	Neighborhood	Neighborhood
Total Students	467	1065	1005	654	609	462
Demographics	85% Black 10% Hispanic 4% White	47% Hispanic 42% Black 5% White	39% Black 31% Hispanic 22% White	57% Black 31% Hispanic 8% White	44% Black 32% Hispanic 9% White	87% Black 6% Hispanic 4% White
4 Year Graduation Rate	56%	66%	98%	84%	72%	67%
% Attending College (2 or 4 year)	23%	34%	82%	41%	27%	26%
Average Composite ACT	13.6 with 61% taking	13.4 with 58% taking	20.8 with 99% taking	14.4 with 85% taking	13.7 with 58% taking	13.6 with 58% taking
Special Education	21%	10%	1%	18%	17%	17%

Table 11: Comparison of KCPS Schools, 2023[772]

In the aftermath of the Court's 2003 order and the dismantling of Kansas City's district-wide magnet program, Central and Lincoln

High Schools took very different paths. Lincoln's college preparatory magnet theme remained intact, while Central's computer and Greek athletic magnet themes were deconstructed. Thus, Lincoln continued to attract district-wide enrollment, appealing to students interested in college readiness through advanced placement courses and a unique International Baccalaureate Diploma program designed to promote critical thinking and college preparation. Central reverted to a neighborhood school, meaning specialized academic programming was removed from the curriculum, and Central's enrollment was confined to district-approved neighborhood attendance boundaries. Lincoln was named a National Blue Ribbon School in 2014, followed by being named the best high school in Missouri in 2015 by *U.S. News and World Report*.[773] Nearly all the news out of Lincoln in the post-magnet years was positive. For every positive storyline emerging out of Lincoln, there was a negative one at Central. Two distinct narratives were unfolding: Lincoln High School became the district's shining star, the premier high school option for college-bound students; Central and other district neighborhood schools were relegated to second-class status.

There is particular irony in the current arrangement of KCPS high schools, which places Lincoln at the top and Central at the bottom (see Table 11). In the late 1970s, Lincoln High School was 100 percent Black and had been since its creation as an all-Black, segregated high school in the late nineteenth century. Lincoln was the only high school option for Black students in Kansas City, Missouri, for more than fifty years. With its history rooted in de jure segregation as a Black institution, even after the destruction of school segregation, White residents were not interested in sending their White children to Lincoln despite its impressive academic record as one of the best high schools in the nation. It was a Black school, after all, which, to the White community, represented inferiority. Thus, Lincoln remained all Black for more than two decades following the *Brown* decision. Then, in 1978, Lincoln was re-envisioned as the district's first magnet school. The district incorporated an intentional college preparatory focus within its magnet curriculum to attract White students. Many argued it would not work, but despite initial skepticism, it did.

Today, almost all of Lincoln's more than one thousand students, with a relatively balanced demographic mix, graduate in four years; just over half of Central's fewer than five hundred mostly Black students do the same. A mere 1 percent of Lincoln students receive special education services; over 20 percent of Central students receive such services. Upon graduation, over 80 percent of Lincoln's students continue on to post-secondary opportunities, while fewer than 25 percent of Central's students do so. Academic performance is similarly dichotomous. There was not a statistically significant number of Central students who scored at the proficient or advanced level on the 2022 Missouri Assessment Program scores in math, English language arts, science, or social studies. Too few students scored in the range to show up on the reported data. That was not how it played out at Lincoln, where over 70 percent scored proficient or advanced in English language arts, and roughly 50 percent of students scored at that level in science and social studies, respectively.[774] The only similarity between the two schools is their notable historic significance.

The accumulated effect of perceived failure at Central has taken its toll. The characterization of Central as dangerous and failing and the growing stratification within urban education in Kansas City has resulted in Central High School taking on the identity of a "bad" school with "bad" kids. Central and its students have long been characterized as such, but within the contemporary educational choice market, the stereotypes have become even more widespread and entrenched. Dr. Allenda Williams, who worked at Central for nearly a decade as a teacher, instructional coach, and vice principal between 2013 and 2022, believes that students have internalized negative messages and that those messages have hampered individual success. Research suggests that students' perceptions of the school environment influence social and academic engagement.[775] The stigma or unwanted identity accompanying the failing urban school is created at the institutional level but is often experienced at the individual level; students internalize notions that lead to feelings of diminishment and shame. There is a genuine racial element to all of this as well. Like Kansas City's Central High School, enrollment within urban neighborhood schools is almost always exclusively Black and Brown. Biases permeate notions of Blackness and associations with violence, chaos, and failure. Compounding the issue further is that selective magnet schools and charter schools continue to trap the most marginalized students within urban neighborhood schools, a far cry from the vision of the neighborhood public school as a democratically constructed, inclusive institution. There are real-life consequences as urban schools consistently underperform in nearly every measure of academic success. The fallout often comes in the form of constant threats of closure. Kansas City's Central High School is no exception.

12 | The Threat of Permanent Closure

Emotions were running high on a mid-October evening in 2022. A standing-room-only crowd piled into Central High School's cafeteria for a listening session, to which KCPS had invited community members to hear about and give input on the potential closure of ten KCPS schools. The mood was tense. Blueprint 2030, the KCPS long-term restructuring plan, involved consolidating or closing schools with low enrollment to free up opportunities to modernize classrooms and expand access to extracurricular activities and academic opportunities.[776]

Blueprint 2030 was the work of Superintendent Mark Bedell, who, in the face of dwindling enrollment, asked:

> How much do you think a high schooler can get in a school where the [enrollment numbers] are under 500? Do you think you can offer band? Do you think you can have debate? Do you think you can fill the football team throughout the whole season? . . . It's not possible.[777]

He continued, "And is that fair to our kids that we continue to offer a system like this that does not give them a true comprehensive experience?"[778]

Bedell, an assistant superintendent in Baltimore, had never held a school district's top post. The stakes were particularly high in Kansas City, where the district was still not fully accredited at the time of Bedell's arrival. No superintendent had remained in Kansas City for more than four years since Robert Wheeler, who had served from 1977 to 1982. Given the context, the skepticism was reasonable. By the time Bedell began publicizing his Blueprint 2030, however, the district was on the verge of full accreditation for the first time in over twenty years, and he was just beginning his sixth year as KCPS Superintendent. On Tuesday, January 11, 2022, Bedell and KCPS learned it had achieved full accreditation.[779] There was not much time to revel in celebration, though. Five months later, on June 9, 2022, Bedell announced his resignation.

Bedell's departure was a surprise and was met with a mix of reactions, from anger and despair to appreciation and pride. Bedell was moving on, headed to Anne Arundel County Public Schools (AACPS), a metropolitan Baltimore, Maryland, district, where he was later named the 2023 National Alliance of Black School Educators Superintendent of the Year.[780] It was a homecoming of sorts for Bedell, a district he knew well, having departed the area in 2016 to lead KCPS. At AACPS, Bedell would oversee the education of more than eighty thousand students, a far cry from the fewer than fifteen thousand KCPS students he was leaving behind.[781]

Students in Kansas City would now be under the leadership of interim superintendent Dr. Jennifer Collier, a twenty-two-year veteran of KCPS. She was the first interim superintendent since 2009, when Clive Coleman served in such a capacity.[782] It was up to Collier to keep KCPS fully accredited and move the district forward, guided by Blueprint 2030. Just four short months after Bedell's exodus, Collier presented to the KCPS School Board about the potential of closing ten KCPS schools. It's not exactly the way a superintendent likes to begin their tenure. The most notable school on the closure list? Central High School.

Saving Central

"This might as well be Blueprint 1977," suggested a community member, Paul Cosby, at one of the district's school closure listening sessions in the fall of 2022.[783] Cosby was referencing district decisions decades before that disproportionately impacted Black and Brown students. It was a sentiment that many Central alumni and community members shared—that notion of "here we go again." To be sure, KCPS found itself in a precarious position. Despite the closure of forty-four buildings between 2007 and 2018, many of the school district's schools were still well under capacity in 2022. Blueprint 2030 proposed closing ten additional schools, bringing that closure total to fifty-four. Critics of the plan worried about building utilization upon closure. Nearly 70 percent of the forty-four schools KCPS had closed in the preceding years remained vacant. Central, it was proposed, would be one of the buildings to be repurposed and used for its athletic facilities, though it was not clear exactly how that would work. But still, the Central community struggled to understand: Why Central?

The school district's reasoning for closing Central was quite simple. It was the numbers. Central can hold 1,200 students, but enrollment had not been near that in more than a decade. In the last five years, total student enrollment had hovered around five hundred students, even dipping below that number during the 2022 and 2023 school years.[784] School district projections predicted continued student population decline over the next decade. Several current Central teachers suggested that the listed numbers were far higher than actual attendance, meaning fewer students than reported were showing up to school. One teacher estimated that school-wide daily attendance was closer to three hundred students. In contrast, another teacher offered that of the average twenty-five students on her roster, daily classroom attendance was often as low as seven. This had affected staffing, course offerings, extracurricular activities, and the like. In 2021, Superintendent Bedell questioned the academic opportunity a high schooler could experience in a school where the enrollment numbers were under five hundred.[785] On a practical level, the question was legitimate. Central already combined some athletic teams with Southeast High School due to low participation, and a lot went in to keeping a school building running. Did it not make sense to close the school if there was consistent under-enrollment and underperformance? Indeed, it did, or at least it might.

Researcher Argun Saatcioglu explored the relationship between school closures, property values, and incidences of crime in Kansas City between 2007 and 2018. What he discovered was that school closures, particularly in high-poverty neighborhoods of color, had adverse effects on both crime and housing prices. So within low-income communities of color—such as those in which Central resides—school closures led to an increase in incidences of crime and a reduction of housing values. This was not true of communities with high social and political capital. School closures within communities with greater levels of wealth benefited from countervailing forces, which reduced the ill effects of a school's closure. For example, a vacant school in an affluent part of the city might be redeveloped as condominiums. Saatcioglu also found that the closure of KCPS buildings led to the growth of charter school density. Thus, the closure of one KCPS school resulted in the addition of 1.2 charter schools.[786] This was not good for a school district already losing a proportion of its students to a growing charter school landscape.

Central High School was newly built in 1991, making it easily the most modern of all current high school buildings. The other KCPS high schools—Lincoln, East, Northeast, Paseo, and Southeast—were all built in the early twentieth century. "We don't understand," asserted Chester Brock, a 1977 Central graduate, "if we have the Central facility with an Olympic pool, football field, auditorium, science labs, and all of that, why would we not keep it open?"[787] The sentiment shared by many was that Central's facilities alone justify its continued use. Central has impressive and unique building features, but it also has $14 million in deferred maintenance costs; at least, that is what MGT Consulting, the group the school district hired to evaluate facilities, concluded. When pressed on the issue, a spokesperson for MGT pointed out that the Central building, though newer than the other district high schools, was thirty years old and the construction was not built to last.

Complicating the matter further, KCPS has struggled to pass bond initiatives. Up until April of 2025, KCPS had not successfully passed a bond issue in fifty-six years. In 1967, Kansas City Voters approved a bond issue. They just did so again in 2025. A remarkable feet given the decades-long drought. Bond initiatives are the most common way for a school district to borrow money to fund building projects. The school district's money in the late 1980s and early 1990s to renovate and newly construct schools resulted from court-ordered funds rather than publicly supported ones like bond issues. When the *Jenkins* money ran out, there was no reserve available. The result: most KCPS schools need repair, but there wasn't a funding source to cover the bill.

KCPS district leaders suggested they were interested in community feedback before making final decisions about closing schools. The district had learned that lesson the hard way. Superintendent Covington's rightsizing plan of 2010 and the closing of twenty-six district schools were not well received at the time. Interim Superintendent Collier would not make the same mistake: ". . . we don't want to just place Central students at Southeast without considering the things that are important to them, the pride that they have in their school."[788] The community outcry was intense, especially after it was made public that the plan for Central students involved attending Southeast High School upon Central's closure. The Central community strongly opposed this plan.

The "Save Our Schools" initiative was born, and community organizers argued the district's school closure plan would represent a "death blow" to neighborhood schools.[789] Combining Central and Southeast seems logical when looking only at the numbers. Still, many were confused by the district's initial push to repurpose Central and use Southeast High School as the combined Southeast/Central school location. Southeast High School's structure is more than fifty years older than Central High School's, but the district claimed that maintenance costs at Southeast were lower than that of Central and that fewer students resided in the Central attendance area. While the two schools are the least populated schools, they are also the only two remaining majority-Black high schools in the district and have the highest proportion of students receiving special education services. Moreover, they have the lowest four-year graduation rates, lowest average ACT scores, and lowest percentage of students attending college.[790] Given the circumstances, the decision to combine the two schools seemed risky and left an important question looming—how does the consolidation of Central and Southeast benefit students, and to what extent would any benefit outweigh the many adverse effects?

The two schools have unique school contexts and proud school traditions. They also are situated roughly five miles apart. Central's closure would require Central students to travel five miles from their neighborhoods surrounding Central High School. "The real story is that there are a lot of neighborhood block-based beefs," claimed Mayor Quinton Lucas, alluding to potential student conflict in merging Central and Southeast. It was possible, since conflict had occurred before when Westport had closed and its students ended up at other district high schools, including Central.

Ultimately, it is not completely clear why—other than community anger, particularly around the potential closing of Central—KCPS considerably scaled back their closure plan from ten schools to two. There is not much in the way of local coverage regarding KCPS's course change, but at the beginning of 2023, the district released an updated plan that included closing two elementary schools, Troost and Longfellow, and keeping the other eight schools, including Central, open. The school board signed off, and just like that, Central was saved.

The news was met with excitement among supporters of Central. "If I was younger, I'd jump in the air," asserted Teola Powell, a 1966 Central graduate.[791] Interim Superintendent Collier provided insight into the decision-making process: "The safety and well-being of our students is one of the highest priorities. And there is a great deal that will need to be addressed and considered if we were to move forward with a secondary school closure."[792] Collier explained that the decision to keep Central (and other district schools) open was not meant to be a long-term solution. Schools like Central must prove their worth by increasing enrollment and improving academic outcomes. KCPS, after all, was still facing a $25 million shortfall and staring down enrollment shortages.

Money and Leadership

The Elementary and Secondary School Emergency Relief Fund (ESSER) was established to assist school districts through the challenges faced during and immediately following the COVID-19 pandemic.[793] KCPS was the beneficiary of such funds in several iterations. A portion of the funding was allocated for academic support (hiring math and reading specialists) and to address deferred building maintenance.[794] This was a considerable amount—tens of millions of dollars—and it has been helpful. But to be sure, school financing is messy, with nearly 80 percent coming from local sources of revenue, namely tax levies and bonds.

In addition to the fifty-eight year bond drought, the dilemma within KCPS is that the tax levy has remained stagnant at just under $4.96 per $100 assessed valuation since 1995.[795] The results have been funding deficits. It is estimated that KCPS and Jackson County charter schools lost roughly $45 million in 2022 funding due to developers receiving tax breaks.[796] As an enticement, cities use tax breaks to waive or defer local tax payments. The deferment can be for years or even decades: "Any unnecessary dollar flowing into a private development project is a dollar that isn't going into our public school classrooms."[797] This is perhaps an oversimplification, but the point is valid—KCPS is short hundreds of millions of dollars in deferred maintenance alone. The district can ill afford to miss out on tens of millions of dollars in re-directed revenue.

There does appear to be opportunity for the district to garner some additional funding through new funding sources. KCPS benefited from a significant increase in property values in 2023. While the KCPS tax levy is the second lowest in Jackson County, the average property tax for 2023 on a home in Jackson County went up by 35 percent. Property tax is a critical funding source for public school districts, especially districts like KCPS that have been unsuccessful in generating public support for tax levy increases and bond initiatives. In KCPS, where capital funds are not available to cover staffing and operational costs, tax levies cover the cost of nearly everything. The increase in Jackson County property tax means a payout for KCPS and additional funding of up to $260 million. This is good news for a district with deferred maintenance costs in the $400 million range.[798]

Like everything involved in school funding, though, it is complicated. A Missouri state law—The Hancock Amendment— requires school districts to lower a tax levy if property tax rates increase faster than inflation. In Jackson County, assessed property values have risen 40 percent since 2021; the consumer price index has increased by 13 percent.[799] In all districts other than KCPS, this would require a tax levy reduction, but that is not so in KCPS. The Hancock Amendment does not apply to KCPS because Judge Russell Clark established the federally mandated tax levy more than twenty-five years ago, another relic from *Jenkins*.

Additionally, KCPS recently ended that fifty-eight year bond initiative drought. In the spring of 2025, the voting public passed a general obligation (GO) bond, which are municipal bonds utilized to raise money for projects that are not direct revenue-generating measures, like schools. As such, KCPS plans to use the bond for constructing three new schools, a primary component of Blueprint 2030. With the passage of the bond, KCPS now has the opportunity to move forward with construction and renovation plans. This is a big win for Superintendent Jennifer Collier.

After Bedell's departure, Kansas City followed the typical process for finding a superintendent. The school board and its search firm conducted a national search and interviewed five candidates. The district had become familiar with the process over the years, as superintendents came and went with great frequency. Former Superintendent Bedell was the exception, having remained longer than all of those before him in recent memory. James Hazlett was the last superintendent with a longer tenure than Bedell, and that was in 1955.

That the district was engaging in a time-consuming and costly national superintendent search was somewhat surprising. After all, as Bedell remarked in his farewell address, "The district is in good hands."[800] He was referring to Collier, his deputy superintendent and interim replacement. Collier had also won the support of local community members, who routinely praised her efforts throughout the difficult school closure process. It is unusual for a superintendent to receive compliments amidst serious discussions about closing schools, but Collier's willingness to listen to community members won her their support. "We have been impressed," stated Gregg Lombardi, executive director of the Lykins Neighborhood, in the northeast part of the city and near Whittier Elementary School, which was among the initial ten schools scheduled to close.[801] In reference to Collier, he complimented her "willingness to listen to difficult feedback and to have frank discussions about really difficult issues."[802]

The KCPS School Board made it official in mid-February 2022, and Collier's interim designation was removed. Dr. Jennifer Collier was the board's unanimous selection as the district's forty-second superintendent. Collier had already navigated her way through difficulty. School closures often represent the end of the line for superintendents. Though counter-intuitive, in Collier's situation, it might have been this very issue that secured her the permanent superintendency due to her willingness to listen to the community and scale back closing ten schools to just two. Perhaps the decision served to appease the public and delay the inevitable. For now, Central and seven additional KCPS schools survived, but the last several years have been anything but easy.

The COVID Years

COVID hit Central hard, as it did most urban schools. There was much uncertainty initially. It was March 16, 2020, when KCPS closed all district schools. Students did not return to school again that academic year. Many high school students would not enter a school building until fall 2022. For seniors like Mikayla Witcher, Central class of 2020, high school as they knew it was over. In that initial period, the spring of 2020, all teaching was remote, which involved students being given packets of work to complete on their own time and having to report to online classes. It did not go well. "I hated it," proclaimed Witcher.[803] Witcher was among the unfortunate 2020 high school graduates who were robbed of their final semester of high school when life essentially stopped in mid-March. Witcher was second in her class and a great student. And although she is a self-described introvert, she did not enjoy online schooling. Unlike many of her classmates, though, she showed up virtually. Nearly half of students district-wide did not. Only 55 percent of KCPS students participated in the district's remote schooling option in the spring of 2020.[804] This occurred for various reasons, not least because of digital equity and issues of Wi-Fi access across the KCPS district.

The digital divide significantly impacts people of color who are concentrated in lower-income communities. According to the Kansas City Connectivity Report, which detailed digital access issues during COVID, roughly 20 percent of the households within Central's attendance area did not have internet access, and 9 percent of households district-wide were without internet access.[805] KCPS did what it could to prioritize Wi-Fi connectivity for families, but a structural issue of such a magnitude is not an easy fix. Progress has been made since the 2020 connectivity report was released, specifically focusing on the third congressional district within which Central is situated. In COVID's aftermath, a Digital Equity Office was created by the city of Kansas City, Missouri, with the explicit purpose of increasing digital equity and working to close the divide. The full extent of the program has yet to be realized, but it does represent limited but meaningful growth. For Central students from the COVID years, however, it is too little, too late.

Lynnica Harley was a junior at Central during the 2019–2020 academic year. She recalled how her life dramatically changed overnight. She was a good student—As and Bs—loved representing her school on the volleyball and basketball court and running track. Abruptly, though, it was all gone, and her grades suffered. "I'm not an online person," Harley remarked, and she was not alone. By the summer, it was clear with COVID still ever-present, online was the only option the district could reasonably undertake in the fall of 2020. There were hopes that in-person schooling would resume for the fall semester, but July 2020 marked another spike in COVID cases, leaving Superintendent Bedell remarking that the "nightmare" would not go away. The logistical challenges were unprecedented.[806]

At home again in the fall of 2020, Harley started prioritizing work over school. Central's principal at the time, Anthony Madry, was alarmed by what he saw, and with good reason. By the end of the fall 2020 semester, enrollment data was extremely disconcerting, showing combined district and charter enrollment down 20 percent.[807] High school students, especially within lower-income communities, were taking on responsibilities of watching over younger siblings at home while parents worked or were working themselves. Leslie Kohlmeyer of Show Me KC Schools, an independent nonprofit organization established to assist parents in navigating Kansas City's public school educational landscape, went so far as to suggest, in reference to Kansas City's public school system, "we are on the verge of total system collapse."[808]

Finally, in March of 2021, students returned to school, but not all did. It had been almost exactly a year since students had last attended school in person. Harley was one of the Central students who returned, and she was glad to leave full-time online schooling behind. To ensure that school buildings would remain at 50 percent capacity for safety, students were allowed to attend school only part time. Thus, a student would spend half of the time within their respective school building and the other half online. Many high school students opted not to return, remaining online for the duration of the 2021 academic year and resulting in a very different in-person school experience for those students who headed back. Harley, who graduated in May of 2022, suggested that after COVID, Central was never the same.

The pandemic harmed students, especially students of color in majority Black and Brown schools and particularly within low-income communities, widening pre-existing opportunity and achievement gaps. Students in majority Black schools ended the 2021 school year six months behind in math and reading. Conversely, students in majority White schools finished the 2021 school year four months behind in math and three months behind in reading. COVID resulted in students within low-income and urban schools falling further behind during the pandemic than their peers in high-income rural and suburban schools.[809]

Within the educational system in Kansas City—traditional public and charter schools—proficiency rates on English Language Arts and Math dropped considerably between 2019 and 2021. They were particularly low among Black and Latinx students.

Year	2019	2021
Black	22%	13%
Latinx	27%	18%
White	60%	47%

Table 12: State Testing and Performance by Race, 2019 and 2021[810]

Each demographic group has rebounded, though no group has recovered to pre-COVID percentages. The Black/White proficiency gap was 38 percent in 2019 and 37 percent in 2022.[811]

The Status Quo

In many ways, COVID was a game-changer, and it might take a generation to rebound. The COVID pandemic profoundly affected students and schools, but COVID did not create school inequity; it merely exacerbated it. A review of the 2022, 2023, and 2024 Annual Performance Report Building-Level Summary reveals nothing new. Among all KCPS schools, Central was the lowest-performing school in the district across all buildings, regardless of grade level. The other district neighborhood high schools—East High School, Northeast High School, and Southeast High School—were not too far behind, ranking among the bottom seven lowest-performing district schools.[812] The highest-performing district high school was the district's signature secondary school, Lincoln College Preparatory Academy.

Standardized testing remains the primary vehicle by which performance and progress of both individual schools and school districts is measured. In Missouri, this is done through the Missouri School Improvement Plan (MSIP), originating in 1991 and now in its sixth iteration.[813] While the focus of MSIP 6 remains academic performance, unlike previous versions, the sixth edition incorporates progress or "improvement" in addition to performance. Importantly, though, the point distribution between performance and improvement is significant, meaning performance is weighed much more heavily than improvement.

The 2021–2022 school year marked a reconceptualization of the Missouri School Improvement Program, which means the data cannot be compared to previous years, given the differences in reporting. However, the 2019 MSIP-5 Annual Performance Report (APR) Building-Level Summary, like the 2022, 2023, and 2024 MSIP-6 APR, classifies Central as the worst-performing school in the district. Among secondary schools, there is one clear outlier: Lincoln College Preparatory Academy. Lincoln's performance outshines the performance of all other district secondary schools, and it is not even close—and it has been this way for the better part of two decades.

So what is next for Central? For now, it remains unclear. The only certainty is that Central is open for now, yet its current existence is under looming threat of closure. Central must prove its worth to remain open, which means it must achieve conventional academic measures of success as calculated through DESE's Missouri School Improvement Program.

School	Year 2022 Total Possible Points: 96	Year 2023 Total Possible Points: 144	Year 2024 Total Possible Points: 140
Central High School	33	49.9	57.5
East High School	35.5	70.1	73
Lincoln College Preparatory	83.5	106.1	102.5
Northeast High School	39	51	80.5
Southeast High School	41	58.9	82.5

Table 13: KCPS MSIP 6 High School Point Distribution, 2022–2024[814]

For Central and the other KCPS schools for which closure was and is a real consideration, MSIP scores might determine whether their doors remain open. Based on the 2022, 2023, and 2024 data, this could present a problem for Central High School proponents, but data also suggest that this is not merely a Central "problem." MSIP 6 data, like previous versions of state-level data reporting, show a clear divide between KCPS secondary neighborhood schools and the selective secondary signature schools, especially Lincoln College Preparatory Academy.

The building-level data for district schools is presented in two categories, performance and improvement, outlined in Table 13. Performance is 70 percent of the total calculation and continuous improvement is 30 percent. The emphasis for individual schools is performance, and performance metrics are largely calculated on academic achievement based on end-of-course standardized tests and the graduation rate.

Table 13 outlines the total scores for all high schools (grades nine through twelve) within KCPS for 2022, 2023, and 2024.[815] Scores are tabulated based on a point scale. Higher scores represent higher performance and greater academic achievement. The most striking outcome from the 2022, 2023 and 2024 APR data is the difference in performance between Lincoln College Preparatory School and the other schools. Central's score is the lowest; Lincoln outperforms them all. By comparison, Lincoln's point differential in 2022 was plus fifty over Central, and in 2023 grew to plus fifty-seven; it dropped slightly to plus forty-five in 2024.

A similar pattern can be seen in tested content areas detailed in table 14, which outlines student proficiency in English language arts, math, science, and social studies. Whereas Lincoln met or exceeded state-level performance indicators in all tested areas, not one KCPS neighborhood high school—Central, East, Northeast, or Southeast— even came close. The number of students at Central and Southeast High Schools showing an "adequate" or "thorough" command of the content and scoring within the "proficient" or "advanced" classification was not statistically significant enough to generate a percentage score. Nearly all students at Central and Southeast across all tested areas scored at "below basic" or "basic levels" and demonstrated only a "partial" or "minimal" command of the state standards within the content area.[816]

	Language Arts	Math	Science	Social Studies
State of Missouri	2023 - 48%	2023 - 25%	2023 - 30%	2023 - 33%
	2024 - 46%	2024 - 26%	2024 - 27%	2024 - 35%
Central High School	2023 - *	2023 - *	2023 - *	2023 - *
	2024 - *	2024 - *	2024 - *	2024 - *
East High School	2023 - *	2023 - *	2023 - *	2023 - 14%
	2024 - *	2024 - *	2024 - 6%	2024 - *
Lincoln College Preparatory School	2023 - 64%	2023 - 22%	2023 - 31%	2023 - 57%
	2024 - 63%	2024 - 27%	2024 - 29%	2024 - 52%
Northeast High School	2023 - *	2023 - *	2023 - *	2023 - *
	2024 - 12%	2024 - *	2024 - 6%	2024 - *
Southeast High School	2023 - *	2023 - *	2023 - *	2023 - *
	2024 - *	2024 - *	2024 - *	2024 - *

* Data is not statistically significant.

Table 14: 2023 and 2024 Student Proficiency by Content[817]

Based on this data, KCPS signature high schools, and notably Lincoln College Preparatory Academy, continue to outperform district neighborhood high schools. Several decades ago, Smrekar and Goldring warned of the dangers of specialty schools creating a two-tiered system, in which low-achieving students would attend poorly functioning traditional schools and academically-oriented magnet schools would house the highest-performing students.[818] Ironically, Kansas City's comprehensive magnet plan of the 1980s and 1990s used this reasoning as justification for intentionally transforming all high schools and middle schools into magnet schools. This was done to avoid an inequitable system (See Chapter 7). While Kansas City no longer uses the terminology of "magnet" school, perhaps due to its controversial magnet school history, today's "signature" school represents a different name for the same concept—a public school with a specialized curricular or academic theme. Whereas magnet schools were initially utilized to bolster efforts of desegregation, today the emphasis has shifted from desegregation to choice and achievement, though race remains a salient feature. For example, schools like Lincoln College Preparatory Academy give KCPS a competitive advantage within the educational choice environment, an outcome of the new educational landscape that has evolved since the creation of charter schools in the late 1990s and the growing emphasis on choice in education. Unfortunately, there is not room for everyone in a choice market. Schools like Central have fulfilled their destiny, set into motion decades ago, as a byproduct of an ongoing system of inequity that advantages some and marginalizes and oppresses others. Those who continue to suffer the most are students of color within the lowest socioeconomic contexts.

Winners and Losers

Magnet schools emerged out of the necessity to desegregate schools through voluntary means. The *Swann v. Charlotte-Mecklenburg Board of Education* case in 1971, in which the Court ruled that segregation in housing in Charlotte, North Carolina, also resulted in racially identifiable schools, provided a glimmer of hope for proponents of mandated desegregation. It did not take long for the pendulum to swing back, as the courts moved away from involuntary desegregation in two very important judicial rulings that followed *Swann*: *Milliken* in Detroit, Michigan, and *Jenkins* in Kansas City, Missouri. Both shaped the trajectory of desegregation to date.

The details of these landmark court cases are covered in earlier chapters; they marked a substantive movement away from federal efforts of desegregation within schools and have led to greater racial and socioeconomic isolation. For example, KCPS is only 10 percent White. If charters are included, the greater KCPES is 11 percent White. Thus, given the context and the fact that the student population within district schools and charter schools is similarly about 90 percent of color, meaningful desegregation is no longer an option within urban communities that remain highly segregated, at least not when schools are structured geographically. That score was settled long ago—beginning in the 1970s—as the judicial retreat from federal forced desegregation continued in the years after *Milliken*. The public school student population is growing in diversity. Projections reveal continued growth among students of color into the future, especially among Latinx students. By 2031, the majority of students within US public schools will be students of color. Despite this, schools remain highly segregated according to race, ethnicity, and socioeconomic status.[819]

Separate has never been and will never be equal: "Separate educational facilities are inherently unequal." That was the Court's unanimous decision in *Brown* seventy years ago. Yet more than a third of students today attend a predominantly same-race school, and roughly 15 percent attend schools where almost the entire student body is of a single race.[820] In particular, it has been the post-*Milliken* and post-*Jenkins* period and the courts' abandonment of involuntary desegregation that has resulted in schools' retreat to greater racial and economic isolation, especially in the North and Midwest—Kansas City included. Instead of desegregation, the federal government's focus became achievement, accountability, and choice. In other words, the emphasis shifted from attempting to integrate our schools to measuring how students performed on standardized tests and promoting high-performing schools within an educational choice market. Those losing the most in such a system remain students in historically underperforming public schools within economically oppressed communities that serve almost exclusively Black and Brown children.[821]

A dominant ideology of market-based principles, which emphasize individual autonomy and competition, has become the primary focus of educational policy. Within this choice system, schools like Central and other urban neighborhood public schools confront longstanding negative stereotypes and stigmas around notions of failure. These schools are forced to compete for enough students to remain open while restricted to traditional geographic neighborhood attendance zones, whereas the competition—charter schools and magnet schools—face no such confines. Urban neighborhood public schools often become the "generic" option for the neediest students, both academically and socioeconomically. Meanwhile, all schools are pressured to meet performance expectations as measured through standardized tests, irrespective of systemic and structural issues that persist unchecked. It is "perform or perish" in the school choice market, laying a ruinous path forward for Central and schools like it across the country.

Conclusion

Central High School shares a lengthy struggle similar to those faced by many other urban public schools around the country, who, like Central, are in a fight for survival, and race is firmly affixed at the center of it all. Urban school enrollment is declining, and most urban students today identify as either Hispanic (38 percent) or Black (22 percent), with the number of students from immigrant households tripling since 1980.[822] This demographic shift is occurring across the country and has been in motion for decades, ever since the *Brown v. Topeka Board of Education* decision in 1954 spurned massive White flight from American cities and city schools. Moreover, data shows that the percentage of students in urban public schools living in poverty is far greater than that of students who do not attend an urban public school.[823] This is the reality of the contemporary urban public school which is powered by a growing emphasis on neoliberalism, prioritizing competition, achievement, and individualism.

The most recent state data, 2023–2024, showed growth at Central High School in the total number of students at 539, which is up from 467 in 2021–2022. It was a modest increase of three students from 536 in 2022–2023. The four-year graduation rate increased as well, up 12 percent from 2022–2023 to 79 percent in 2023–2024; but it is an impressive 23 percent increase in the last two years.[824] It is too early to know if this is a mere blip or represents a persistent change, but it does signify progress for a school desperate for something positive. Unfortunately, student achievement reigns supreme in the neoliberal school environment, and student achievement data at

Central does not indicate similar growth. Central students continue to perform among the lowest in the district and the state. Central has fulfilled its prescribed destiny, one school among many in an inequitable system that churns out winners and losers. Central has been losing for decades, but let's be clear—this is most certainly not rooted within the individual student.

Public perception holds steady that the urban public school is inherently flawed and full of apathetic Black and Brown students who come from homes that don't value education and hard work, and that this is just the way things are. Not so. "Deficits are not in the students," suggests David Paunesku of Stanford University; "they are in the systems that are supposed to serve them."[825] This is an important distinction. Again, Paunesku says, "When data reveal students' shortcomings without revealing the shortcomings of the systems intended to serve them, it becomes easier to treat students as deficient."[826] While the vision of schools as the great equalizer is the prevailing narrative of American education, it is flawed. This is not to say that a student's hard work cannot or will not lead to individual success; it just might. However, the presumption that academic achievement occurs exclusively at the individual level and is rooted in biology, genetic variation, or culture is untrue. Such ways of thinking do not take into consideration the powerful influences of social institutions that have been structured in ways that advantage some and oppress others.

Schools in the United States were constructed on the notion of White supremacy, built on the idea that Black and White children should not learn together but separately in segregated settings. We have been told that schooling opens up opportunities for all students, regardless of race or class, and that one's success is predicated on individualism and meritocracy, in which individual effort ultimately leads to achievement.

This brings me back to my "why" and the importance of this book. Yes, Central's institutional history is fascinating. It is also an example of how American education is failing students; well, certain students—students within low-performing schools like Central, often situated within urban communities of color. Only through a comprehensive history can one understand the long struggle, particularly within urban education. Most importantly, this might encourage discourse around meaningful systemic change.

While this book is not a policy initiative, it is shortsighted to ignore the value of Central's institutional history in improving urban education and the lives of students in Kansas City and beyond. Though I do not have the answers, I firmly believe that historical perspective is integral to finding those solutions. Following one single institution over time provides valuable insight and perspective. Solving the education puzzle and lifting schools, especially schools like Central that have long been marginalized, is a book in itself. For now, the focus is on Central's institutional history, a comprehensive history from 1867 to 2024. I am honored to tell its story and grateful to those who helped me do so.

Appendices

Appendix 1: Acronyms

OCR	Office for Civil Rights
CCC	Citizens Coordinating Committee
CORE	Congress of Racial Equality
CUA	Council for United Action
HEW	Department of Health, Education, and Welfare
ESAA	Emergency School Aid Act
NAACP	National Association for the Advancement of Colored People
SCLC	Southern Christian Leadership Conference
HUD	Housing and Urban Development
DOT	Department of Transportation
MMAT	Missouri Mastery and Achievement Test
TAP	Tests of Academic Proficiency
ESEA	Elementary and Secondary Education Act
BEST	Basic Essential Skills Test
DMC	Desegregation Monitoring Committee
CEEJ	Coalition for Education and Economic Justice
MAP	Missouri Assessment Program
KCNA	Kansas City Neighborhood Academy
KCMSD	Kansas City, Missouri School District (to 2013)
KCPS	Kansas City Public Schools (from 2013)
KCPES	Kansas City Public Education System
DESE	Department of Elementary and Secondary Education

AACPS   Anne Arundel County Public Schools
ESSER   Elementary and Secondary School Emergency Relief Fund

Appendix 2: Chronology of Central's Principals

Principal	Dates of Service
J.B. Bradley	1867–1871
W.G. Pratt	1871–1873
C.L. Sheffield	1873–1876
E.C. White	1876–1887
J.J. Buchanan	1887–1897
E.C. White	1897–1901
I.I. Cammack	1901–1911
E.M. Bainter	1911–1912
H.H. Holmes	1912–1920
Otto F. Dubach	1920–1946
W.W. Clement	1946–1952
Paul M. Marshall	1952–1960
James F. Boyd	1960–1969
C.S. Settles	1969–1971
D.W. Porter	1971
D.L Britton (Acting)	1971–1972
D.L. Britton	1972–1982
Melvin Franklin	1982–1988
Robert Jackson (Interim)	1988–1989
Arthur Rainwater	1989–1990
Robert Jackson	1990–1993
Emmerson Payne	1993–1996
Willie Bowie	1996–2001
William McClendon	2001–2006
Glenn Mitchell	2006–2008
Deborah McGill	2008–2010
Derek Jordan (Acting)	2010

(continued next page)

Linda Collins	2010-2013
Larry Garry	2013-2016
Anthony Madry	2016-2022
Anthony Holland	2022-Present

Appendix 3: Chronology of Superintendents of the Kansas City, Missouri School District/KCPS

Superintendent	Dates of Service
J.B. Bradley	1867-1868
E.P. Tucker	1868-1869
John R. Phillips	1869-1874
James M. Greenwood	1874-1913
I.L. Cammack	1913-1928
George Melcher	1928-1940
Herold C. Hunt	1940-1947
Roscoe V. Shores (Acting)	1947-1948
Harold E. Moore	1948-1950
Roscoe V. Shores (Acting)	1950-1952
Mark W. Bills	1952-1955
Roscoe V. Shores (Acting)	1955
James A. Hazlett	1955-1969
Donald Hair (Acting)	1969-1970
J. Glenn Travis (Acting)	1970
Andrew S. Adams	1970-1973
J. Glenn Travis (Acting)	1973
Robert Medcalf	1973-1975
Edward E. Fields (Interim)	1975-1977
Robert Wheeler	1977-1982
John A. Minor	1982-1985
Eugene E. Eubanks (Interim)	1985
Claude G. Perkins	1985-1986
Jasper W. Harris (Interim)	1986-1987

(continued next page)

George F. Garcia	1987-1991
Dr. Walter Marks	1991-1995
Dr. Willie Giles (Interim)	1995-1996
Dr. Ida Love (Interim)	1996
Dr. Henry P. Williams	1996-1998
Dr. Phillis Chase (Interim)	1998
Bonnie McKelvy (Interim)	1998
Benjamin Demps	1999-2001
Dr. Bernard Taylor, Jr.	2001-2006
Anthony Amato	2006-2008
Dr. John Martin (Interim)	2008
Dr. Clive H. Coleman (Interim)	2008-2009
Dr. John Covington	2009-2011
Dr. Stephen Green	2011-2015
Al Tunis	2015-2016
Dr. Mark Bedell	2016-2022
Dr. Jennifer Collier (Interim)	2022
Dr. Jennifer Collier	2023-Present

Endnotes

1   Kevin Gotham, *Race, Real Estate, and Uneven Development: The Kansas City Experience, 1900–2000* (Albany: State University Press, 2002).

2   Joshua Dunn, *Complex Justice: The Case of Missouri v. Jenkins* (Chapel Hill: University of North Carolina Press, 2008).

3   Sherry Schirmer, *A City Divided: The Racial Landscape of Kansas City, 1900-1960* (Columbia: University of Missouri Press, 2016); G. S. Griffin, *Racism in Kansas City: A Short History* (Traverse City: Chandler Lake Books, 2015); Tanner Colby, *Some of My Best Friends are Black: The Strange Story of Integration in America* (New York: Penguin Books, 2013); Margie Carr, *Kansas City's Montgall Avenue: Black Leaders and the Street they Called Home* (Lawrence: University of Kansas Press, 2023); Gotham, *Race, Real Estate, and Uneven Development.*

4   Kansas City, Missouri School District changed its name in 2013 to Kansas City Public Schools to emphasize the district's role as a public educational institution and the district's commitment to serving the entire community. It was in essence a rebranding during a time when public perception was quite negative.

5   Loyce Caruthers, Jennifer Friend, and Candace Schlein, "School Desegregation as Multi-generational Narratives of Afropessimism," *Educational Studies* 58, no. 1 (2021): 33-49.

6   H. Richard Milner, "But What is Urban," *Urban Education* 47, no. 3 (2021): 556-61.

7   Milner, "But What is Urban."

8   Robert Tabscott, "Commentary: A Look Back: Early African-American Education in St. Louis," St. Louis Public Radio, September 20, 2009.

9   Nathan Parker, *Missouri as It Is in 1867: An Illustrated Historical Gazetteer of Missouri* (Philadelphia: J. B. Lippincott & Co., 1867), 424.

10   Henry S. Williams, "The Development of the Negro Public School System in Missouri," *The Journal of Negro History* 5, no. 2 (1920): 137-65.

11   "Kansas City's First High School, Central at 11th and Locust Was Opened in 1867," Missouri Valley Special Collections, Vertical (Old) Files.

12   De jure is a formal term often used to refer to legal separation of the races. The Jim Crow era (1880s–1954) is an example of de jure segregation.

13 Loyce Caruthers and Bradley Poos, "Narratives of Lincoln High School African American Graduates in Kansas City, Missouri: 1955-1985," *Journal of Black Studies* 46, no. 6 (2015): 626-49.

14 Vanessa Siddle Walker, "Valued Segregated Schools for African American Children in the South, 1935–1969: A Review of Common Themes and Characteristics," *Review of Educational Research* 70, no. 3 (2000): 235-85, 277.

15 James D. Anderson, *The Education of Blacks in the South, 1860-1935* (Chapel Hill: University of North Carolina Press, 1988).

16 Charles E. Coulter, *"Take Up the Black Man's Burden"*: Kansas City's African American Communities, 1865–1939 (Columbia: University of Missouri Press, 2006).

17 Nineteenth Annual Report on Desegregation in the Kansas City Public Schools (1973–1974), State Historical Society of Missouri, Arthur A. Benson II, Box 452; Social Explorer Professional, 1940–1960, accessed October 12, 2013, www.socialexplorer.com.

18 Gotham, *Race, Real Estate, and Uneven Development.*

19 Stephen Menendian, Samir Gambhir, and Arthur Gailes, "The Roots of Structural Racism Project: Twenty-First Century Racial Residential Segregation in the United States," June 21, 2021, https://belonging.berkeley.edu/roots-structural-racism.

20 U.S. Government Accountability Office, "K-12: Student Population has Significantly Diversified, but many Schools Remain Divided Along Racial, Ethnic, and Economic Lines," June 16, 2022.

21 U.S. Government Accountability Office, "K-12: Student Population has Significantly Diversified."

22 Thomas Gillette, *Santa Fe: A Study of the Effects of Negro Invasion on Property Values* (Master's thesis, 1954), 3.

23 Gotham, *Race, Real Estate, and Uneven Development.*

24 Gotham, *Race, Real Estate, and Uneven Development.*

25 *Centralian*, 1913, Missouri Valley Special Collections.

26 *Centralian*, 1913, Missouri Valley Special Collections.

27 *Central Luminary,* May 26, 1921, Missouri Valley Special Collections.

28 *Central Luminary,* February 12, 1925, Missouri Valley Special Collections, 1.

29 *Kansas City Star,* October 9, 1938, Missouri Valley Special Collections, Schools-Public Central High. History, Early.

30 Rollins Bingham, "Alumni Article," *Central Luminary,* January 9, 1906, Missouri Valley Special Collections.

31 *Kansas City Star,* October 9, 1938.

32 "Kansas City's First High School, Central at 11th and Locust Was Opened in 1867."

33 *Central Luminary,* May 1898, Missouri Valley Special Collections.

34 *Central Luminary,* October 1893, Missouri Valley Special Collections.

35 *Kansas City Star,* May 8, 1938, Missouri Valley Special Collections, Schools-Public Central High History, Early.

36 *Kansas City Star,* May 8, 1938.

37 *Central Luminary,* May 26, 1921, Missouri Valley Special Collections.

38 *Central Luminary,* May 26, 1921, Missouri Valley Special Collections.

39 Rollins Bingham, "Alumni Article," *Central Luminary,* January 9, 1906.

40 Bingham, "Alumni Article," *Central Luminary,* January 9, 1906.

41 Law of 1889, Revised Statutes (1889), 1861, State Historical Society of Missouri, Arthur A. Benson II, Box 303.

42 Carmen Jones, "Lincoln First Schools for Blacks in Kansas City," *Kansas City Star,* 2000, Missouri Valley Special Collections, Vertical File, Lincoln.

43 Annual Report of the Superintendent of Schools, 1867–1947, Missouri Valley Special Collections.

44 *Central Luminary,* May 24, 1985, Missouri Valley Special Collections.

45 *Central Luminary,* December 1898, Missouri Valley Special Collections.

46 *Central Luminary,* December 1898; *Central Luminary,* February 1890, Missouri Valley Special Collections.

47 "The Opening of the Schools," *Kansas City Star,* 16 December 1895, 4.

48 Ella Wiberg, *The History of the Development of Public Education in Kansas City, Missouri* (Master's thesis, University of Wisconsin, 1925).

49 *Central Luminary,* May 24, 1985, Missouri Valley Special Collections.

50 *Central Luminary,* November 1893, Missouri Valley Special Collections.

51 "Sunset Glow on Old Central High," *Kansas City Star,* August 31, 1952, Missouri Valley Special Collections, Schools-Public Central High History, Early.

52 Annual Report of the Superintendent of Schools, 1894, Missouri Valley Special Collections.

53 Annual Report of the Superintendent of Schools, 1895, Missouri Valley Special Collections, 18.

54 *Central Luminary,* Missouri Valley Special Collections.

55 *Central Luminary,* May 1897, Missouri Valley Special Collections.

56 *Central Luminary,* March 1894, Missouri Valley Special Collections.

57 *Central Luminary,* February 1897, Missouri Valley Special Collections.

58 *Centralian,* 1934, Missouri Valley Special Collections.

59 "Dr. Butler of New York Pays Tribute to the Kansas City Educator," *Kansas City Star,* May 9, 1897, 1.

60 "Central High School Report," *Kansas City Star,* December 11, 1896, 2.

61 *Central Luminary,* December 1896, Missouri Valley Special Collections.

62 *Central Luminary,* September 1897, Missouri Valley Special Collections.

63 *Central Luminary,* May 1897, Missouri Valley Special Collections.

64 *Central Luminary,* September 1897, Missouri Valley Special Collections.

65 *Central Luminary,* May 1898, Missouri Valley Special Collections.

66 *Central Luminary,* March 1899, Missouri Valley Special Collections.

67 *Central Luminary,* January 1901, Missouri Valley Special Collections, 1.

68 Sam Ray. "A Postcard from Old Kansas City," *Kansas City Star,* May 11, 1968, Missouri Valley Special Collections, Central (Old) Vertical File.

69 *Kansas City Star,* December 12, 1908, Missouri Valley Special Collections, Central (New) Vertical File.

70 L.W. Fifield, *Central Luminary,* December 1907, 25.

71 Annual Report of the Superintendent of Schools, 1905–1906, Missouri Valley Special Collections; *Kansas City Journal,* December 9, 1906, Missouri Valley Special Collections, Schools-Public, Night Schools.

72   *Kansas City Times,* December 9, 1911, Missouri Valley Special Collections, Schools-Public, Night Schools.

73   *Kansas City Times,* December 9, 1911.

74   *Kansas City Star,* October 28, 1913, Missouri Valley Special Collections; *Kansas City Times,* October 15, 1912, Missouri Valley Special Collections, Schools-Public, Night Schools.

75   Annual Report of the Superintendent of Schools, 1913–1914, Missouri Valley Special Collections.

76   *Kansas City Star,* November 11, 1915, Missouri Valley Special Collections, Schools-Public, Central High.

77   "Rush to Enter High School," *Kansas City Star,* August 31, 1911, 7.

78   "Asks for Eleven New Schools," *Kansas City Star,* June 8, 1913, 2.

79   Asa E. Martin, *Our Negro Population: A Sociological Study of the Negroes of Kansas City,* Missouri (Franklin Hudson Publishing Company, c. 1913), https://www.loc.gov/item/13023501/, 171.

80   Coulter, *"Take Up the Black Man's Burden."*

81   *Kansas City Star,* 12 September 1915, Missouri Valley Special Collections, Schools-Public, Buildings New, 18.

82   *Central Luminary,* March 1913, Missouri Valley Special Collections, 27.

83   *Kansas City Star,* November 11, 1915, Missouri Valley Special Collections, Schools-Public, Central High.

84   "E. M. Bainter to Porto Rico," *Kansas City Star,* April 8, 1912, 1.

85   In 1953, the old building at 11th and Locust was razed and used as a parking lot, later to become the site of Kansas City's Municipal Courts building in the early 1970s.

86   *Central Luminary,* March 1915, Missouri Valley Special Collections, 6.

87   *Central Luminary,* December 1915, Missouri Valley Special Collections, 29.

88   *Kansas City Star,* November 11, 1915, Missouri Valley Special Collections, Schools-Public, Central High.

89   *Kansas City Star,* November 11, 1915.

90   "A Large Senior Enrollment," *Kansas City Star,* December 2, 1919, 6.

91   *Central Luminary,* April 1894, Missouri Valley Special Collections.

92   *Central Luminary,* March 1915, Missouri Valley Special Collections, 6.

93   *Central Luminary,* November 1912, Missouri Valley Special Collections, 20.

94   *Central Luminary,* January 19, 1922, Missouri Valley Special Collections, 1.

95   *Kansas City Post,* May 17, 1918, Missouri Valley Special Collections, Schools-Public, German Language.

96   *Central Luminary,* February 1919, Missouri Valley Special Collections, 2.

97   *Central Luminary,* February 1919, Missouri Valley Special Collections, 27.

98   "Central to Graduate 270," *Kansas City Star,* June 5, 1920, 2; "Central to Graduate 407," *Kansas City Star,* June 3, 1922, 4.

99   *Central Luminary,* March 24, 1921, Missouri Valley Special Collections, 2.

100   *Central Luminary,* March 24,1921.

101   *Central Luminary,* 22 September 1921, Missouri Valley Special Collections, 1.

102   *Central Luminary,* February 21, 1922, Missouri Valley Special Collections, 1.

103   *Kansas City Star,* December 14, 1924, Missouri Valley Special Collections, Schools-Public, Junior High, Central.

104   *Central Luminary,* November 12, 1922, Missouri Valley Special Collections, 1.

105   Phillip O'Connor, "Finding a Solution to Lincoln's Future," *Kansas City Star,* March 11, 1990, 10.

106   *Central Luminary,* October 13, 1921, Missouri Valley Special Collections.

107   By 1922, establishments included the following: Mann Bros Market (East Thirty-first), Just-rite (Twenty-seventh and Prospect), Lucky's Bakery (Twenty-sixth and Prospect), Japan Florist (Thirty-fourth and Prospect), Wolfe's Modern Dance Studio (Twenty-ninth and Brooklyn), T.A. Link Drug Company (Thirty-first and Prospect), Myerson Book Store (Thirty-first and Indiana), Indiana Cleaners and Tailors (Twenty-eighth and Linwood), Kaifetz Delicatessen (East Thirty-first Street), Model Cleaners (Thirty-third and Prospect), Justus Plumbing Company (East Thirty-first), K.L. Perkins Prescription Specialist (Thirty-first and Indiana), Stamp Photos (Thirtieth and Prospect), TA Link Drug Company (Thirty-first and Prospect), Greens School Supplies and Food (Thirty-first and Agnes), Southeast State Bank (Thirty-first and Prospect), Mitchell's Drugstore (Twenty-ninth and Prospect), K.L. Perkins Prescription Specialist (Thirty-first and Indiana), Schneider Dry Goods Company (Thirty-first and Indiana), and Lott and Von Drug Store (Thirty-first and Brooklyn). *Central Luminary,* 1920–1922, Missouri Valley Special Collections.

108   Douglas S. Massey and Nancy A. Denton, *American Apartheid: Segregation and the Making of the Underclass* (Cambridge: Harvard University Press, 1993); Gotham, *Race, Real Estate, and Uneven Development.*

109   Schirmer, *A City Divided.*

110   "Divided We Fall," *Kansas City Call,* July 3, 1925, State Historical Society of Missouri, Arthur A. Benson II, Box 303.

111   Gotham, *Race, Real Estate, and Uneven Development.*

112   "Improvement Association Moves to Restrict against Colored Owners," *Kansas City Call,* December 24, 1926, State Historical Society of Missouri, Arthur A. Benson II, Box 343.

113   "Linwood Association Takes Lead in National Association," *Kansas City Call,* July 29, 1927, State Historical Society of Missouri, Arthur A. Benson II, Box 343.

114   Gotham, *Race, Real Estate, and Uneven Development,* 34.

115   Stanley McMichael and Robert Bingham, *City Growth and Values* (Cleveland: The Stanley McMichael Publishing Organization, 1923).

116   Schirmer, *A City Divided.*

117   *Central Luminary,* September 25, 1924, Missouri Valley Special Collections, 2.

118   *Central Luminary,* September 18, 1924, Missouri Valley Special Collections, 1.

119   *Central Luminary,* November 12, 1925, Missouri Valley Special Collections, 4.

120   *Central Luminary,* November 12, 1925.

121   *Kansas City Star,* December 15, 1931, Missouri Valley Special Collections, School-Public, Junior High Schools.

122   *Central Luminary,* December 11, 1924, Missouri Valley Special Collections, 1.

123   *Central Luminary,* January 28, 1926, Missouri Valley Special Collections, 1.

124   "Pay-as-you-go Plan," *Kansas City Star,* January 24, 1928, Missouri Valley Special Collections, Schools-Revenue.

125   *Kansas City Star,* January 3, 1929, Missouri Valley Special Collections, Schools-Revenue.

126   *Kansas City Star,* January 3, 1929, Missouri Valley Special Collections, Schools-Revenue.

127   Kansas City Service Bulletin, Executive Department of the Kansas City, Missouri Public Schools (November 1932), Missouri Valley Special Collections, 14.

128   *Central Luminary,* March 14, 1930, 1.

129   Kansas City Service Bulletin, Executive Department of the Kansas City, Missouri Public Schools, Missouri Valley Special Collections (November 1932), 13.

130   Kansas City Service Bulletin, Executive Department of the Kansas City, Missouri Public Schools (April 1939), Missouri Valley Special Collections, 262.

131   Kansas City Service Bulletin, Executive Department of the Kansas City, Missouri Public Schools (November 1932), Missouri Valley Special Collections, 16.

132   Kansas City Service Bulletin (November 1935), Missouri Valley Special Collections, 18.

133   *Central Luminary,* November 5, 1937, 1.

134   Schirmer, *A City Divided.*

135   Andrew Theodore Brown and Lyle W. Dorsett, *K.C.: A History of Kansas City, Missouri* (Pruett Publishing Company, 1978).

136   *Kansas City Star,* May 15, 1938, Missouri Valley Special Collections, Schools-Public.

137   "Survey of Financial Situation in K.C. Schools," *Kansas City Star,* November 9, 1938, Missouri Valley Special Collections, Schools-Public.

138   *Central Luminary,* March 20, 1942, Missouri Valley Special Collections, 1.

139   *Central Luminary,* April 10, 1942, Missouri Valley Special Collections, 1.

140   *Central Luminary,* September 25, 1942, October 2, 1942; October 16, 1942; November 6, 1942, Missouri Valley Special Collections.

141   *Central Luminary,* January 20, 1943, 1; December 1, 1944, 1; *Centralian,* 1945, Missouri Valley Special Collections, 1.

142   *Centralian,* 1945, Missouri Valley Special Collections, 42.

143   "The Spirit of Freedom: A Profile of the History of Blacks in Kansas City, Missouri," Missouri Valley Special Collections.

144   "Is Kansas City North or South," *Kansas City Call,* November 29, 1946, State Historical Society of Missouri, Arthur A. Benson II, Box 303.

145   "Another Step Nearer to Real Democracy," *Kansas City Call,* April 18, 1952, State Historical Society of Missouri, Arthur A. Benson II, Box 303.

146   Nichols was one of the first developers of planned all-White residential communities in the country.

147   William S. Worley, *J.C. Nichols and the Shaping of Kansas City: Innovation in Planned Residential Communities* (Columbia: University of Missouri Press, 1993).

148   Gotham, *Race, Real Estate, and Uneven Development.*

149   "The Spirit of Freedom."

150   *Shelley v. Kraemer,* 334 U.S. 1 (1948).

151   "Delay in Home Suit," *Kansas City Star,* June 14, 1948, State Historical
       Society of Missouri, Arthur A. Benson II, Box 343.
152   "To Appeal Housing Decision," *Kansas City Call,* December 23, 1949, State
       Historical Society of Missouri, Arthur A. Benson II, Box 343.
153   "Sues over Home Sale," *Kansas City Call,* December 31, 1949, State
       Historical Society of Missouri, Arthur A. Benson II, Box 343.
154   Alvin Brooks, Conversation with Author, October 31, 2012.
155   "The Spirit of Freedom."
156   Gotham, *Race, Real Estate, and Uneven Development.*
157   "The Spirit of Freedom," 38.
158   Gotham, *Race, Real Estate, and Uneven Development.*
159   Alvin Brooks, Conversation with Author, October 31, 2012.
160   "Inventory of Intergroup Education Problems," paper presented at the Kansas
       City Conference on Human Relations (March 1953), State Historical Society
       of Missouri, Arthur A. Benson II, Box 306.
161   "Another Step Nearer to Real Democracy," *Kansas City Call,* April 18, 1952.
162   "City Sets Poor Example for Citizens," *Kansas City Call,* June 6, 1952, State
       Historical Society of Missouri, Arthur A. Benson II, Box 303.
163   "All Pools Are Open," *Kansas City Call,* May 27, 1955, State Historical
       Society of Missouri, Arthur A. Benson II, Box 303.
164   *Brown v. Board of Education,* 347 U.S. 483 (1954).
165   James T. Patterson, *Brown v. Board of Education: A Civil Rights Milestone
       and its Troubled Legacy (Pivotal Moments in American History)* (New York:
       Oxford University Press, 2001).
166   W. E. B. Du Bois, "Does the Negro Need Separate Schools," *Journal of Negro
       Education* 4, no. 3 (July 1935): 328.
167   *McLaurin v. Oklahoma State Regents* 339 U.S. 627 (1950); *Sweatt v. Painter,*
       339 U.S. 629 (1950).
168   Peter W. Moran, *Race, Law, and the Desegregation of Public Schools* (New
       York: LFB Publishing, 2005).
169   Michael L. Levine, *African Americans and Civil Rights: From 1619 to
       the Present* (Phoenix: Oryx Press, 1996), https://archive.org/details/
       africanamericans00levi.
170   *Brown v. Board of Education,* 347 U.S. 483 (1954).
171   Walter Stephan, "A Brief Historical Overview of School Desegregation," in
       School Desegregation: Past, Present, and Future, eds. Walter Stephan and Joe
       Feagin (New York: Plenum Press, 1980), 3-22.
172   "Mississippi Governor 'Sad, Disappointed,'" *Kansas City Call,* May 21,
       1954, 1.
173   "Mississippi Governor 'Sad, Disappointed.'"
174   Brian J. Daugherity and Charles C. Bolton, *With All Deliberate Speed:
       Implementing Brown v. Board of Education* (Fayetteville: University of
       Arkansas Press, 2008).
175   *Brown v. Board of Education,* 349 U.S. 294 (1955).
176   *Briggs v. Elliott,* 132 F. Supp. 776 (1955), 777.
177   Raymond Wolters, *The Burden of Brown: Thirty Years of School
       Desegregation* (Knoxville: University of Tennessee Press, 1984).
178   Moran, *Race, Law, and the Desegregation of Public Schools.*

179   Hubert Wheeler, "U.S. Supreme Court Ruling on Segregation in the Public Schools" (March 1954), State Historical Society of Missouri, Arthur A. Benson II, Box 310.

180   Hubert Wheeler, Missouri State Commissioner of Education, to District and County Superintendents (June 15, 1954), State Historical Society of Missouri, Arthur A. Benson II, Box 310.

181   Hubert Wheeler, Missouri State Commissioner of Education memo to District and County Administrators, regarding "Opinion of Attorney General John M. Dalton in Reference to Decision of U.S. Supreme Court on Segregation in the Public Schools" (July 1, 1954), State Historical Society of Missouri, Arthur A. Benson II, Box 310.

182   Moran, *Race, Law, and the Desegregation of Public Schools.*

183   "A Study in the Problems Involved in the Desegregation in the Public Schools of Kansas City," Kansas City, Missouri School District Research Department (July 1954), State Historical Society of Missouri, Arthur A. Benson II, Box 310.

184   Moran, *Race, Law, and the Desegregation of Public Schools,* 14.

185   Policies for Transition from Separate Schools to Desegregated School System, Superintendent's Office (March 6, 1955), State Historical Society of Missouri, Arthur A. Benson II, Box 310, 4.

186   Policies for Transition from Separate Schools to Desegregated School System.

187   Gwendolyn Adams, Conversation with Author, September 18, 2012.

188   Gwendolyn Adams, Conversation with Author, September 18, 2012.

189   "A Task for Each City," *Kansas City Times*, September 19, 1954, 18.

190   "Time to Hire Teachers," *Kansas City Call,* January 24, 1955, State Historical Society of Missouri, Arthur A. Benson II, Box 306.

191   "Are Our Teachers 'Frozen' Out," *Kansas City Call,* July 8, 1955, State Historical Society of Missouri, Arthur A. Benson II, Box 306.

192   "All Kinds of Tricks against Teachers," *Kansas City Call,* May 6, 1955, State Historical Society of Missouri, Arthur A. Benson II, Box 306.

193   "Central High Sets an Example in Integration," *Time,* July 29, 1961, Missouri Valley Special Collections, Schools-Central.

194   "A Big Year for the Schools," *Kansas City Star,* June 4, 1956, Missouri Valley Special Collections, Schools-Public.

195   "43 Integrated Schools," *Kansas City Call,* September 22, 1955, State Historical Society of Missouri, Arthur A. Benson II, Box 306.

196   *Central Luminary,* September 23, 1955, Missouri Valley Special Collections, 1.

197   *Central Luminary,* September 23, 1955, Missouri Valley Special Collections, 1.

198   Dual attendance zones refer to the system of racial segregation in which schools were allocated to different racial groups. For example, White students would attend schools in one zone while Black students would attend schools in another zone, often underfunded and unequal.

199   Alvin Brooks, Conversation with Author, October 31, 2012.

200   Policies for Transition from Separate Schools to Desegregated School System.

201   Policies for Transition from Separate Schools to Desegregated School System, 29.

202   Moran, *Race, Law, and the Desegregation of Public Schools.*

203 Kansas City, Missouri School District Enrollment by School, 1954-1955–1983-1984, Arthur Benson, unpublished demographic data, State Historical Society of Missouri, Arthur A. Benson II, Box 567.

204 Nineteenth Annual Report on Desegregation in the Kansas City Public Schools (1973-1974), State Historical Society of Missouri, Arthur A. Benson II, Box 452.

205 Social Explorer Professional, 1940-1960, accessed October 12, 2013, www.socialexplorer.com.

206 Alvin Brooks, Conversation with Author, October 31, 2012.

207 Gillette, *Santa Fe*, 1.

208 "Santa Fe Neighborhood Assessment Report," Kansas City, City Planning and Development Department, City of Kansas City, Missouri (July 2001), Missouri Valley Special Collections.

209 Gotham, *Race, Real Estate, and Uneven Development*, 95.

210 Gillette, *Santa Fe*, 3.

211 Gotham, *Race, Real Estate, and Uneven Development*.

212 Gotham, *Race, Real Estate, and Uneven Development*.

213 "A Good Plan Sabotaged," *Kansas City Call*, October 7, 1955, 20.

214 Brown and Dorsett, *K.C.: A History of Kansas City, Missouri*.

215 Brown and Dorsett, *K.C.: A History of Kansas City, Missouri*, 256.

216 Brown and Dorsett, *K.C.: A History of Kansas City, Missouri*, 256.

217 *Central Luminary*, March 23, 1956, Missouri Valley Special Collections, 3.

218 *Central Luminary*, March 23, 1956, Missouri Valley Special Collections, 3.

219 *Central Luminary*, March 23, 1956, Missouri Valley Special Collections, 3.

220 Lyle Davis, Jr., Conversation with Author, November 7, 2012.

221 Lyle Davis, Jr., Conversation with Author, November 7, 2012.

222 Lyle Davis, Jr., Conversation with Author, November 7, 2012.

223 "Central High Sets an Example in Integration," *Time*, July 29, 1961.

224 *Central Luminary*, April 1, 1960, Missouri Valley Special Collections, 1.

225 *Central Luminary*, October 23, 1959, 1; November 6, 1959, Missouri Valley Special Collections, 2.

226 *Central Luminary*, February 14, 1958, Missouri Valley Special Collections, 3.

227 *Central Luminary*, November 6, 1959, Missouri Valley Special Collections, 2.

228 Kansas City, Missouri School District Enrollment by School, 1954-1955–1983-1984, Arthur Benson.

229 *Central Luminary*, September 19, 1958, Missouri Valley Special Collections, 1.

230 *Central Luminary*, September 25, 1959, Missouri Valley Special Collections, 1.

231 *Central Luminary*, September 25, 1959, Missouri Valley Special Collections, 1.

232 Loretta Stewart, Conversation with Author, November 2, 2012.

233 Loretta Stewart, Conversation with Author, November 2, 2012.

234 Loretta Stewart, Conversation with Author, November 2, 2012.

235 Loretta Stewart, Conversation with Author, November 2, 2012.

236 Loretta Stewart, Conversation with Author, November 2, 2012.

237 *Central Luminary*, 25 September 1959; September 26, 1969, 1.

238 *Central Luminary*, May 11, 1962, 1.

239 *Central Luminary*, September 21, 1962, 1.

240 *Central Luminary*, September 21, 1962, 1.

[241] Martin Mayer, "The Good Slum Schools," *Harper's Magazine* (April 1961), 46-52, Missouri Valley Special Collections, SC 73; "Everything's Up to Date in Kansas City," *Time Magazine* 78, no. 4 (July 1961): 38, Missouri Valley Special Collections, SC 73.

[242] Martin Mayer, "The Good Slum Schools."

[243] Forestal Lawton, Conversation with Author, November 7, 2012.

[244] Martin Mayer, "The Good Slum Schools."

[245] Mary Beveridge, "Biography of Jeremiah Cameron," *Kansas City Star,* 2009, Missouri Valley Special Collections.

[246] Loretta Stewart, Conversation with Author, November 2, 2012.

[247] Forestal Lawton, Conversation with Author, November 2, 2012.

[248] Loretta Stewart, Conversation with Author, November 2, 2012.

[249] Forestal Lawton, Conversation with Author, November 2, 2012.

[250] "Everything's Up to Date in Kansas City."

[251] *Central Luminary,* May 8, 1964, 5.

[252] *Central Luminary,* October 9, 1964, 1.

[253] *Central Luminary,* September 26, 1969, 1.

[254] Current and Proposed Status of Faculty Integration, July 25, 1963, State Historical Society of Missouri, Arthur A. Benson II, Box 311.

[255] Current and Proposed Status of Faculty Integration, July 25, 1963.

[256] "Capacity Compared to Membership, Actual 1963, Estimated 1967 and 1972," Office of the Superintendent, Kansas City, Missouri School District (1963), State Historical Society of Missouri, Arthur A. Benson II, Box 313.

[257] Kansas City, Missouri School District Board Minutes (1963), State Historical Society of Missouri, Arthur A. Benson II, Box 313.

[258] "A Danger of School Resegregation Grows," *Kansas City Star,* October 27, 1965, Missouri Valley Special Collections, Schools-Public.

[259] Gotham, Race, *Real Estate, and Uneven Development,* 101.

[260] Study of Human Rights in Missouri, Missouri Commission on Human Rights (1960), State Historical Society of Missouri, Arthur A. Benson II, Box 312, 1.

[261] Study of Human Rights in Missouri, Missouri Commission on Human Rights (1960).

[262] Levine, *African Americans and Civil Rights.*

[263] Levine, *African Americans and Civil Rights.*

[264] Forrest Carson to Superintendent of Public Schools (March 20, 1968), State Historical Society of Missouri, Arthur A. Benson II, Box 315.

[265] Revisions to Title VI, Department of Health, Education, and Welfare (February 1966), State Historical Society of Missouri, Arthur A. Benson II, Box 315.

[266] Enrollment of Negro Pupils in Southern and Border States, Office of Education (December 1966), State Historical Society of Missouri, Arthur A. Benson II, Box 314.

[267] Harold Howe, U.S. Commissioner of Education, to Phil Landrum, House of Representatives (April 5, 1967), State Historical Society of Missouri, Arthur A. Benson II, Box 314.

[268] Thelma King, Council for United Action, to T. Johnson, Office of Civil Rights (June 23, 1967), State Historical Society of Missouri, Arthur A. Benson II, Box 314.

269   Statement by the Kansas City, Missouri School District Board of Education (July 1963), State Historical Society of Missouri, Arthur A. Benson II, Box 313.

270   Transcript of Procedures, March to Protest Resegregation (July 1963), State Historical Society of Missouri, Arthur A. Benson II, Box 313.

271   "Citizens Want a New School," *Kansas City Times,* October 26, 1960, 22.

272   "A School Waits on Race Issue," *Kansas City Times,* October 10, 1964, 1-2.

273   Deprivations of bused students cited by the CCC included the following: (1) required to be at their sending school at least twenty minutes earlier than other pupils, often in winter months leaving during darkness (2) loaded into buses and required to sit three to a seat and stand (3) denied opportunity to go home for a hot lunch (4) deprived of opportunity to attend many of the cultural activities which are a part of the enrichment program provided other pupils (5) subjected to total segregation from all activities of the school they attend and do not play, eat, or participate in normal regular activities with the school's other pupils (6) teacher of bused pupil is required to utilize her time and energy to assume additional responsibilities for supervision during recess, lunch, and transportation (7) full responsibility of bused pupils remains vested in the principal of the sending school (8) parent of bused pupil who does not have transportation is severely handicapped in visiting child and classroom (Report to the Kansas City, Missouri Board of Education, Citizens Coordinating Committee, State Historical Society of Missouri, Arthur A. Benson II, Box 313).

274   "School Parents Disturbed by Integration Move," *The Wednesday Magazine* (September 1965), State Historical Society of Missouri, Arthur A. Benson II, Box 314, 12.

275   Patricia Doyle, "For Education 3 to 1," *Kansas City Times,* February 1965, 1-2.

276   Rex Stout and John King, "Background Information on the Problems of Overcrowding and Integration in the Kansas City, Missouri District, League of Women Voters of Kansas City, Missouri" (September 1967), State Historical Society of Missouri, Arthur A. Benson II, Box 314.

277   Some Questions and Answers: Regarding Citizens Coordinating Committee Policy, Citizens Coordinating Committee (July 1965), State Historical Society of Missouri, Arthur A. Benson II, Box 314.

278   Some Questions and Answers: Regarding Citizens Coordinating Committee Policy.

279   Some Questions and Answers: Regarding Citizens Coordinating Committee Policy.

280   "Coordinating Committee Opposes School Sites," *Kansas City Call,* June 9, 1965, State Historical Society of Missouri, Arthur A. Benson II, Box 314.

281   Citizen's Coordinating Committee memo to James Hazlett (n.d.), State Historical Society of Missouri, Arthur A. Benson II, Box 315.

282   "New Site Study for 3 Schools," *Kansas City Times,* July 31, 1965, 1-2.

283   Robert Havighurst, William Cobb, and Norman Drachler, "Problems of Integration in the Kansas City Public Schools" (November 1965), State Historical Society of Missouri, Arthur A. Benson II, Box 514.

284   Havighurst, Cobb, and Drachler, "Problems of Integration in the Kansas City Public Schools."

285   James Hazlett to the Board of Education (June 14, 1967), State Historical
      Society of Missouri, Arthur A. Benson II, Box 315.
286   James Hazlett to the Board of Education (June 14, 1967).
287   James Hazlett to the Board of Education (June 14, 1967).
288   Thelma King, "Statement to Board of Education" (July 6, 1967), Missouri
      Valley Special Collections, James A. Hazlett Papers.
289   Stout and King, "Background Information on the Problems of Overcrowding
      and Integration."
290   Thelma King to T. Johnson, Office of Civil Rights (June 23, 1967), State
      Historical Society of Missouri, Arthur A. Benson II, Box 314; Theron
      Johnson, Special Assistant to the Assistant Commissioner to Dr. Holloway,
      Acting Chief Title IV (June 30, 1967), State Historical Society of Missouri,
      Arthur A. Benson II, Box 314.
291   Harold Williams memo to Theron Johnson, July 12, 1967, State Historical
      Society of Missouri, Arthur A. Benson II, Box 314.
292   Paul Fairly and Gerald Sroufe, "Review of Kansas City, Missouri Schools"
      (1967), State Historical Society of Missouri, Arthur A. Benson II, Box 315.
293   Fairly and Sroufe, "Review of Kansas City, Missouri Schools" (1967).
294   Karen Krueger, "Preliminary Review of the Kansas City, Missouri Schools,
      July 17-21, 1967, Curriculum, Pupil Assignment and Transfer," State
      Historical Society of Missouri, Arthur A. Benson II Papers, Box 315.
295   "Concepts for Changing Times: Proposals Offered for Public Examination,
      Dealing with Educational Equity in the Kansas City, Missouri, School
      District," Office of the Superintendent, The School District of Kansas City,
      Missouri (March 1968), Missouri Valley Special Collections, James A Hazlett
      Papers.
296   "Concepts for Changing Times."
297   The Title 1 Program was established in 1965 as part of the Elementary
      and Secondary Education Act to provide supplemental federal aid to local
      education agencies (school districts) with a high concentration of students in
      high poverty schools.
298   Alvin Brooks, Conversation with Author, October 31, 2012.
299   Alvin Brooks, Conversation with Author, October 31, 2012.
300   "Final Report: Mayor's Commission on Civil Disorder" Mayor's Commission
      on Civil Disorder (August 1968), State Historical Society of Missouri, Arthur
      A. Benson II, Box 514, 3.
301   "Arrest Twelve Youths in Disturbance," Kansas City Times, November 11,
      1967, Missouri Valley Special Collections, Schools-Public, Central High.
302   "Final Report: Mayor's Commission on Civil Disorder," 5.
303   "Final Report: Mayor's Commission on Civil Disorder," 9.
304   "Final Report: Mayor's Commission on Civil Disorder," 10.
305   "Final Report: Mayor's Commission on Civil Disorder," 12-13.
306   J. Anthony Snorgrass, Conversation with Author, February 20, 2013.
307   Alvin Brooks, Conversation with Author, October 31, 2012.
308   Alvin Brooks, Conversation with Author, October 31, 2012.
309   "Final Report: Mayor's Commission on Civil Disorder," 20.
310   Alvin Brooks, Conversation with Author, October 31, 2012.
311   "Final Report: Mayor's Commission on Civil Disorder," 23.

312   "Final Report: Mayor's Commission on Civil Disorder," 25.

313   "Police, Fireman, and Guardsmen Praised for Riot Performance," *Kansas City Star,* May 5, 1968, 1.

314   "Final Report: Mayor's Commission on Civil Disorder."

315   "Negroes Still Angry at Police," *Kansas City Star,* May 5, 1968, 15A.

316   "Negroes Still Angry at Police," *Kansas City Star,* May 5, 1968, 15A.

317   "Negroes Still Angry at Police," *Kansas City Star,* May 5, 1968, 15A.

318   "Equal Treatment to Equals: A New Structure for Public Schools in the Kansas City and St. Louis Metropolitan Areas," Missouri School District Reorganization Commission (June 1969), State Historical Society of Missouri, Arthur A. Benson II, Box 315, 1.

319   "Concepts for Changing Times."

320   James Hazlett to the Board of Directors (July 18, 1969), State Historical Society of Missouri, Arthur A. Benson II, Box 315.

321   Center for the Study of Metropolitan Problems in Education, UMKC, *Public Schools of the Southeast Side: A Report to the Community* (Kansas City: University of Missouri-Kansas City, 1970).

322   Kansas City, Missouri School District Enrollment by School, 1954-1955–1983-1984, Arthur Benson.

323   Kansas City, Missouri School District Enrollment by School, 1954-1955–1983-1984, Arthur Benson.

324   Kansas City, Missouri School District Enrollment by School, 1954-1955–1983-1984, Arthur Benson.

325   Rajiv Sethi and Rohini Somanathan, "Inequality and Segregation," *Journal of Political Economy* 112, no. 6 (2004), 1296-321.

326   Myron Orfield, "Segregation and Environmental Justice," *Minnesota Journal of Law, Science and Technology* 7, no. 1 (2005), 147-60.

327   Melvin Oliver and Thomas Shapiro, *Black Wealth/White Wealth* (New York: Routledge, 1995).

328   Oliver and Shapiro, *Black Wealth/White Wealth.*

329   Kevin Gotham, "Separate and Unequal: The Housing Act of 1968 and the Section 235 Program," *Sociological Forum* 15, no. 1 (November 2000): 13-37.

330   Gotham, "Separate and Unequal."

331   *Kansas City Star,* January 26, 1971, 6A, Missouri Valley Special Collections.

332   "Raytown Comprehensive Plan," Raytown Planning and Zoning Commission, October 2002, www.raytown.mo.us.; Social Explorer Professional, United States Census (1970), www.socialexplorer.com.

333   "Population Characteristics: 2011 Annual Development Report," Overland Park Planning and Development Services Department, March 2012, www.opkans.org; Social Explorer Professional, United States Census (1970), www.socialexplorer.com.

334   *Central Luminary,* November 24, 1967, Missouri Valley Special Collections, 1.

335   *Central Luminary,* November 24, 1967, Missouri Valley Special Collections, 1.

336   "Arrest Twelve Youths in Disturbance," *Kansas City Times.*

337   "Arrest Twelve Youths in Disturbance," *Kansas City Times.*

338   *Central Luminary,* November 24, 1967, Missouri Valley Special Collections, 1.

339   "Hold Youth in Tourney Fight," *Kansas City Star,* March 14, 1969, Missouri
      Valley Special Collections, Schools-Public, Central High.
340   *Central Luminary,* March 1, 1968, 1.
341   "Vandals Rake Central High," *Kansas City Times,* February 24, 1969, 1, 3.
342   "New Breed of Student at Central Aims to Change School's Image," *Kansas
      City Times,* May 24, 1969, 3E.
343   "New Breed of Student at Central."
344   *Central Luminary,* September 26, 1969, 2.
345   "Outbreaks at Schools Here," *Kansas City Star,* February 13, 1970;
      "Resorting to Guards with Guns in the Public Schools," *Kansas City Star,*
      February 14, 1970, Missouri Valley Special Collections, Schools-Public,
      Central High.
346   "Armed Guards Concern Students," *Kansas City Star,* February 17, 1970,
      Missouri Valley Special Collections, Schools-Public, Central High.
347   *Central Luminary,* March 6, 1970, Missouri Valley Special Collections, 1.
348   Marion Halim, Conversation with Author, October 2, 2012.
349   Arthur Jackson, Conversation with Author, October 2, 2012.
350   "Violence Condemned by Central High School Students," *Kansas City Call,*
      February 20, 1970.
351   "Violence Condemned by Central High School Students."
352   Mrs. Edward C. Warren, "Parent Complains of Central," *Kansas City Call,*
      January 29, 1971.
353   Warren, "Parent Complains of Central."
354   "David Porter Resigns as Central Principal at Parents' Meeting," *Kansas City
      Call,* February 4, 1972.
355   "Week of Uncertainty at Central," *Kansas City Star,* November 21, 1972,
      Missouri Valley Special Collections, Schools-Public, Central High.
356   "Central Principal Receives New Job," *Kansas City Star,* February 17, 1972,
      Missouri Valley Special Collections, Schools-Public, Central High.
357   "Week of Uncertainty at Central," *Kansas City Star.*
358   "Basketball Fight Studied," *Kansas City Times,* March 10, 1972, Missouri
      Valley Special Collections, Schools-Public, Central High.
359   Arthur Jackson, Conversation with Author, October 2, 2012.
360   Arthur Jackson, Conversation with Author, October 2, 2012.
361   Arthur Jackson, Conversation with Author, October 2, 2012.
362   "Action Against Central," *Kansas City Star,* March 10, 1972, Missouri Valley
      Special Collections, Schools-Public, Central High.
363   "Central is Barred," *Kansas City Star,* March 27, 1972, Missouri Valley
      Special Collections, Schools-Public, Central High.
364   *Central Luminary,* February 8, 1973, 3.
365   *Central Luminary,* February 8, 1973, 3.
366   Henry Givens, "A Report to the State Board of Education Concerning the
      Desegregation of the Kansas City Public School District" (August 1975), State
      Historical Society of Missouri, Arthur A. Benson II, Box 514.
367   Warner and Warner, *Three Year Report.*
368   Warner and Warner, *Three Year Report.*
369   Warner and Warner, *Three Year Report.*

370 Warner and Warner, *Three Year Report.*
371 Missouri Department of Health, Education, and Welfare News Release (January 1971), State Historical Society of Missouri, Arthur A. Benson II, Box 315.
372 Missouri Department of Health, Education, and Welfare News Release (January 1971).
373 118 Cong. Rec. S 2524-S 2543, February 24, 1972, in David Henderson, *Integration in Missouri Public Schools: Faculty and Students Twenty Years after* Brown (Jefferson City, MO: Commission on Human Rights, 1974).
374 United States Commission on Human Rights, Statement of the United States Commission on Civil Rights Concerning the Statement by the President on Elementary and Secondary School Desegregation (Washington, DC: Center for Human Relations, National Education Association, 1970).
375 Michael Brogan, "Ineligibility under the Emergency School Aid Act: A Disparate Impact Standard," *Nebraska Law Review* 59, no. 4 (1980), 1127-42.
376 Emergency School Aid Act: Final Report to Task Force, National Advisory Council on Equality of Educational Opportunity (June 1977), State Historical Society of Missouri, Arthur A. Benson II, Box 316.
377 "City Schools: A Racial Dilemma," *Kansas City Star,* February 28, 1973, State Historical Society of Missouri, Arthur A. Benson II, Box 462.
378 *Adams v. Richardson,* 356 F. Supp. 92 (1973).
379 *Swann v. Charlotte-Mecklenburg Board of Education,* 402 U.S. 1 (1971).
380 *Swann v. Charlotte-Mecklenburg Board of Education,* 402 U.S. 1 (1971).
381 John Egerton, "*Adams v. Richardson*: Can Separate Be Equal?" *Change* 6, no. 10 (Winter 1974/1975): 29-36.
382 Warner and Warner, *Three Year Report.*
383 Warner and Warner, *Three Year Report.*
384 Peter Holmes, Director of the Office of Civil Rights, to Superintendent Adams (April 17, 1973), State Historical Society of Missouri, Arthur A. Benson II, Box 316.
385 Glenn Travis, Acting Superintendent to Peter Holmes, Director of the Office of Civil Rights (April 30,1973), State Historical Society of Missouri, Arthur A. Benson II, Box 316.
386 Resolution Regarding the Current State of Education in Kansas City, Missouri, Commission on Human Relations (March 1973), State Historical Society of Missouri, Arthur A. Benson II, Box 322.
387 Moran, *Race, Law, and the Desegregation of the Public Schools.*
388 Moran, *Race, Law, and the Desegregation of the Public Schools.*
389 "Parents Oppose Integration Options," *Kansas City Times,* March 27, 1973, State Historical Society of Missouri, Arthur A. Benson II, Box 462.
390 "Van Horn School Group Oppose Bussing Options," *Kansas City Times,* March 28, 1973, State Historical Society of Missouri, Arthur A. Benson II, Box 462.
391 Chief Education Branch Office for Civil Rights, memo to Kansas City School District (April 2, 1973), State Historical Society of Missouri, Arthur A. Benson II, Box 317.
392 Moran, *Race, Law, and the Desegregation of the Public Schools.*

393   Kansas City, Missouri School District Enrollment by School, 1954-1955–
1983-1984, Arthur Benson.

394   Kansas City, Missouri School District Enrollment by School, 1954-1955–
1983-1984, Arthur Benson.

395   "Schools Here May Hire 100," *Kansas City Times,* April 28, 1966, Schools-
Public.

396   Kansas City, Missouri School District Enrollment by School, 1954-1955–
1983-1984, Arthur Benson.

397   Kansas City, Missouri School District Enrollment by School, 1954-1955–
1983-1984, Arthur Benson.

398   John Scheldrup, Regional Representative to the Director, OCR memo to W.P.
Hefley, Regional Commissioner, Office of Education, regarding "Eligibility of
the School District of Kansas City, Missouri, ESAA Application," May 29,
1973, State Historical Society of Missouri, Arthur A. Benson II, Box 317.

399   Phillip Hersley, Regional Commissioner, Office of Education to
Superintendent Medcalf (April 3, 1974), State Historical Society of Missouri,
Arthur A. Benson II, Box 317.

400   Phillip Hersley, Regional Commissioner, Office of Education to
Superintendent Medcalf.

401   Edward Fields internal memo to Robert Medcalf, August 20, 1974, State
Historical Society of Missouri, Arthur A. Benson II, Box 317.

402   "Medcalf Denies Noncompliance," *Kansas City Star,* January 26, 1975, 3A.

403   "U.S. Again Halts School Grant," *Kansas City Times,* April 18, 1975, State
Historical Society of Missouri, Arthur A. Benson II, Box 402.

404   "Suit Asks Schools to Repay U.S. Aid," *Kansas City Times,* May 29, 1975,
State Historical Society of Missouri, Arthur A. Benson II, Box 402.

405   "Education Board Orders Staff to Implement Integration Plan," *Kansas City
Times,* July 17, 1975, State Historical Society of Missouri, Arthur A. Benson
II, Box 402.

406   "Leaders Seek Acceptance of Bussing Plan," *Kansas City Times,* July 14,
1975, State Historical Society of Missouri, Arthur A. Benson II, Box 462.

407   "SCLC Drafting School Plan," *Kansas City Times,* June 13, 1975, State
Historical Society of Missouri, Arthur A. Benson II, Box 402.

408   SCLC Drafting School Plan."

409   "Board Members Say HEW Can't Stop Plan," *Kansas City Times,* July 11,
1975, State Historical Society of Missouri, Arthur A. Benson II, Box 462.

410   "Board Members Say HEW Can't Stop Plan."

411   Taylor August, Director of Office of Civil Rights, to Superintendent Medcalf, July
14, 1975, State Historical Society of Missouri, Arthur A. Benson II, Box 317.

412   "HEW Blocks School Grant," *Kansas City Times,* September 19, 1975, State
Historical Society of Missouri, Arthur A. Benson II, Box 402.

413   "Desegregation Now Up to Board," *Kansas City Star,* October 3, 1976, State
Historical Society of Missouri, Arthur A. Benson II, Box 462.

414   "Desegregation Now Up to Board."

415   "School Plan Termed Racist," *Kansas City Times,* March 18, 1977, B36.

416   "Mixed Reactions to Plan," *Kansas City Star,* March 18, 1977, B36.

417   Kathleen Nutter, "'Militant Mothers: Boston, Busing, and the Bicentennial,
1976," *Historic Journal of Massachusetts* (Fall 2010), 52-74.

418   David Tatel, Director, Office of Civil Rights, to Superintendent Wheeler, July 7, 1977, State Historical Society of Missouri, Arthur A. Benson II, Box 316.

419   David Tatel, Director, Office of Civil Rights, to Superintendent Wheeler.

420   Samuel Carpenter, President of the Board, to David Tatel, Director of Office of Civil Rights (February 22, 1978), State Historical Society of Missouri, Arthur A. Benson II, Box 316.

421   "Concepts for Changing Times."

422   Gary Orfield and Susan Eaton, *Dismantling Desegregation: The Quiet Reversal of Brown v. Board of Education* (New York: The New Press, 1996).

423   *Milliken v. Bradley,* 418 U.S. 717 (1974).

424   Kansas City, Missouri School District Enrollment by School, 1954-1955–1983-1984, Arthur Benson.

425   "Total Student Enrollment, 1955-1984," Kansas City, Missouri, School District, Western Historical Manuscript Collection, Arthur Benson Papers, Box 567.

426   Johnson County, Kansas, was 99.2 percent White in 1960 and 97.2 percent White in 1980. Social Explorer Professional, United States Census (1960, 1980), www.socialexplorer.com.

427   Clay County, Missouri, was 99.1 percent White in 1960 and 97.5 percent White in 1980. Social Explorer Professional, United States Census (1960, 1980), www.socialexplorer.com.

428   "Crisis and Opportunity: Education in Greater Kansas City," Bi-State Committee on Education, Missouri Advisory Committee (January 1977), Missouri Valley Special Collections, 1.

429   "Crisis and Opportunity: Education in Greater Kansas City," vi.

430   "Crisis and Opportunity: Education in Greater Kansas City," 5.

431   "Crisis and Opportunity: Education in Greater Kansas City," 6.

432   "Chronology," *Kansas City Times,* September 1, 1977, B4.

433   *Green v. New Kent County School Board,* 391 U.S. 430 (1968); *Keyes v. Denver School District,* 413 U.S. 189 (1973).

434   Orfield and Eaton, *Dismantling Desegregation.*

435   Orfield and Eaton, *Dismantling Desegregation.*

436   Stephen Winn, "Effect on Suit Here Unclear to Lawyers," *Kansas City Star,* July 3, 1979, A4.

437   Moran, *Race, Law, and the Desegregation of Public Schools.*

438   Dunn, *Complex Justice.*

439   This was in stark contrast to Judge Oliver, who was originally assigned to the case. Oliver was appointed by President Kennedy and was known as one of the most activist judges in the country. The case was transferred from Oliver to Clark, however, after the defendants challenged Oliver's impartiality due to his representation of the school district fifteen years earlier.

440   Phillip O'Connor and Lynn Horsley, "Guardian or Glory Hound? Arthur A. Benson II Has Been Called Many Things During KC Schools Case," *Kansas City Star,* July 14, 1996, A1.

441   Arthur Benson, Conversation with Author, October 23, 2013.

442   Arthur Benson, Conversation with Author, October 23, 2013.

443   Arthur Benson, Conversation with Author, October 23, 2013.

444   Arthur Benson, Conversation with Author, October 23, 2013.

445   Moran, *Race, Law, and the Desegregation of Public Schools.*

446   Arthur Benson, Conversation with Author, October 23, 2013.

447   Rick Abel, "'Push for Excellence,' Rev. Jesse Jackson Urges Students, Leaders," *Kansas City Call*, October 15, 1976, 1.

448   "Brief History," Rainbow PUSH Coalition, www.rainbowpush.org.

449   "Full-Time Director for EXCEL," *Kansas City Call*, August 19, 1977.

450   "Jesse Jackson to Speak at Excel Kick-off Banquet, *Kansas City Call*, October 7, 1977.

451   Terminate PUSH/EXCEL Program at East High," *Kansas City Call*, March 5, 1982, 1.

452   "D. F. Stewart, "Warm Farewell Given to Central High Principal," *Kansas City Call*, June 12, 1981.

453   See Chapter 5 for further discussion.

454   Gotham, *Race, Real Estate, and Uneven Development.*

455   William J. Wilson, *The Truly Disadvantaged: The Inner City, the Underclass, and Public Policy* (Chicago: University of Chicago Press, 1987).

456   Social Explorer Professional, United States Census (1940-1970), www.socialexplorer.com.

457   Social Explorer Professional, United States Census (1970-1990), www.socialexplorer.com.

458   Connie Wright, Conversation with Author, November 12, 2012.

459   Connie Wright, Conversation with Author, November 12, 2012.

460   Connie Wright, Conversation with Author, November 12, 2012.

461   Lee Barnes, Jr., Conversation with Author, November 12, 2012.

462   Lee Barnes, Jr., Conversation with Author, November 12, 2012.

463   Kansas City, Missouri School District Enrollment by School, 1954-1955– 1983-1984, Arthur Benson, unpublished demographic data.

464   Jeremiah Cameron, "N.A.A.C.P. in Action," *Kansas City Call*, March 12, 1981.

465   Social Explorer Professional, United States Census (1970), www.socialexplorer .com.

466   Lee Barnes, Jr., Conversation with Author, November 12, 2012.

467   Kansas City, Missouri School District Enrollment by School, 1954-1955– 1983-1984, Arthur Benson.

468   "Crisis and Opportunity: Education in Greater Kansas City," Bi-State Committee on Education, Missouri Advisory Committee (January 1977), Missouri Valley Special Collections, 5.

469   David Tatel, Director, Office of Civil Rights, to Samuel Carpenter, President of the Board (February 22, 1978), State Historical Society of Missouri, Arthur A. Benson II, Box 316.

470   Note: The name was changed back to Lincoln High School in May of 1978 as a result of protests among Lincoln High School alumni.

471   "'Lincoln Plan OK': Eagleton School Tour," *Kansas City Times*, March 29, 1978, State Historical Society of Missouri, Arthur A. Benson II, Box 462.

472   "'Lincoln Plan OK': Eagleton School Tour."

473   "Four All-Day Kindergartens Part of Magnet School Plan," *Kansas City Times*, May 4, 1978, State Historical Society of Missouri, Arthur A. Benson II, Box 316.

474   Ronald Szczypkowski and Marilyn Musumeci, "New York State Evaluation Study," in *Magnet School Policy Studies and Evaluations,* eds. Donald R. Waldrip, Walter L. Marks, and Nolan Estes (Austin: Morgan Printing and Publishing, 1993), 103-256.

475   *Morgan v. Kerrigan,* 530 F.2d 431(1976).

476   Susan E. Eaton and Elizabeth Crutcher, "Magnets, Media, and Mirages: Prince George's County's Miracle Cure," in *Dismantling Desegregation: The Quiet Reversal of Brown v. Board of Education,* eds. Gary Orfield and Susan E. Eaton (New York: The New Press, 1996), 265-89.

477   Thomas Eagleton, U.S. Senate, to Hale Champion, HEW, May 23, 1978, State Historical Society of Missouri, Arthur A. Benson II, Box 319.

478   Mary A. Raywid, "The Accomplishments of Schools of Choice," in *Magnet Schools: Recent Developments and Perspectives,* eds. Nolan Estes, Daniel U. Levine, and Donald R. Waldrip (Austin: Morgan Printing and Publishing, 1990), 31-47.

479   Marilyn Musumeci and Ronald Szczypkowski, *New York Magnet School Evaluation Study: Final Report* (New York: Magi Educational Services, 1991).

480   Daniel U. Levine and Eugene E. Eubanks, "Desegregation and Regional Magnetization," in *Magnet Schools: Recent Developments and Perspectives,* eds. Nolan Estes, Daniel U. Levine, and Donald R. Waldrip (Austin: Morgan Printing and Publishing, 1990), 49-57.

481   Levine and Eubanks, "Desegregation and Regional Magnetization."

482   Ellen B. Goldring and Claire Smrekar, "Magnet Schools and the Pursuit of Racial Balance," *Education and Urban Society* 33, no. 17 (2000): 17-35.

483   Claire Smrekar and Ellen B. Goldring, *School Choice in Urban America: Magnet Schools and the Pursuit of Equity* (New York: Teachers College Press, 1999).

484   Arthur Benson, Conversation with Author, October 23, 2013.

485   Levine and Eubanks, "Desegregation and Regional Magnetization," 55-6.

486   Daniel U. Levine and Connie C. Moore, "Considerations in Developing and Implementing Big City Magnet Programs," State Historical Society of Missouri, Arthur A. Benson II, Box 514.

487   Arthur Benson, Conversation with Author, October 23, 2013.

488   Arthur Benson, Conversation with Author, October 23, 2013.

489   *Jenkins v. Missouri,* 639 F. Supp. 19 (W.D. Mo. 1985).

490   Alison Morantz, "Money and Choice in Kansas City: Major Investments with Modest Returns," in *Dismantling Desegregation: The Quiet Reversal of Brown v. Board of Education,* eds. Gary Orfield and Susan E. Eaton (New York: The New Press, 1996), 241-63.

491   Kansas City, Missouri School District Enrollment by School, 1954-1955–1983-1984, Arthur Benson.

492   *Jenkins v. Missouri,* 593 F. Supp. 1485 (W.D. Mo. 1984), 36.

493   Dunn, *Complex Justice.*

494   "Judge Throws Out District's Desegregation Plan," United Press International, January 28, 1985.

495   Arthur Benson, Conversation with Author, October 23, 2013.

[496]   Mark C. Vopat, "Magnet Schools, Innate Talent, and Social Justice," *Theory and Research in Education* 9, no. 1 (2011), 59-72.

[497]   Vopat, "Magnet Schools, Innate Talent, and Social Justice."

[498]   *Chronology of Jenkins,* Missouri Valley Special Collections, Schools-Public, Kansas City, Vertical File.

[499]   Phale D. Hale and Daniel U. Levine, *Long Range Magnet School Plan* (Kansas City, MO: Kansas City, Missouri School District, 1986), State Historical Society of Missouri, Arthur A. Benson II, Box D503.

[500]   "Effective Schools," *Education Week*, May 1, 1992.

[501]   "Black corridor schools" appears to have been the prevailing term for these eighteen schools, though such a term was not identified in school documents.

[502]   Loyce Caruthers, Conversation with Author, April 12, 2014.

[503]   Court Order, November 12, 1986.

[504]   Court Order, November 12, 1986.

[505]   Hale and Levine, *Long Range Magnet School Plan.*

[506]   Hale and Levine, *Long Range Magnet School Plan.*

[507]   Court Order, November 12, 1986.

[508]   Court Order, November 12, 1986.

[509]   Richard C. Hunter Deposition (November 11, 1988), State Historical Society of Missouri, Arthur A. Benson II, Box D162.

[510]   Richard C. Hunter, "Kansas City, Missouri School District Long-Range Capital Improvement Plan" (January 1987), State Historical Society of Missouri, Arthur A. Benson II, Box 618.

[511]   Hunter, "Kansas City, Missouri School District Long-Range Capital Improvement Plan."

[512]   Hunter, "Kansas City, Missouri School District Long-Range Capital Improvement Plan."

[513]   Richard C. Hunter Deposition.

[514]   Richard C. Hunter Deposition.

[515]   Arthur Rainwater, Conversation with Author, July 29, 2013.

[516]   Court Order, September 17, 1987.

[517]   Court Order, September 17, 1987.

[518]   Court Order, September 17, 1987.

[519]   "Central High School Academic Program," Central High School Task Force (January 1988), State Historical Society of Missouri, Arthur A. Benson II, Box D153.

[520]   *Jenkins v. Missouri,* "Plaintiff's Post-Hearing Brief and Suggested Findings of Fact" (March 31, 1989), State Historical Society of Missouri, Arthur A. Benson II, Box D237.

[521]   Design Program Analysis for the New Kansas City Central High School, Kansas City, Missouri," Councilman/Hunsaker & Associates (March 1988), State Historical Society of Missouri, Arthur A. Benson II, Box D503.

[522]   Thomas Eaton Meeting Notes (March 2, 1988), State Historical Society of Missouri, Arthur A. Benson II, Box D503.

[523]   Arthur Rainwater Deposition, November 2, 1988, State Historical Society of Missouri, Arthur A. Benson II, Box D174.

[524]   Final Site Report, Kansas City, Missouri School District (August 1988), State Historical Society of Missouri, Arthur A. Benson II, D503.

525   Court Order, April 26, 1989.

526   *Jenkins v. Missouri,* "State's Opposition to the Motion of the Kansas City, Missouri School District for Approval of a Site for Central High School and for Increases and Modifications in the Budgets for Building Construction and Equipment for the Magnet; Alternative Request for a Hearing" (December 1988), State Historical Society of Missouri, Arthur A. Benson II, Box D503.

527   Arthur Rainwater, Conversation with Author, July 29, 2013.

528   Arthur Rainwater, Conversation with Author, July 29, 2013.

529   Hale and Levine, *Long Range Magnet School Plan.*

530   Hale and Levine, *Long Range Magnet School Plan.*

531   "Central High School Academic Program."

532   "Central High School Academic Program."

533   "Central High School Academic Program."

534   Hale and Levine, *Long Range Magnet School Plan.*

535   "Central High School Classical Greek Preliminary Program Narrative," Central High School Task Force (n.d.), State Historical Society of Missouri, Arthur A. Benson II, Box D153.

536   "Central High School Classical Greek Preliminary Program Narrative."

537   Hale and Levine, *Long Range Magnet School Plan.*

538   Arthur Rainwater Deposition,

539   "Central High School Classical Greek Preliminary Program Narrative."

540   "Central High School Classical Greek Preliminary Program Narrative."

541   Arthur Rainwater Deposition.

542   Daniel Levine Deposition, February 16, 1989, State Historical Society of Missouri, Arthur A. Benson II, Box D174.

543   "Central High School Classical Greek Preliminary Program Narrative."

544   Elizabeth L. Spaid, "'Magnets' Attract in Kansas City," *Christian Science Monitor,* June 15, 1992, 12.

545   Formative Evaluation of the Central Senior Magnet School Computers Unlimited, 1988-1989," Evaluation Office, School District of Kansas City, Missouri, State Historical Society of Missouri, Arthur A. Benson II Papers, Box 511.

546   Formative Evaluation of the Central Senior Magnet School Computers Unlimited, 1988-1989.

547   Hale and Levine, *Long Range Magnet School Plan.*

548   Formative Evaluation of the Central Senior Magnet School Computers Unlimited, 1988-1989.

549   Formative Evaluation of the Central Senior Magnet School Computers Unlimited, 1988-1989.

550   *Jenkins v. Missouri,* "Motion for Approval of the Kansas City, Missouri School District Long-Range Capital Improvement Plan" (1987), State Historical Society of Missouri, Arthur A. Benson II Papers, Box 511.

551   Crystal Shakur, Conversation with Author, December 5, 2013.

552   Daryl Norton, Conversation with Author, September 27, 2013.

553   Hale and Levine, "Longterm Magnet School Plan."

554   Daryl Norton, Conversation with Author, September 27, 2013.

555   Daryl Norton, Conversation with Author, September 27, 2013.

556   Formative Evaluation of the Central Senior Magnet School Computers Unlimited, 1989-1990.

557   Formative Evaluation of the Central Senior Magnet School Computers Unlimited, 1989-1990.

558   Social Explorer Professional, 1990, accessed May 15, 2023, www.socialexplorer.com.

559   Dunn, *Complex Justice.*

560   Lynn Horsley, "Brand-new Year Opens with Four Brand-new Schools," *Kansas City Star*, September 4, 1991.

561   Tim O'Connor, "New Central High to Cost $32 Million," *Kansas City Star,* n.d., A9, Missouri Valley Special Collections, Schools-Public, Central.

562   Mike DeArmond, "Central Hopes to Draw Students with New Facility," *Kansas City Star*, June 2, 1991.

563   Jim Mosley, "Stunning: Kansas City's New Central High Has It," *St. Louis Post-Dispatch,* February 9, 1992, 4A.

564   Lynn Horsley, "KC's Central High: The School Some Love and Some Love to Hate," *Kansas City Star,* May 10, 1992, A1, A14.

565   Bruce Rodgers, "A Good Guy Leaving a Tough Job," *Kansas City View,* November 2, 1990, Missouri Valley Special Collections, Kansas City, Missouri Superintendents, Vertical File.

566   Art Brisbane, "Nominee is a Man for His Era," *Kansas City Star*, July 5, 1991.

567   Kansas City, Missouri School District Enrollment by School, 1954-1955–1983-1984, Arthur Benson.

568   Central High School Classical Greek Program Narrative.

569   Christopher Slaughter, Conversation with Author, September 30, 2013.

570   Arthur Benson, Conversation with Author, October 23, 2013.

571   Kansas City, Missouri School District Enrollment by School, 1954-1955–1983-1984, Arthur Benson.

572   "Summative Evaluation of the Central Computers Unlimited Magnet High School, 1988-1992," Evaluation Office, School District of Kansas City, Missouri; "Formative Evaluation of the Central Classical Greek Magnet High School, 1991-1992," Evaluation Office, School District of Kansas City, Missouri, State Historical Society of Missouri, Arthur A. Benson II Papers, Box 511.

573   *Centralian*, 1993, Missouri Valley Special Collections, Digital Archive.

574   Willie Mahone, Conversation with Author, October 24, 2012.

575   John Garrity, "From Russia With Love: Vladimir Nazlymov, Former Coach of the Soviet Saber Team, Now Teaches Fencing in a Kansas City High School," *Sports Illustrated,* June 1, 1992.

576   Vladimir Nazlymov, Conversation with Author, July 22, 2013.

577   Walter Marks memo to the Board, November 9, 1993, State Historical Society of Missouri, Arthur A. Benson II Papers, Box 185D.

578   United States Fencing Press Release, March 2, 1993, State Historical Society of Missouri, Arthur A. Benson II Papers, Box 185D.

579   "Olympic Style Weightlifting Program, Central Senior High," Press Release, December 23, 1993.

580   "Suit Says Magnet Schools Bar Black Children," *New York Times,* August 3, 1989, A14.

581   "Summative Evaluation of the Central Computers Unlimited Magnet High School, 1988-1992"; "Formative Evaluation of the Central Classical Greek Magnet High School, 1991-1992."

582   "Report of the Progress of Desegregation in the Kansas City, Missouri Public Schools 1985-1986 through 2000-2001," Kansas City, Missouri School District.

583   "Report of the Progress of Desegregation in the Kansas City, Missouri Public Schools 1985-1986 through 2000-2001."

584   "Long Range Magnet Plan: Elementary through Secondary Schools," Missouri Valley Special Collections, Schools-Central.

585   "Long Range Magnet Plan: Elementary through Secondary Schools."

586   Scott Thompson, "Missouri's Statewide BEST Test Helps Shape 'Basics' Curriculum," Special to the *Christian Science Monitor,* August 23, 1985.

587   "A Missouri History of Assessment and Accountability," Department of Elementary and Secondary Education, www.dese.mo.gov.

588   James Bliss and David Honeyman, "A Legislative Report in the Excellence in Education Act of 1985," *Journal of Education Finance* 11, no. 4 (Spring 1986): 480-9.

589   Tim O'Connor, "KC Offers Good Schools, but Pupils Don't Learn, Panel Says," *Kansas City Star,* August 31, 1991, A1.

590   Lynn Horsley, "Goals Elude KC Magnets: Enrollment and Achievement Lag Despite Years of Effort, Money," *Kansas City Star,* August 10, 1992.

591   Horsley, "Goals Elude KC Magnets."

592   Dunn, *Complex Justice.*

593   "Central High School Places in Computer Science Olympiad Programming Competition," *Kansas City Call,* March 22, 1996; "Central Aquatics Club to Host Swim Meet," *Kansas City Call,* March 7, 1997; "Eleven Central Weightlifters Qualify for Junior National Weightlifting Championships," *Kansas City Call,* March 26, 1993.

594   Christopher Slaughter, Conversation with Author, September 30, 2013.

595   USA Fencing, "Dr. Jeremy Summers Steps Down as USA Fencing Director of Sports Medicine," accessed June 12, 2023, usafencing.org.

596   Kevin Stankiewicz, "Fencing: 'He's a Legend': Vladimir Nazlymov Retires After 19 Seasons as Ohio State Head Coach," *The Lantern,* April 17, 2018.

597   Vladimir Nazlymov, Conversation with Author, July 22, 2013.

598   *Jenkins v. Missouri,* 515 U.S. 70 (1995).

599   *Jenkins v. Missouri,* 515 U.S. 70 (1995).

600   Arthur Benson, Conversation with Author, October 23, 2013.

601   "Suburban Kansas City Students Are Leaving Magnet Schools," *St. Louis Post-Dispatch,* April 27, 1995, 4D.

602   During the magnet era, tuition waivers were provided by the state of Missouri to cover the cost of attendance by out-of-district students.

603   Arthur Benson, "Chronology of the Kansas City, Missouri, Desegregation Case." Missouri Valley Special Collections, Schools-Public, Kansas City Desegregation.

604   Donna McGuire, "Schools See Loss from Suburbs – Desegregation Ruling's Fallout Begins to Settle on the KC Magnet Program," *Kansas City Star,* August 23, 1995, A1.

605   McGuire, "Schools See Loss from Suburbs."

606   McGuire, "Schools See Loss from Suburbs."

607   Dennis Farney, "Fading Dream? Integration Is Faltering in Kansas City Schools as Priorities Change," *Wall Street Journal,* September 26, 1995, n.p.

608   Dunn, *Complex Justice.*

609   Emily Langer, "John Murphy, Pr. George's Superintendent Who Helped Bridge Racial Gap, Dies," *Washington Post,* August 24, 2011.

610   Benson, "Chronology of the Kansas City, Missouri, Desegregation Case."

611   Benson, "Chronology of the Kansas City, Missouri, Desegregation Case."

612   Lynn Horsley and Philip O'Connor, "School Chief Quits: Judge is Asked to Suspend KC," *Kansas City Star,* June 15, 1996, A1.

613   Dunn, *Complex Justice.*

614   Lynn Horsley and Philip O'Connor, "Clark will Relinquish Desegregation Case," *Kansas City Star,* January 28, 1997, A1.

615   Phillip O'Connor and Lynn Horsley, "Judge Chosen to Oversee Desegregation Lawsuit," *Kansas City Star,* March 29, 1997, C8.

616   "KCMSD Plan for Transition to Unitary Status," Kansas City, Missouri School District, August 15, 1987, State Historical Society of Missouri, Arthur A. Benson II Papers, Box 587.

617   "KCMSD Plan for Transition to Unitary Status."

618   Christine H. Rossell, "The Desegregation of the Kansas City, Missouri School District from Brown to 2000-2001," State Historical Society of Missouri, Arthur A. Benson II Papers, Box 585.

619   Arthur Benson, Conversation with Author, June 19, 2023.

620   "Total Student Membership: School Years 1955-1956 through 1999-2000," Kansas City, Missouri School District, Arthur A. Benson II Papers, Box 567.

621   Rossell, "The Desegregation of the Kansas City, Missouri School District."

622   Rossell, "The Desegregation of the Kansas City, Missouri School District."

623   Desegregation Monitoring Committee, "DMC Report to the Court," October 14, 1998, State Historical Society of Missouri, Arthur A. Benson II Papers, Box 587.

624   Interoffice Memo from Dr. Margaret Seever to Kathy Walter-Mack, "DMC Request," September 9, 1999, Arthur A Benson II Papers, Box 573.

625   Interoffice Memo from Dr. Margaret Seever to Kathy Walter-Mack.

626   Tanika White, "Exams to Put KC Students, District to Exam Scores," *Kansas City Star,* April 18, 1999, B1.

627   Phillip O'Connor, "State Pulls KC School Certification," *Kansas City Star,* October 22, 1999, A1.

628   Phillip O'Connor, "Benson Appeals Ruling on Desegregation Lawsuit," *Kansas City Star,* December 17, 1999, A1.

629   Donna McGuire, "Judge Ends Desegregation Case After 26 Years and $2 Billion," *Kansas City Star,* August 14, 2003, A1.

630   "Report of the Progress of Desegregation in the Kansas City, Missouri Public Schools 1985-1986 through 2000-2001," Kansas City, Missouri School District.

631   "Report of the Progress of Desegregation in the Kansas City, Missouri Public Schools."

632   Arthur Rainwater, Conversation with Author, July 29, 2013.

633   William Celis, III, "Kansas City's Widely Debated Desegregation Experiment Reaches the Supreme Court," *New York Times,* January 11, 1995, B7.

634   Joe Robertson, "Remnants of Magnet Program Persist in KC Schools," *Kansas City Star*, November 2, 2006, A1.

635   McGuire, "Judge Ends Desegregation Case."

636   McGuire, "Judge Ends Desegregation Case."

637   Barbara Shelly, "Schools Offer Promise and Peril," *Kansas City Star,* January 6, 1999, B1.

638   "Reclaiming the Promise of Public Charter Schools through Rigorous Authorizer Reform," American Federation of Teachers, accessed July 18, 2023, aft.org.

639   Diane Ravitch, "The Myth of Charter Schools," The Brookings Institute, November 11, 2010.

640   Charles J. McClain memo to Judge Whipple, "Implementation Monitor," September 22, 2000, State Historical Society of Missouri, Arthur A. Benson II Papers, Box 568.

641   Revised Statute Missouri Charter Schools, RSMo, Section 160.400.2.

642   School District of Kansas City, Missouri Executive Summary, "Fiscal Year 2003 Comprehensive Budget," June 11, 2002, State Historical Society of Missouri, Arthur A. Benson II Papers, Box 568.

643   Charles J. McClain memo to Judge Whipple.

644   School District of Kansas City, Missouri Executive Summary.

645   Frederic Pierce, "Charter School Firm Loses Work Across Nation-Problems, Criticisms Not New for Management Company of Failed Syracuse School," *Post-Standard*, August 28, 2005, A1.

646   Lynn Franey, "KC District Locks Doors to Charter-Two Westport Buildings are Regained after Court Ruling Favors School Board," *Kansas City Star*, August 19, 2004, A1.

647   Benjamin Demps, Jr., "From the Superintendent: An Open Letter about Schools," *Kansas City Star,* October 23, 1999, State Historical Society of Missouri, Arthur A. Benson II, Box 573.

648   "Demps Says Takeover Might Be Best Option," *Kansas City Star*, April 26, 2001, A8.

649   Jermaine Wilson, Conversation with Author, July 10, 2013.

650   Dean Smith, "State Declares Five KC Schools Deficient – District to get Money, Professional Help," *Kansas City Star*, September 21, 2001.

651   Smith, "State Declares Five KC Schools Deficient."

652   Smith, "State Declares Five KC Schools Deficient."

653   Joe Miller, "The Long Walk Home," *Pitch*, May 23, 2002.

654   Deann Smith, "Central in KC will Require Uniforms," *Kansas City Star*, December 4, 2001, B1.

655   Joe Robertson, "School Year Brings New Attitude at Central," *Kansas City Star,* August 25, 2008, A1.

656   Joe Robertson, "Reform Plan Founders at KC's Central High School," *Kansas City Star*, April 12, 2009, C1.

657   Robertson, "Reform Plan Founders."

658   Joe Robertson, "Ragsdale, Pelofsky Won't Seek Re-election to KC School Board," *Kansas City Star*, January 7, 2010, A4.

659   "U.S. American Community Surveys, 2005-2009," Social Explorer Professional, accessed August 2, 2023, www.socialexplorer.com.

660   "Census 2020 – Preliminary Data," Social Explorer Professional, accessed August 2, 2023, www.socialexplorer.com.

661   "Building Demographic Data, 2022," Missouri Department of Elementary and Secondary Education, accessed August 2, 2023, www.dese.mo.gov.

662   "U.S. Decennial Census, 1970, 1980, 1990, 2000, 2010, 2020," Social Explorer Professional, accessed August 2, 2023, www.socialexplorer.com.

663   Project WNYC, accessed September 25, 2023, projectwnyc.org.

664   "Central High School Report Card, Historical," Missouri Department of Elementary and Secondary Education, accessed August 2, 2023, www.dese. mo.gov.

665   "Census 2020 – Preliminary Data," Social Explorer Professional, accessed August 2, 2023, www.socialexplorer.com.

666   *Cross-X follows the Central debate team and their teacher as they experience success during their championship 2002 season.* Joe Miller, *Cross-X: The Amazing True Story of How the Most Unlikely Team from the Most Unlikely of Places Overcame Staggering Obstacles at Home and at School to Challenge the Debate Community on Race, Power, and Education* (New York: Farrar, Straus and Giroux, 2006).

667   *Craig Dydell vs. Bernard Taylor,* SC90912 (MO 2011).

668   "Penalty Leads Teachers to Stage 'Sick Out,'" *Columbia Daily Tribune*, November 20, 2005, 1.

669   Joe Robertson, "Teachers Defend 'Sick Out' Strategy," *Kansas City Star*, December 1, 2005, B3.

670   Robertson, "Teachers Defend 'Sick Out' Strategy."

671   Robertson, "Teachers Defend 'Sick Out' Strategy."

672   Eric Zorn, "Thug is a Problem Word, Even if It Didn't Used to Be," *Chicago Tribune,* March 3, 2021.

673   "Black on Black Crime is Still a Plague," *Kansas City Call*, June 4, 2004; "Student Arrested After Taking Gun to School," *Kansas City Star*, December 15, 2005; "Wounded Boy Dies at Help's Door," *Kansas City Star*, June 16, 2005; "Gangs' Reach Extends Clear into Eighth Grade," *Kansas City Star*, December 2, 2007; "Mentors Needed at Central High School," *Kansas City Star*, October 23, 2008; "Shots Fired Near Central High; One Wounded," *Kansas City Star*, March 10, 2011, 1; "Police Investigate Shooting that Killed Teen," *Kansas City Star*, March 11, 2008, B2.

674   Joe Robertson, "Long-term Solution Sought after Central High," *Kansas City Star*, November 11, 2009, A11.

675   Robertson, "Long-term Solution Sought."

676   Tonya Mosley, "Why the Crack Cocaine Epidemic Hit the Black Communities 'First and Worst,'" July 13, 2023.

677   Donovan X. Ramsey, *When Crack Was King: A People's History of a Misunderstood Era* (One World, 2023).

678   Alvin Brooks, Conversation with Author, October 12, 2023.

679   Ed Chung, Betsy Pearl, and Lea Hunter, "The 1994 Crime Bill Continues to Undercut Justice Reform—Here's How to Stop It," Center for American Progress, March 26, 2019.

680   Chung et al., "The 1994 Crime Bill."

681   "Central High School Report Card, Historical," Missouri Department of Elementary and Secondary Education.

682   "Lincoln College Preparatory Academy Report Card, Historical," Missouri Department of Elementary and Secondary Education, accessed September 8, 2023, www.dese.mo.gov.

683   "Building Report Card, 2021-2022," Missouri Department of Elementary and Secondary Education, www.dese.mo.gov.

684   "Required Documentation," Lincoln College Preparatory Academy, accessed August 14, 2023, pa/kcpublicschools.edu/enroll.

685   Kayla Neal, Conversation with Author, May 5, 2023.

686   Joe Robertson, "KC Scores Fall Short," *Kansas City Star*, December 5, 2006, B10.

687   "KC Leaders Face Slur Claims," *Columbia Daily Tribune,* December 16, 2007.

688   Joe Robertson, "KC School Board Hires Colorado Educator as Superintendent," *Kansas City Star*, May 1, 2009, A1.

689   Joe Robertson, "Meetings to Focus on School Consolidations," *Kansas City Star*, October 4, 2006, B5.

690   Kansas City, Missouri School District Enrollment by School, 1954-1955–1983-1984, Arthur Benson.

691   John Michaels, "U.S. School Superintendents: Handling Political Divisions is Toughest Part of Job," EAB, February 17, 2022.

692   KC School District Budget Cuts Unpopular but Crucial," *Kansas City Star*, November 28, 2009, A20.

693   Tina Kells, "Kansas City School Closures," *Kansas City Examiner*, March 11, 2010, 11-12.

694   Tina Kells, "School Board Votes to Close 29 of 61 Schools," *Kansas City Examiner*, March 11, 2010.

695   Council of Great City Schools, "Urban School Superintendents: Characteristics, Tenure, and Salary," Fall 2014.

696   Chris Blank, "Kansas City School District Loses Accreditation," *Associated Press*, September 20, 2011.

697   Kansas City Schools Superintendent Honored, Says He Plans to Stay as the District's Leader," *Kansas City Star*, April 1, 2015.

698   Linda Collins, Conversation with Author, October 19, 2023.

699   Linda Collins, Conversation with Author, October 19, 2023.

700   Linda Collins, Conversation with Author, October 19, 2023.

701   Linda Collins, Conversation with Author, October 19, 2023.

702   Linda Collins, Conversation with Author, October 19, 2023.

703   Linda Collins, Conversation with Author, October 19, 2023.

704   Linda Collins, Conversation with Author, October 19, 2023.

705   Joe Robertson, "Ambitious School Reform Relies on the Personal Touch," *Kansas City Star*, June 27, 2011, 1A.

706   Robertson, "Ambitious School Reform."

707   Joe Robertson, "A School by Another Name," *Kansas City Star,* June 28, 2012, 1.

708   Robertson, "A School by Another Name."

709   "System Analysis," Kansas City Public Schools, May 9, 2019.

710   Robertson, "A School by Another Name."

711   Robertson, "A School by Another Name."

712   John Papay, Andrew Backer-Hicks, Lindsay Page, and William Marinell, "The Challenge of Teacher Retention in Urban Schools: Evidence of Variation from a Cross-Site Analysis," *Educational Researcher*, 46, no. 8 (2017): 434-48.

713   "Race and Ethnicity of Public School Teachers and their Students," National Center for Education Statistics (September 2020).

714   Jared Kastelein, Conversation with Author, December 1, 2023.

715   "KC's Central High School Renamed," *Kansas City Star,* July 25, 2012.

716   "KC's Central High School Renamed."

717   Joe Robertson, "Kansas City District will Reconsider Central High School Name Change," *Kansas City Star,* November 11, 2012.

718   Note: There is little formal coverage of the forum, but I attended the 2012 meeting.

719   Lynne Shipley, Conversation with Author, May 15, 2023.

720   Leslie Collins, "Central High Principal Proposes Changing Name," *Northeast News,* July 10, 2012, 1.

721   Collins, "Central High Principal Proposes."

722   Linda Collins, Conversation with Author, October 19, 2023.

723   Lynne Shipley, Conversation with Author, May 15, 2023.

724   Sarah Clark, "What It's Like to Live Inside the Murder Factory," *Fox 4 News*, November 8, 2011.

725   "Kansas City Murders Reached Record High in 2023," *Associated Press*, January 2, 2023.

726   "Kansas City, Missouri Murder/Homicide Rate, 1999-2018," Macrotrends, accessed September 13, 2023, www.macrotrends.net.

727   Tim Rizzo, "Murder Factory: Part 1: 64130, The Zip Code of Notoriety," *Kansas City Star*, January 25, 2009, A1; Tim Rizzo, "Murder Factory: Part 2, Murder Factory: Decades of Blight Leave Zip Code 64130 Reeling in Violence," *Kansas City Star*, January 26, 2009, A1; Tim Rizzo, "Murder Factory: Part 3: Kansas City Needs to Fight Back and Close the 'Factory,'" January 27, 2009, A1; *Kansas City Murder Factory*, directed by Mike Rollen (IMDb Pro, 2011), 1:13, https://www.imdb.com/title/tt1728241/.

728   Opportunity Atlas, accessed September 14, 2023, www.opportunityatlas.org.

729   Elizabeth Orosco, "15-Year-Old Victim in Shooting at Central Academy of Excellence has been Identified," *Northeast News*, February 14, 2019.

730   Melissa Greenstein and Tom Dempsey, "KCPD Looking for Man in Connection to Teen's Fatal Shooting at Gas Station," KSHB, October 22, 2018.

731   Orosco, "15-Year-Old Victim in Shooting."

732   "Two Kansas City Women have been Arrested, Charged in Connection in Tuesday's Shooting at Central High School," *Northeast News*, February 14, 2019.

733   Anthony Madry, Conversation with Author, November 14, 2023.

734   Anthony Madry, Conversation with Author, November 14, 2023.
735   Anthony Madry, Conversation with Author, November 14, 2023.
736   Anthony Madry, Conversation with Author, November 14, 2023.
737   Rizzo, "Murder Factory: Part 1"; Rizzo, "Murder Factory: Part 2"; Rizzo, "Murder Factory: Part 3."
738   *Kansas City Murder Factory*, directed by Mike Rollen.
739   Rizzo, "Murder Factory: Part 1."
740   Rizzo, "Murder Factory, Part 3."
741   Rizzo, "Murder Factory, Part 3."
742   "System Analysis," Kansas City Public Schools.
743   Paul Thompson, "Back to School 2016: Q&A with new KCPS Superintendent," *Northeast News*, August 3, 2016.
744   "New Kansas City Charter School Holds Promise," *Kansas City Star*, August 27, 2015.
745   Cynthia Yueting Xu, "Where are All of the Charter Schools Located?" *National Alliance for Public Charter Schools*, December 6, 2022.
746   Argun Saatcioglu and Anthony Snethen, "Preference Compromise and Parent Satisfaction with Schools in Choice Markets: Evidence from Kansas City, Missouri," *Educational Evaluation and Policy Analysis* 45, no. 3 (2023): 367-98.
747   Saatcioglu and Snethen, "Preference Compromise."
748   African-Centered College Preparatory Academy (9-12), African-Centered College Preparatory Academy (PK-8), Border Star Montessori (PK-6), Foreign Language Academy (K-8), George Washington Carver Dual Language School (K-6), Harold Holliday Montessori (Pre-K-6), Lincoln College Preparatory Academy (9-12), Lincoln College Preparatory Academy Middle School (6-8), Paseo Academy of Fine and Performing Arts (7-12).
749   Saatcioglu and Snethen, "Preference Compromise."
750   Saatcioglu and Snethen, "Preference Compromise."
751   Tim Walker, "A 'Choice' Grounded in Exclusion and Inequality," *neaToday*, August 19, 2021.
752   Jon Hale, *The Choice We Face: How Segregation, Race, and Power have Shaped America's Most Controversial Reform Movement* (Boston: Beacon Press, 2021).
753   "System Analysis," Kansas City Public Schools.
754   "System Analysis," Kansas City Public Schools.
755   "Kansas City Data Summit: Data for Action," UMKC Urban Education Research Center, February 8, 2023.
756   "Kansas City Data Summit: Data for Action."
757   "Kansas City Data Summit: Data for Action."
758   "Kansas City Data Summit: Data for Action."
759   Michael DeArmond, Alice Opalka, and Patrick Denise, "Student Mobility in Kansas City," Turn the Page KC, June 2019.
760   Patrick Gill, Mauricio Molina, and Daniel Potter, "The Relationship Between School-Year Mobility and School Performance in the Houston Area," Houston Education Research Consortium, December 2021.
761   Sarah Sparks, "Student Mobility: How it Affects Learning," *Education Week*, August 2016.
762   Sparks, "Student Mobility."

763   "System Analysis," Kansas City Public Schools.

764   "System Analysis," Kansas City Public Schools.

765   "System Analysis," Kansas City Public Schools.

766   "System Analysis," Kansas City Public Schools.

767   "Kansas City Data Summit: Data for Action."

768   "Kansas City Data Summit: Data for Action."

769   "District Demographic Data." Missouri Department of Elementary and Secondary Education, accessed October 16, 2023, apps.dese.mo.gov.

770   "District Demographic Data."

771   Loyce Caruthers, Brad Poos, and Jennifer Friend, "Transitory Voices: The Journey from Urban High School to an Early College Program," *Urban Education* 56, no. 2 (2021): 289-317.

772   "District Demographic Data." Missouri Department of Elementary and Secondary Education, accessed October 16, 2023, apps.dese.mo.gov.

773   "Lincoln College Prep Named Missouri's Top High School," *Northeast News,* May 13, 2015.

774   "School Report Card," Missouri Department of Elementary and Secondary Education, accessed October 10, 2023, https://dese.mo.gov/.

775   Julia Ann McWilliams, "The Neighborhood School Stigma: School Choice, Stratification, and Shame," *Policy Futures in Education* 15, no. 2 (2017): 221-38.

776   *Blueprint 2030*, Kansas City Public Schools, December 7, 2022.

777   Sarah Ritter, "Kansas City Schools May Close, Consolidate Schools After Years of Enrollment Decline," *Kansas City Star*, October 12, 2021.

778   Ritter, "Kansas City Schools May Close."

779   Sarah Ritter, "Accreditation is Only the Start for Kansas City Schools. Here's the Plan for What's Next," *Kansas City Star*, January 11, 2022.

780   "Dr. Bedell Named Superintendent of the Year by NABSE," eyeonannapolis. net, October 2, 2023.

781   Anne Arundel County Public Schools, aacps.org, accessed October 10, 2023.

782   "History of KCPS," KCPS, accessed August 2, 2023, kcpublicschools.org.

783   Sarah Ritter, "'We Don't Understand': Emotional Alums Plead to Keep KC's Central High from Closing," *Kansas City Star*, October 17, 2022.

784   "Report – Public Final," 2022 and 2023, Missouri Department of Elementary and Secondary Education, https://dese.mo.gov/; "School Report Card," Missouri Department of Elementary and Secondary Education, accessed October 10, 2023, https://dese.mo.gov/.

785   Ritter, "Kansas City Schools May Close."

786   Argun Saatcioglu, *The Relationship of Public School Closures with Property Values and Crime Incidences in Kansas City Public School District, 2007-2018.* Report Commissioned by BlaqueKC, 2022, Kansas City, MO.

787   Ritter, "'We Don't Understand.'"

788   Maria Benevento, "Proposal to Close 10 Schools in Kansas City, Improve Academics Hinges on Community Support," *Griffon News: Missouri Western State College*, October 17, 2022.

789   Sarah Ritter, "Is Plan to Close KC Schools 'Academic Vision' or 'Death Blow'? Neighbors Fear Fallout, *Kansas City Star*, December 5, 2022.

790   "School Report Card, 2022," (Central and Southeast), Missouri Department of Elementary and Secondary Education, www.dese.mo.gov.

791   Sarah Ritter, "After Community Outcry, Kansas City District Now Proposes Closing Far Fewer Schools," *Kansas City Star*, January 11, 2023.

792   Ritter, "After Community Outcry."

793   "Covid Relief Federal Fund Priorities," Missouri Department of Elementary and Secondary Education, May 5, 2021, www.dese.mo.gov.

794   "Covid Relief Federal Fund Priorities."

795   Jodi Fortino, "Kansas City Schools Missed Out on $45 Million Last Year Due to Tax Breaks for Developers," National Public Radio, January 23, 2023.

796   Fortino, "Kansas City Schools Missed Out."

797   Fortino, "Kansas City Schools Missed Out."

798   Dave D'Marko, "KCPS Hosts Listening Session as it Considers Keeping Windfall from Property Assessments," *Missouri News*, September 7, 2023.

799   Jodi Fortino, "Kansas City Public Schools will Maintain Tax Levy to Deal with $400 million in Maintenance Needs," National Public Radio, September 28, 2023.

800   "KC Public Schools Must Listen to Community in Superintendent Search," *Kansas City Star*, December 15, 2022.

801   Abby Hoover, "Blueprint 2030 Approved, Collier Calls Community to Action," *Northeast News*, February 1, 2023.

802   Hoover, "Blueprint 2030 Approved."

803   Mikayla Witcher, Conversation with Author, November 9, 2023.

804   Abby Hoover, "KCPS Board Discusses Reopening Options," *Northeast News*, July 17, 2020.

805   Stephen Hardy, "KC Connectivity Report," May 19, 2020, mysidewalk.com.

806   Kera Mashek, "KCPS Leaders Scrambling After Health Department Raises Concerns about In-person Classes," *Fox-4*, July 20, 2020.

807   Joe Robertson, "Calling all KC Hands to Rescue Education System 'On Verge of Collapse,'" *Local Investment Commission*, December 1, 2020.

808   Robertson, "Calling all KC Hands."

809   Emma Dorn, Bryan Hancock, Jimmy Sarakatsannis, and Ellen Viruleg, "Covid 19 and Education: The Lingering Effects of Unfinished Learning," McKinsey and Company, July 27, 2021.

810   "Education Data for Action Summit," UMKC Urban Education Research Center, June 22, 2023.

811   "Education Data for Action Summit."

812   "Missouri 2022 APR Summary by Building," Missouri Department of Elementary and Secondary Education, www.dese.mo.gov.

813   MSIP 6 School APR Summary Report – Public Final" (2022 and 2023). Missouri Department of Elementary and Secondary Education.

814   Paseo Academy of Performing Arts is calculated on a grades 7-12 scale, and the Missouri Department of Elementary and Secondary Education warns against comparing buildings with different grade spans.

815   "MSIP 6 School APR Summary Report–Public Final" (2022, 2023, and 2024), Missouri Department of Elementary and Secondary Education.

816   The data is not comparable for Paseo because it is reported for grades 7-12 as a collective. The others are reported as grades 9-12.

817   "MSIP 6 School APR Summary Report–Public Final" (2023 and 2024), Missouri Department of Elementary and Secondary Education

818   Claire Smrekar and Ellen B. Goldring, *School Choice in Urban America: Magnet Schools and the Pursuit of Equity* (New York: Teachers College Press, 1999).

819   "K-12: Student Population has Significantly Diversified, but many Schools Remain Divided Along Racial, Ethnic, and Economic Lines," U.S. Government Accountability Office, June 16, 2022.

820   "K-12: Student Population has Significantly Diversified."

821   Bryan Duarte, "The Effects of School Choice Competition on an Underserved Neighborhood Public School," *Educational Policy* 37, no. 7 (2023): 1950-88.

822   "Urban Student Characteristics and Urban School Challenges: What High-Quality Education for Every Student Means," Center for Public Education Report (2024), National School Boards Association.

823   "Urban Student Characteristics and Urban School Challenges."

824   "Central Building Report Card," Missouri Department of Middle and Secondary Education, 2023.

825   David Paunesku, "The Deficit Lens of the Achievement Gap Needs to be Flipped: Here's How," *Education Week,* July 9, 2019.

826   Paunesku, "The Deficit Lens of the Achievement Gap."

Works Cited

118 Cong. Rec. S 2524-S 2543, February 24, 1972. In David Henderson, *Integration in Missouri Public Schools: Faculty and Students Twenty Years after* Brown. Jefferson City, MO: Commission on Human Rights, 1974.

"43 Integrated Schools." *Kansas City Call*, September 22, 1955. State Historical Society of Missouri, Arthur A. Benson II, Box 306.

Abel, Rick. "'Push for Excellence,' Rev. Jesse Jackson Urges Students, Leaders." *Kansas City Call*, 15 October 1976, 1.

"A Big Year for the Schools." *Kansas City Star*, June 4, 1956. Missouri Valley Special Collections, Schools-Public.

"Action Against Central." *Kansas City Star*, March 10, 1972. Missouri Valley Special Collections, Schools-Public, Central High.

Adams v. Richardson, 356 F. Supp. 92 (1973).

"A Danger of School Resegregation Grows." *Kansas City Star*, October 27, 1965. Missouri Valley Special Collections, Schools-Public.

"A Good Plan Sabotaged." *Kansas City Call*, October 7, 1955, 20.

"A Large Senior Enrollment." *Kansas City Star*, December 2, 1919, 6.

"All Kinds of Tricks against Teachers." *Kansas City Call*, May 6, 1955. State Historical Society of Missouri, Arthur A. Benson II, Box 306.

"All Pools Are Open." *Kansas City Call*, May 27, 1955. State Historical Society of Missouri, Arthur A. Benson II, Box 303.

American Federation of Teachers. "Reclaiming the Promise of Public Charter Schools through Rigorous Authorizer Reform." Accessed July 18, 2023, aft.org.

Anderson, James D. *The Education of Blacks in the South, 1860-1935*. Chapel Hill: University of North Carolina Press, 1988.

Anne Arundel County Public Schools, Aacps.org. Accessed October 10, 2023.

Annual Report of the Superintendent of Schools, 1867-1947. Missouri Valley Special Collections.

Annual Report of the Superintendent of Schools, 1894. Missouri Valley Special Collections.

Annual Report of the Superintendent of Schools, 1895. Missouri Valley Special Collections.

Annual Report of the Superintendent of Schools, 1905-1906. Missouri Valley Special Collections

Annual Report of the Superintendent of Schools, 1913-1914. Missouri Valley Special Collections.

"Another Step Nearer to Real Democracy." *Kansas City Call*, April 18, 1952. State Historical Society of Missouri, Arthur A. Benson II, Box 303.

"Are Our Teachers 'Frozen' Out." *Kansas City Call*, July 8, 1955. State Historical Society of Missouri, Arthur A. Benson II, Box 306.

"Armed Guards Concern Students." *Kansas City Star*, February 17, 1970. Missouri Valley Special Collections, Schools-Public, Central High.

"Arrest Twelve Youths in Disturbance." *Kansas City Times*, November 11, 1967. Missouri Valley Special Collections, Schools-Public, Central High.

Arthur Rainwater Deposition, 2 November 1988. State Historical Society of Missouri, Arthur A. Benson II, Box D174.

"A School Waits on Race Issue." *Kansas City Times*, October 10, 1964, 1-2.

"Asks for Eleven New Schools." *Kansas City Star*, June 8, 1913, 2.

"A Study in the Problems Involved in the Desegregation in the Public Schools of Kansas City." Kansas City, Missouri School District Research Department (July 1954). State Historical Society of Missouri, Arthur A. Benson II, Box 310.

"A Task for Each City." *Kansas City Times*, September 19, 1954, 18.

August, Taylor, Director of Office of Civil Rights, to Superintendent Medcalf, July 14, 1975. State Historical Society of Missouri, Arthur A. Benson II, Box 317.

"Basketball Fight Studied." *Kansas City Times*, March 10, 1972. Missouri Valley Special Collections, Schools-Public, Central High.

Benevento, Maria. "Proposal to Close 10 Schools in Kansas City, Improve Academics Hinges on Community Support." *Griffon News: Missouri Western State College*, October 17, 2022.

Benson, Arthur. Chronology of the Kansas City, Missouri, Desegregation Case. Missouri Valley Special Collections, Schools-Public, Kansas City Desegregation.

Beveridge, Mary. "Biography of Jeremiah Cameron." *Kansas City Star*, 2009. Missouri Valley Special Collections.

Bingham, Rollins. "Alumni Article." *Central Luminary*, January 9, 1906. Missouri Valley Special Collections.

"Black on Black Crime is Still a Plague." *Kansas City Call*, June 4, 2004.

Blank, Chris. "Kansas City School District Loses Accreditation." *Associated Press*, September 20, 2011.

Bliss, James and David Honeyman, "A Legislative Report in the Excellence in Education Act of 1985." *Journal of Education Finance* 11, no. 4 (Spring 1986): 480-9.

Blueprint 2030, Kansas City Public Schools, December 7, 2022.

"Board Members Say HEW Can't Stop Plan." *Kansas City Times*, July 11, 1975. State Historical Society of Missouri, Arthur A. Benson II, Box 462.

Briggs v. Elliott, 132 F. Supp. 776 (1955), 777.

Brisbane, Art. "Nominee is a Man for His Era." *Kansas City Star*, July 5, 1991.

Brogan, Michael. "Ineligibility under the Emergency School Aid Act: A Disparate Impact Standard." *Nebraska Law Review* 59, no. 4 (1980), 1127-42.

Brown, Andrew Theodore and Lyle W. Dorsett, *K.C.: A History of Kansas City, Missouri*. Pruett Publishing Company, 1978.

Brown v. Board of Education, 347 U.S. 483 (1954).

Brown v. Board of Education, 349 U.S. 294 (1955).

"Capacity Compared to Membership, Actual 1963, Estimated 1967 and 1972." Office of the Superintendent, Kansas City, Missouri School District (1963). State Historical Society of Missouri, Arthur A. Benson II, Box 313.

Carpenter, Samuel, President of the Board, to David Tatel, Director of Office of Civil Rights (February 22, 1978). State Historical Society of Missouri, Arthur A. Benson II, Box 316.

Carr, Margie. *Kansas City's Montgall Avenue: Black Leaders and the Street they Called Home*. Lawrence: University of Kansas Press, 2023.

Carson, Forrest to Superintendent of Public Schools (March 20, 1968). State Historical Society of Missouri, Arthur A. Benson II, Box 315.

Caruthers, Loyce and Bradley Poos, "Narratives of Lincoln High School African American Graduates in Kansas City, Missouri: 1955-1985." *Journal of Black Studies* 46, no. 6 (2015): 626-49.

Caruthers, Loyce, Brad Poos, and Jennifer Friend, "Transitory Voices: The Journey from Urban High School to an Early College Program." *Urban Education* 56, no. 2 (2021): 289-317.

Caruthers, Loyce, Jennifer Friend, and Candace Schlein, "School Desegregation as Multi-generational Narratives of Afropessimism." *Educational Studies* 58, no. 1 (2021): 33-49.

Celis, III, William. "Kansas City's Widely Debated Desegregation Experiment Reaches the Supreme Court." *New York Times*, January 11, 1995, B7.

Center for the Study of Metropolitan Problems in Education, UMKC, *Public Schools of the Southeast Side: A Report to the Community*. Kansas City: University of Missouri-Kansas City, 1970.

"Central Aquatics Club to Host Swim Meet." *Kansas City Call*, March 7, 1997.

"Central High School Academic Program." Central High School Task Force (January 1988). State Historical Society of Missouri, Arthur A. Benson II, Box D153.

"Central High School Classical Greek Preliminary Program Narrative." Central High School Task Force (n.d.). State Historical Society of Missouri, Arthur A. Benson II, Box D153.

"Central High School Places in Computer Science Olympiad Programming Competition." *Kansas City Call*, March 22, 1996.

"Central High School Report." *Kansas City Star*, December 11, 1896, 2.

"Central High Sets an Example in Integration." *Time*, July 29, 1961. Missouri Valley Special Collections, Schools-Central.

Centralian, 1913. Missouri Valley Special Collections.

Centralian, 1934. Missouri Valley Special Collections.

Centralian, 1945. Missouri Valley Special Collections, 42.

Centralian, 1993. Missouri Valley Special Collections, Digital Archive.

"Central is Barred." *Kansas City Star*, March 27, 1972. Missouri Valley Special Collections, Schools-Public, Central High.

Central Luminary, 1920–1922. Missouri Valley Special Collections.

Central Luminary, April 10, 1942. Missouri Valley Special Collections.

Central Luminary, April 1, 1960. Missouri Valley Special Collections.

Central Luminary, April 1894. Missouri Valley Special Collections.

Central Luminary, December 1, 1944. Missouri Valley Special Collections.

Central Luminary, December 11, 1924. Missouri Valley Special Collections.

Central Luminary, December 1896. Missouri Valley Special Collections.

Central Luminary, December 1898. Missouri Valley Special Collections.

Central Luminary, December 1915. Missouri Valley Special Collections.

Central Luminary, February 12, 1925. Missouri Valley Special Collections.

Central Luminary, February 14, 1958. Missouri Valley Special Collections.

Central Luminary, February 1890. Missouri Valley Special Collections.

Central Luminary, February 1897. Missouri Valley Special Collections.

Central Luminary, February 1919. Missouri Valley Special Collections.

Central Luminary, February 21, 1922. Missouri Valley Special Collections.

Central Luminary, February 8, 1973. Missouri Valley Special Collections.

Central Luminary, January 1901. Missouri Valley Special Collections.

Central Luminary, January 19, 1922. Missouri Valley Special Collections.

Central Luminary, January 20, 1943. Missouri Valley Special Collections.

Central Luminary, January 28, 1926. Missouri Valley Special Collections.

Central Luminary, March 1, 1968. Missouri Valley Special Collections.

Central Luminary, March 14, 1930. Missouri Valley Special Collections.

Central Luminary, March 1894. Missouri Valley Special Collections.

Central Luminary, March 1899. Missouri Valley Special Collections.

Central Luminary, March 1913. Missouri Valley Special Collections.

Central Luminary, March 1915. Missouri Valley Special Collections.

Central Luminary, March 20, 1942. Missouri Valley Special Collections.

Central Luminary, March 23, 1956. Missouri Valley Special Collections.

Central Luminary, March 24, 1921. Missouri Valley Special Collections.

Central Luminary, March 4, 1921. Missouri Valley Special Collections.

Central Luminary, March 6, 1970. Missouri Valley Special Collections.

Central Luminary, May 11, 1962. Missouri Valley Special Collections.

Central Luminary, May 1897. Missouri Valley Special Collections.

Central Luminary, May 1898. Missouri Valley Special Collections.

Central Luminary, May 24, 1985. Missouri Valley Special Collections.

Central Luminary, May 25, 1921. Missouri Valley Special Collections.

Central Luminary, May 8, 1964. Missouri Valley Special Collections.

Central Luminary, November 12, 1922. Missouri Valley Special Collections.

Central Luminary, November 12, 1925. Missouri Valley Special Collections.

Central Luminary, November 1893. Missouri Valley Special Collections.

Central Luminary, November 1912. Missouri Valley Special Collections.

Central Luminary, November 24, 1967. Missouri Valley Special Collections.

Central Luminary, November 5, 1937. Missouri Valley Special Collections.

Central Luminary, November 6, 1942. Missouri Valley Special Collections.

Central Luminary, November 6, 1959. Missouri Valley Special Collections.

Central Luminary, October 13, 1921. Missouri Valley Special Collections.

Central Luminary, October 16, 1942. Missouri Valley Special Collections.

Central Luminary, October 1893. Missouri Valley Special Collections.

Central Luminary, October 2, 1942. Missouri Valley Special Collections.

Central Luminary, October 23, 1959. Missouri Valley Special Collections.

Central Luminary, October 9, 1964. Missouri Valley Special Collections.

Central Luminary, September 1897. Missouri Valley Special Collections.

Central Luminary, September 18, 1924. Missouri Valley Special Collections.

Central Luminary, September 19, 1958. Missouri Valley Special Collections.

Central Luminary, September 1955. Missouri Valley Special Collections.

Central Luminary, September 21, 1962. Missouri Valley Special Collections.

Central Luminary, September 22, 1921. Missouri Valley Special Collections.

Central Luminary, September 25, 1924. Missouri Valley Special Collections.

Central Luminary, September 25, 1942. Missouri Valley Special Collections.

Central Luminary, September 25, 1959. Missouri Valley Special Collections.

Central Luminary, September 26, 1969. Missouri Valley Special Collections.

"Central Principal Receives New Job." *Kansas City Star*, 17 February 1972. Missouri Valley Special Collections, Schools-Public, Central High.

"Central to Graduate 270." *Kansas City Star*, 5 June 1920, 2.

"Central to Graduate 407." *Kansas City Star*, 3 June 1922, 4.

Charles J. McClain memo to Judge Whipple, "Implementation Monitor." September 22, 2000. State Historical Society of Missouri, Arthur A. Benson II Papers, Box 568.

Chief Education Branch Office for Civil Rights, memo to Kansas City School District (2 April 1973). State Historical Society of Missouri, Arthur A. Benson II, Box 317.

"Chronology." *Kansas City Times*, September 1, 1977, B4.

Chronology of Jenkins. Missouri Valley Special Collections, Schools-Public, Kansas City, Vertical File.

Chung, Ed, Betsy Pearl, and Lea Hunter, "The 1994 Crime Bill Continues to Undercut Justice Reform—Here's How to Stop It." Center for American Progress, March 26, 2019.

Citizen's Coordinating Committee memo to James Hazlett (n.d.). State Historical Society of Missouri, Arthur A. Benson II, Box 315.

"Citizens Want a New School." *Kansas City Times*, October 26, 1960, 22.

"City Schools: A Racial Dilemma." *Kansas City Star*, February 28, 1973. State Historical Society of Missouri, Arthur A. Benson II, Box 462.

"City Sets Poor Example for Citizens." *Kansas City Call*, June 6, 1952. State Historical Society of Missouri, Arthur A. Benson II, Box 303.

Clark, Sarah. "What it's Like to Live Inside the Murder Factory." *Fox 4 News*, 8 November 2011.

Colby, Tanner. *Some of My Best Friends are Black: The Strange Story of Integration in America*. New York: Penguin Books, 2013.

Collins, Leslie. "Central High Principal Proposes Changing Name." *Northeast News*, July 10, 2012, 1.

"Concepts for Changing Times: Proposals Offered for Public Examination, Dealing with Educational Equity in the Kansas City, Missouri, School District." Office of the Superintendent, The School District of Kansas City, Missouri (March 1968). Missouri Valley Special Collections, James A Hazlett Papers.

"Coordinating Committee Opposes School Sites." *Kansas City Call*, June 9, 1965. State Historical Society of Missouri, Arthur A. Benson II, Box 314.

Coulter, Charles E. *"Take Up the Black Man's Burden": Kansas City's African American Communities, 1865-1939*. Columbia: University of Missouri Press, 2006.

Council of Great City Schools, "Urban School Superintendents: Characteristics, Tenure, and Salary." Fall 2014.

Court Order, April 26, 1989.

Court Order, November 12, 1986.

Court Order, September 17, 1987.

Craig Dydell vs. Bernard Taylor, SC90912 (MO 2011).

"Crisis and Opportunity: Education in Greater Kansas City." Bi-State Committee on Education, Missouri Advisory Committee (January 1977). Missouri Valley Special Collections, 1.

Current and Proposed Status of Faculty Integration, July 25, 1963. State Historical Society of Missouri, Arthur A. Benson II, Box 311.

Daniel Levine Deposition, 16 February 1989. State Historical Society of Missouri, Arthur A. Benson II, Box D174.

Daugherity, Brian J. and Charles C. Bolton, *With All Deliberate Speed: Implementing Brown v. Board of Education.* Fayetteville: University of Arkansas Press, 2008.

"David Porter Resigns as Central Principal at Parents' Meeting." *Kansas City Call*, February 4, 1972.

DeArmond, Michael, Alice Opalka, and Patrick Denise. "Student Mobility in Kansas City." Turn the Page KC, June 2019.

DeArmond, Michael. "Central Hopes to Draw Students with New Facility." *Kansas City Star*, June 2, 1991.

"Delay in Home Suit." *Kansas City Star*, June 14, 1948. State Historical Society of Missouri, Arthur A. Benson II, Box 343.

Demps, Jr., Benjamin. "From the Superintendent: An Open Letter about Schools." *Kansas City Star*, October 23, 1999. State Historical Society of Missouri, Arthur A. Benson II, Box 573.

"Demps Says Takeover Might Be Best Option." *Kansas City Star*, April 26, 2001, A8.

Desegregation Monitoring Committee, "DMC Report to the Court." 14 October 1998. State Historical Society of Missouri, Arthur A. Benson II Papers, Box 587.

"Desegregation Now Up to Board." *Kansas City Star*, October 3, 1976. State Historical Society of Missouri, Arthur A. Benson II, Box 462.

"Design Program Analysis for the New Kansas City Central High School, Kansas City, Missouri." Councilman/Hunsaker & Associates (March 1988). State Historical Society of Missouri, Arthur A. Benson II, Box D503.

"Divided We Fall." *Kansas City Call*, July 3, 1925. State Historical Society of Missouri, Arthur A. Benson II, Box 303.

D'Marko, Dave. "KCPS Hosts Listening Session as it Considers Keeping Windfall from Property Assessments." *Missouri News*, September 7, 2023.

Dorn, Emma, Bryan Hancock, Jimmy Sarakatsannis, and Ellen Viruleg, "Covid 19 and Education: The Lingering Effects of Unfinished Learning." McKinsey and Company, July 27, 2021.

Doyle, Patricia. "For Education 3 to 1." *Kansas City Times*, February 1965, 1-2.

"Dr. Bedell Named Superintendent of the Year by NABSE." eyeonannapolis.net, October 2, 2023.

"Dr. Butler of New York Pays Tribute to the Kansas City Educator." *Kansas City Star*, May 9, 1897, 1.

Duarte, Bryan. "The Effects of School Choice Competition on an Underserved Neighborhood Public School." *Educational Policy* 37, no. 7 (2023): 1950-88.

Du Bois, W. E. B. "Does the Negro Need Separate Schools." *Journal of Negro Education* 4, no. 3 (July 1935): 328.

Dunn, Joshua. *Complex Justice: The Case of Missouri v. Jenkins*. Chapel Hill: University of North Carolina Press, 2008.

Eagleton, Thomas, U.S. Senate, to Hale Champion, HEW, May 23, 1978. State Historical Society of Missouri, Arthur A. Benson II, Box 319.

Eaton, Susan E. and Elizabeth Crutcher, "Magnets, Media, and Mirages: Prince George's County's Miracle Cure." In *Dismantling Desegregation: The Quiet Reversal of Brown v. Board of Education*, edited by Gary Orfield and Susan E. Eaton, 265-89. New York: The New Press, 1996.

Eaton, Thomas Meeting Notes (2 March 1988). State Historical Society of Missouri, Arthur A. Benson II, Box D503.

"Education Board Orders Staff to Implement Integration Plan." *Kansas City Times*, July 17, 1975. State Historical Society of Missouri, Arthur A. Benson II, Box 402.

"Education Data for Action Summit." UMKC Urban Education Research Center, June 22, 2023.

"Effective Schools." Education Week, May 1, 1992.

Egerton, John. "*Adams v. Richardson*: Can Separate Be Equal?" *Change* 6, no. 10 (Winter 1974/1975): 29-36.

"Eleven Central Weightlifters Qualify for Junior National Weightlifting Championships." *Kansas City Call*, March 26, 1993.

"E. M. Bainter to Porto Rico." *Kansas City Star*, April 8, 1912, 1.

Emergency School Aid Act: Final Report to Task Force, National Advisory Council on Equality of Educational Opportunity (June 1977). State Historical Society of Missouri, Arthur A. Benson II, Box 316.

Enrollment of Negro Pupils in Southern and Border States, Office of Education (December 1966). State Historical Society of Missouri, Arthur A. Benson II, Box 314.

"Equal Treatment to Equals: A New Structure for Public Schools in the Kansas City and St. Louis Metropolitan Areas." Missouri School District Reorganization Commission (June 1969). State Historical Society of Missouri, Arthur A. Benson II, Box 315.

"Everything's Up to Date in Kansas City." *Time Magazine* 78, no. 4 (July 1961): 38. Missouri Valley Special Collections, SC 73.

Fairly, Paul and Gerald Sroufe, "Review of Kansas City, Missouri Schools" (1967). State Historical Society of Missouri, Arthur A. Benson II, Box 315.

Farney, Dennis. "Fading Dream? Integration Is Faltering in Kansas City Schools as Priorities Change." *Wall Street Journal*, September 26, 1995.

Fields, Edward, internal memo to Robert Medcalf, August 20, 1974. State Historical Society of Missouri, Arthur A. Benson II, Box 317.

Fifield, L. W. *Central Luminary*, December 1907, 25.

"Final Report: Mayor's Commission on Civil Disorder" Mayor's Commission on Civil Disorder (August 1968). State Historical Society of Missouri, Arthur A. Benson II, Box 514.

Final Site Report, Kansas City, Missouri School District (August 1988). State Historical Society of Missouri, Arthur A. Benson II, D503.

"Formative Evaluation of the Central Classical Greek Magnet High School, 1991-1992." Evaluation Office, School District of Kansas City, Missouri. State Historical Society of Missouri, Arthur A. Benson II Papers, Box 511.

"Formative Evaluation of the Central Senior Magnet School Computers Unlimited, 1988-1989." Evaluation Office, School District of Kansas City, Missouri. State Historical Society of Missouri, Arthur A. Benson II Papers, Box 511.

"Formative Evaluation of the Central Senior Magnet School Computers Unlimited, 1989-1990." Evaluation Office, School District of Kansas City, Missouri. State Historical Society of Missouri, Arthur A. Benson II Papers, Box 511.

Fortino, Jodi. "Kansas City Public Schools will Maintain Tax Levy to Deal with $400 million in Maintenance Needs." National Public Radio, September 28, 2023.

Fortino, Jodi. "Kansas City Schools Missed Out on $45 Million Last Year Due to Tax Breaks for Developers." National Public Radio, January 23, 2023.

"Four All-Day Kindergartens Part of Magnet School Plan." *Kansas City Times*, May 4, 1978. State Historical Society of Missouri, Arthur A. Benson II, Box 316.

Franey, Lynn. "KC District Locks Doors to Charter-Two Westport Buildings are Regained after Court Ruling Favors School Board." *Kansas City Star*, August 19, 2004, A1.

"Full-Time Director for EXCEL." *Kansas City Call*, August 19, 1977.

"Gangs' Reach Extends Clear into Eighth Grade." *Kansas City Star*, December 2, 2007.

Garrity, John. "From Russia With Love: Vladimir Nazlymov, Former Coach of the Soviet Saber Team, Now Teaches Fencing in a Kansas City High School." *Sports Illustrated*, June 1, 1992.

Gillette, Thomas. *Santa Fe: A Study of the Effects of Negro Invasion on Property Values*. Master's thesis, 1954.

Gill, Patrick, Mauricio Molina, and Daniel Potter, "The Relationship Between School-Year Mobility and School Performance in the Houston Area." Houston Education Research Consortium, December 2021.

Givens, Henry. "A Report to the State Board of Education Concerning the Desegregation of the Kansas City Public School District" (August 1975). State Historical Society of Missouri, Arthur A. Benson II, Box 514.

Goldring, Ellen B. and Claire Smrekar, "Magnet Schools and the Pursuit of Racial Balance." *Education and Urban Society* 33, no. 17 (2000): 17-35.

Gotham, Kevin. *Race, Real Estate, and Uneven Development: The Kansas City Experience, 1900-2000*. Albany: State University Press, 2002.

Gotham, Kevin. "Separate and Unequal: The Housing Act of 1968 and the Section 235 Program." *Sociological Forum* 15, no. 1 (November 2000): 13-37.

Greenstein, Melissa and Tom Dempsey, "KCPD Looking for Man in Connection to Teen's Fatal Shooting at Gas Station." KSHB, October 22, 2018.

Green v. New Kent County School Board, 391 U.S. 430 (1968).

Griffin, G. S. *Racism in Kansas City: A Short History*. Traverse City: Chandler Lake Books, 2015.

Hale, Jon. *The Choice We Face: How Segregation, Race, and Power have Shaped America's Most Controversial Reform Movement.* Boston: Beacon Press, 2021.

Hale, Phale D. and Daniel U. Levine. *Long Range Magnet School Plan.* Kansas City, MO: Kansas City, Missouri School District, 1986). State Historical Society of Missouri, Arthur A. Benson II, Box D503.

Hardy, Stephen. "KC Connectivity Report." May 19, 2020, mysidewalk.com.

Havighurst, Robert, William Cobb, and Norman Drachler. "Problems of Integration in the Kansas City Public Schools" (November 1965). State Historical Society of Missouri, Arthur A. Benson II, Box 514.

Hazlett, James to the Board of Directors (July 18, 1969). State Historical Society of Missouri, Arthur A. Benson II, Box 315.

Hazlett, James to the Board of Education (June 14, 1967). State Historical Society of Missouri, Arthur A. Benson II, Box 315.

Hersley, Phillip, Regional Commissioner, Office of Education to Superintendent Medcalf (April 3, 1974). State Historical Society of Missouri, Arthur A. Benson II, Box 317.

"HEW Blocks School Grant." *Kansas City Times*, September 19, 1975. State Historical Society of Missouri, Arthur A. Benson II, Box 402.

"Hold Youth in Tourney Fight." *Kansas City Star*, March 14, 1969. Missouri Valley Special Collections, Schools-Public, Central High.

Holmes, Peter, Director of the Office of Civil Rights, to Superintendent Adams (April 17, 1973). State Historical Society of Missouri, Arthur A. Benson II, Box 316.

Hoover, Abby. "Blueprint 2030 Approved, Collier Calls Community to Action." *Northeast News*, February 1, 2023.

Hoover, Abby. "KCPS Board Discusses Reopening Options." *Northeast News*, July 17, 2020.

Horsley, Lynn. "Brand-new Year Opens with Four Brand-new Schools." *Kansas City Star*, September 4, 1991.

Horsley, Lynn. "Goals Elude KC Magnets: Enrollment and Achievement Lag Despite Years of Effort, Money." *Kansas City Star*, August 10, 1992.

Horsley, Lynn. "KC's Central High: The School Some Love and Some Love to Hate." *Kansas City Star*, May 10, 1992, A1, A14.

Horsley, Lynn and Philip O'Connor, "Clark will Relinquish Desegregation Case." *Kansas City Star*, 28 January 1997, A1.

Horsley, Lynn and Philip O'Connor, "School Chief Quits: Judge is Asked to Suspend KC." *Kansas City Star*, June 15, 1996, A1.

Howe, Harold, U.S. Commissioner of Education, to Phil Landrum, House of Representatives (April 5, 1967). State Historical Society of Missouri, Arthur A. Benson II, Box 314.

Hunter, Richard C. "Kansas City, Missouri School District Long-Range Capital Improvement Plan" (January 1987). State Historical Society of Missouri, Arthur A. Benson II, Box 618.

"Improvement Association Moves to Restrict against Colored Owners." *Kansas City Call*, December 24, 1926. State Historical Society of Missouri, Arthur A. Benson II, Box 343.

Interoffice Memo from Dr. Margaret Seever to Kathy Walter-Mack, "DMC Request." September 9, 1999, Arthur A Benson II Papers, Box 573.

"Inventory of Intergroup Education Problems." Paper presented at the Kansas City Conference on Human Relations (March 1953). State Historical Society of Missouri, Arthur A. Benson II, Box 306.

"Is Kansas City North or South." *Kansas City Call*, November 29, 1946. State Historical Society of Missouri, Arthur A. Benson II, Box 303.

Jenkins v. Missouri, 515 U.S. 70 (1995).

Jenkins v. Missouri, 593 F. Supp. 1485 (W.D. Mo. 1984).

Jenkins v. Missouri, 639 F. Supp. 19 (W.D. Mo. 1985).

Jenkins v. Missouri, "Motion for Approval of the Kansas City, Missouri School District Long-Range Capital Improvement Plan" (1987). State Historical Society of Missouri, Arthur A. Benson II Papers, Box 511.

Jenkins v. Missouri, "Plaintiff's Post-Hearing Brief and Suggested Findings of Fact" (March 31, 1989). State Historical Society of Missouri, Arthur A. Benson II, Box D237.

Jenkins v. Missouri, "State's Opposition to the Motion of the Kansas City, Missouri School District for Approval of a Site for Central High School and for Increases and Modifications in the Budgets for Building Construction and Equipment for the Magnet; Alternative Request for a Hearing" (December 1988). State Historical Society of Missouri, Arthur A. Benson II, Box D503.

Jeremiah Cameron, "N.A.A.C.P. in Action." *Kansas City Call,* March 13, 1981.

"Jesse Jackson to Speak at Excel Kick-off Banquet, *Kansas City Call,* October 7, 1977.

Johnson, Theron, Special Assistant to the Assistant Commissioner to Dr. Holloway, Acting Chief Title IV (June 30, 1967). State Historical Society of Missouri, Arthur A. Benson II, Box 314.

Jones, Carmen. "Lincoln First Schools for Blacks in Kansas City." *Kansas City Star,* 2000. Missouri Valley Special Collections, Vertical File, Lincoln.

"Judge Throws Out District's Desegregation Plan." United Press International, January 28, 1985.

"K-12: Student Population has Significantly Diversified, but many Schools Remain Divided Along Racial, Ethnic, and Economic Lines." June 16, 2022, U.S. Government Accountability Office.

"Kansas City Data Summit: Data for Action." UMKC Urban Education Research Center, February 8, 2023.

Kansas City Journal, December 9, 1906. Missouri Valley Special Collections, Schools-Public, Night Schools.

Kansas City, Missouri. "General Obligation (GO) Bonds." Accessed October 23, 2023. www.kcmo.gov.

"Kansas City Murders Reached Record High in 2023." *Associated Press,* January 2, 2023.

Kansas City Post, May 17, 1918. Missouri Valley Special Collections, Schools-Public, German Language.

"Kansas City Schools Superintendent Honored, Says He Plans to Stay as the District's Leader." *Kansas City Star*, April 1, 2015.

Kansas City Service Bulletin. Executive Department of the Kansas City, Missouri Public Schools (April 1939). Missouri Valley Special Collections.

Kansas City Service Bulletin, Executive Department of the Kansas City, Missouri Public Schools (November 1932). Missouri Valley Special Collections.

Kansas City Service Bulletin. Executive Department of the Kansas City, Missouri Public Schools (November 1935). Missouri Valley Special Collections.

Kansas City Star, December 12, 1908. Missouri Valley Special Collections, Central (New) Vertical File.

Kansas City Star, December 14, 1924. Missouri Valley Special Collections, Schools-Public, Junior High, Central.

Kansas City Star, December 15, 1931. Missouri Valley Special Collections, School-Public, Junior High Schools.

Kansas City Star, January 26, 1971, 6A. Missouri Valley Special Collections.

Kansas City Star, January 3, 1929. Missouri Valley Special Collections, Schools-Revenue.

Kansas City Star, May 15, 1938. Missouri Valley Special Collections, Schools-Public.

Kansas City Star, May 8, 1938. Missouri Valley Special Collections, Schools-Public Central High History, Early.

Kansas City Star, November 11, 1915. Missouri Valley Special Collections, Schools-Public, Central High.

Kansas City Star, October 28, 1913. Missouri Valley Special Collections.

Kansas City Star, October 9, 1938. Missouri Valley Special Collections, Schools-Public Central High. History, Early.

Kansas City Star, September 12,1915. Missouri Valley Special Collections, Schools-Public, Buildings New.

Kansas City Times, December 9, 1911. Missouri Valley Special Collections, Schools-Public, Night Schools.

Kansas City Times, October 15, 1912. Missouri Valley Special Collections, Schools-Public, Night Schools.

Kansas City, Missouri School District Board Minutes (1963). State Historical Society of Missouri, Arthur A. Benson II, Box 313.

Kansas City, Missouri School District Enrollment by School, 1954-1955–1983-1984, Arthur Benson, unpublished demographic data. State Historical Society of Missouri, Arthur A. Benson II, Box 567.

"Kansas City's First High School, Central at 11th and Locust Was Opened in 1867." Missouri Valley Special Collections, Vertical (Old) Files.

"KC Leaders Face Slur Claims." *Columbia Daily Tribune*, December 16, 2007.

"KCMSD Plan for Transition to Unitary Status." Kansas City, Missouri School District, August 15, 1987. State Historical Society of Missouri, Arthur A. Benson II Papers, Box 587.

KCPS. "History of KCPS." Accessed August 2, 2023, kkcpublicschools.org.

"KC Public Schools Must Listen to Community in Superintendent Search." *Kansas City Star*, December 15, 2022.

"KC's Central High School Renamed." *Kansas City Star*, July 25, 2012.

"KC School District Budget Cuts Unpopular but Crucial." *Kansas City Star*, November 28, 2009, A20.

Kells, Tina. "Kansas City School Closures." *Kansas City Examiner*, March 11, 2010, 11-12.

Kells, Tina. "School Board Votes to Close 29 of 61 Schools." *Kansas City Examiner*, March 11m 2010.

Keyes v. Denver School District, 413 U.S. 189 (1973).

King, Thelma, Council for United Action, to T. Johnson, Office of Civil Rights (June 23, 1967). State Historical Society of Missouri, Arthur A. Benson II, Box 314.

King, Thelma. "Statement to Board of Education" (July 6, 1967). Missouri Valley Special Collections, James A. Hazlett Papers.

King, Thelma to T. Johnson, Office of Civil Rights (June 23, 1967). State Historical Society of Missouri, Arthur A. Benson II, Box 314.

Krueger, Karen. "Preliminary Review of the Kansas City, Missouri Schools, July 17-21, 1967, Curriculum, Pupil Assignment and Transfer." State Historical Society of Missouri, Arthur A. Benson II Papers, Box 315.

Langer, Emily. "John Murphy, Pr. George's Superintendent Who Helped Bridge Racial Gap, Dies." *Washington Post*, August 24, 2011.

Law of 1889, Revised Statutes (1889), 1861. State Historical Society of Missouri, Arthur A. Benson II, Box 303.

"Leaders Seek Acceptance of Bussing Plan." *Kansas City Times*, July 14, 1975. State Historical Society of Missouri, Arthur A. Benson II, Box 462.

Levine, Daniel U. and Connie C. Moore, "Considerations in Developing and Implementing Big City Magnet Programs." State Historical Society of Missouri, Arthur A. Benson II, Box 514.

Levine, Daniel U. and Eugene E. Eubanks, "Desegregation and Regional Magnetization." In *Magnet Schools: Recent Developments and Perspectives*, edited by Nolan Estes, Daniel U. Levine, and Donald R. Waldrip, 49-57. Austin: Morgan Printing and Publishing, 1990.

Levine, Michael L. African Americans and Civil Rights: From 1619 to the Present. Phoenix: Oryx Press, 1996. https://archive.org/details/africanamericans00levi.

Lincoln College Preparatory Academy. "Required Documentation." Accessed August 14, 2023, pa/kcpublicschools.edu/enroll.

"Lincoln College Prep Named Missouri's Top High School." *Northeast News*, May 13, 2015.

"'Lincoln Plan OK': Eagleton School Tour." *Kansas City Times*, March 29, 1978. State Historical Society of Missouri, Arthur A. Benson II, Box 462.

"Linwood Association Takes Lead in National Association." *Kansas City Call*, July 29, 1927. State Historical Society of Missouri, Arthur A. Benson II, Box 343.

"Long Range Magnet Plan: Elementary through Secondary Schools." Missouri Valley Special Collections, Schools-Central.

Macrotrends. "Kansas City, Missouri Murder/Homicide Rate, 1999-2018." Accessed September 13, 2023. www.macrotrends.net.

Marks, Walter memo to the Board, 9 November 1993. State Historical Society of Missouri, Arthur A. Benson II Papers, Box 185D.

Martin, Asa E. *Our Negro Population: A Sociological Study of the Negroes of Kansas City*, Missouri. Franklin Hudson Publishing Company, c. 1913. https://www.loc.gov/item/13023501/.

Mashek, Kera. "KCPS Leaders Scrambling After Health Department Raises Concerns about In-person Classes." *Fox-4*, July 20, 2020.

Massey, Douglas S. and Nancy A. Denton, *American Apartheid: Segregation and the Making of the Underclass*. Cambridge: Harvard University Press, 1993.

Mayer, Martin. "The Good Slum Schools." *Harper's Magazine* (April 1961), 46-52. Missouri Valley Special Collections, SC 73.

McGuire, Donna. "Judge Ends Desegregation Case After 26 Years and $2 Billion." *Kansas City Star*, August 14, 2003, A1.

McGuire, Donna. "Schools See Loss from Suburbs – Desegregation Ruling's Fallout Begins to Settle on the KC Magnet Program." *Kansas City Star*, August 23, 1995, A1.

McLaurin v. Oklahoma State Regents. 339 U.S. 627 (1950).

McMichael, Stanley and Robert Bingham. *City Growth and Values*. Cleveland: The Stanley McMichael Publishing Organization, 1923.

McWilliams, Julia Ann. "The Neighborhood School Stigma: School Choice, Stratification, and Shame." *Policy Futures in Education* 15, no. 2 (2017): 221-38.

"Medcalf Denies Noncompliance." *Kansas City Star*, January 26, 1975, 3A.

Menendian, Stephen, Samir Gambhir, and Arthur Gailes, "The Roots of Structural Racism Project: Twenty-First Racial Residential

Segregation in the United States." June 21, 2021. https://belonging. berkeley.edu/roots-structural-racism.

"Mentors Needed at Central High School." *Kansas City Star*, October 23, 2008.

Michaels, John. "U.S. School Superintendents: Handling Political Divisions is Toughest Part of Job." EAB, February 17, 2022.

Miller, Joe. *Cross-X: The Amazing True Story of How the Most Unlikely Team from the Most Unlikely of Places Overcame Staggering Obstacles at Home and at School to Challenge the Debate Community on Race, Power, and Education.* New York: Farrar, Straus and Giroux, 2006.

Miller, Joe. "The Long Walk Home." *Pitch*, May 23, 2002.

Milliken v. Bradley. 418 U.S. 717 (1974).

Milner, H. Richard. "But What is Urban." Urban Education 47, no. 3 (2021): 556-61.

"Mississippi Governor 'Sad, Disappointed.'" *Kansas City Call*, May 21, 1954, 1.

Missouri Department of Elementary and Secondary Education. "A Missouri History of Assessment and Accountability." www.dese. mo.gov.

Missouri Department of Elementary and Secondary Education. "Building Demographic Data, 2022." Accessed August 2, 2023. www.dese.mo.gov.

Missouri Department of Elementary and Secondary Education. "Building Report Card, 2021-2022." www.dese.mo.gov.

Missouri Department of Elementary and Secondary Education. "Central High School Report Card, Historical." Accessed August 2, 2023. www.dese.mo.gov.

Missouri Department of Elementary and Secondary Education. "Covid Relief Federal Fund Priorities." May 5, 2021. www.dese. mo.gov.

Missouri Department of Elementary and Secondary Education. "District Demographic Data." Accessed October 16, 2023, apps. dese.mo.gov.

Missouri Department of Elementary and Secondary Education. "Lincoln College Preparatory Academy Report Card, Historical." Accessed 8 September 2023. www.dese.mo.gov.

Missouri Department of Elementary and Secondary Education. "Missouri 2022 APR Summary by Building." www.dese.mo.gov.

Missouri Department of Elementary and Secondary Education. "Report – Public Final," 2022 and 2023. https://dese.mo.gov/

Missouri Department of Elementary and Secondary Education. "School Report Card, 2022." (Central and Southeast). www.dese.mo.gov.

Missouri Department of Elementary and Secondary Education. "School Report Card, Historical." Accessed August 2, 2023. www.dese.mo.gov.

Missouri Department of Health, Education, and Welfare News Release (January 1971). State Historical Society of Missouri, Arthur A. Benson II, Box 315.

Missouri Department of Elementary and Secondary Education. "School Report Card." Accessed October 10, 2023. https://dese.mo.gov/.

Missouri Department of Middle and Secondary Education. "Central Building Report Card." 2023. www.dese.mo.gov.

"Mixed Reactions to Plan." *Kansas City Star*, March 18, 1977, B36.

Moran, Peter W. *Race, Law, and the Desegregation of Public Schools.* New York: LFB Publishing, 2005.

Morantz, Alison. "Money and Choice in Kansas City: Major Investments with Modest Returns." In *Dismantling Desegregation: The Quiet Reversal of Brown v. Board of Education,* edited by Gary Orfield and Susan E. Eaton, 241-63. New York: The New Press, 1996.

Morgan v. Kerrigan, 530 F.2d 431(1976).

Mosley, Jim. "Stunning: Kansas City's New Central High Has It." *St. Louis Post-Dispatch*, February 9, 1992, 4A.

Mosley, Tonya. "Why the Crack Cocaine Epidemic Hit the Black Communities 'First and Worst.'" July 13, 2023.

"MSIP 6 School APR Summary Report – Public Final" (2022 and 2023). Missouri Department of Elementary and Secondary Education.

Musumeci, Marilyn and Ronald Szczypkowski, *New York Magnet School Evaluation Study: Final Report*. New York: Magi Educational Services, 1991.

"Negroes Still Angry at Police." *Kansas City Star*, May 5, 1968, 15A.

"New Breed of Student at Central Aims to Change School's Image." *Kansas City Times*, May 24, 1969, 3E.

"New Kansas City Charter School Holds Promise." *Kansas City Star*, August 27, 2015.

"New Site Study for 3 Schools." *Kansas City Times*, July 31, 1965, 1-2.

Nineteenth Annual Report on Desegregation in the Kansas City Public Schools (1973-1974). State Historical Society of Missouri, Arthur A. Benson II, Box 452.

Nutter, Kathleen. "'Militant Mothers: Boston, Busing, and the Bicentennial, 1976." *Historic Journal of Massachusetts* (Fall 2010), 52-74.

O'Connor, Phillip and Lynn Horsley. "Guardian or Glory Hound? Arthur A. Benson II Has Been Called Many Things During KC Schools Case." *Kansas City Star*, July 14, 1996, A1.

O'Connor, Phillip and Lynn Horsley. "Judge Chosen to Oversee Desegregation Lawsuit." *Kansas City Star*, March 29, 1997, C8.

O'Connor, Phillip. "Benson Appeals Ruling on Desegregation Lawsuit." *Kansas City Star*, December 17, 1999, A1.

O'Connor, Phillip. "Finding a Solution to Lincoln's Future." *Kansas City Star*, March 11, 1990, 10.

O'Connor, Phillip. "State Pulls KC School Certification." *Kansas City Star*, October 22, 1999, A1.

O'Connor, Tim. "KC Offers Good Schools, but Pupils Don't Learn, Panel Says." *Kansas City Star*, August 31, 1991, A1.

O'Connor, Tim. "New Central High to Cost $32 Million." *Kansas City Star*, n.d., A9. Missouri Valley Special Collections, Schools-Public, Central.

Oliver, Melvin and Thomas Shapiro, *Black Wealth/White Wealth*, New York: Routledge, 1995.

"Olympic Style Weightlifting Program, Central Senior High." Press Release, December 23, 1993.

Opportunity Atlas. Accessed 14 September 2023. www.opportunity-atlas.org.

Orfield, Gary and Susan Eaton, Dismantling Desegregation: The Quiet Reversal of *Brown v. Board of Education*. New York: The New Press, 1996.

Orfield, Myron. "Segregation and Environmental Justice." *Minnesota Journal of Law, Science and Technology* 7, no. 1 (2005), 147-60.

Orosco, Elizabeth. "15 year-old Victim in Shooting at Central Academy of Excellence has been Identified." *Northeast News*, February 14, 2019.

"Outbreaks at Schools Here." *Kansas City Star*, February 13, 1970.

Overland Park Planning and Development Services Department. "Population Characteristics: 2011 Annual Development Report." March 2012. www.opkans.org.

Papay, John, Andrew Backer-Hicks, Lindsay Page, and William Marinell. "The Challenge of Teacher Retention in Urban Schools: Evidence of Variation from a Cross-Site Analysis." *Educational Researcher*, 46, no. 8 (2017): 434-48.

"Parents Oppose Integration Options." *Kansas City Times*, March 27, 1973. State Historical Society of Missouri, Arthur A. Benson II, Box 462.

Parker, Nathan. *Missouri as It Is in 1867: An Illustrated Historical Gazetteer of Missouri*. Philadelphia: J. B. Lippincott & Co., 1867.

Patterson, James T. *Brown v. Board of Education: A Civil Rights Milestone and its Troubled Legacy (Pivotal Moments in American History)*. New York: Oxford University Press, 2001.

Paunesku, David. "The Deficit Lens of the Achievement Gap Needs to be Flipped: Here's How." *Education Week*, July 9, 2019.

"Pay-as-you-go Plan." *Kansas City Star*, January 24, 1928. Missouri Valley Special Collections, Schools-Revenue.

"Penalty Leads Teachers to Stage 'Sick Out,'" *Columbia Daily Tribune*, November 20, 2005, 1.

Pierce, Frederic. "Charter School Firm Loses Work Across Nation-Problems, Criticisms Not New for Management Company of Failed Syracuse School." *Post-Standard*, August 28, 2005, A1.

"Police, Fireman, and Guardsmen Praised for Riot Performance." *Kansas City Star*, May 5, 1968, 1.

"Police Investigate Shooting that Killed Teen." *Kansas City Star*, March 11, 2008, B2.

Policies for Transition from Separate Schools to Desegregated School System, Superintendent's Office (6 March 1955). State Historical Society of Missouri, Arthur A. Benson II, Box 310, 4.

Project WNYC. Accessed September 25, 2023. projectwnyc.org.

"Race and Ethnicity of Public School Teachers and their Students." National Center for Education Statistics (September 2020).

Rainbow PUSH Coalition. "Brief History." www.rainbowpush.org.

Ramsey, Donovan X. *When Crack Was King: A People's History of a Misunderstood Era*. One World, 2023.

Ravitch, Diane. "The Myth of Charter Schools." The Brookings Institute, November 11, 2010.

Ray, Sam. "A Postcard from Old Kansas City." *Kansas City Star*, May 11, 1968. Missouri Valley Special Collections, Central (Old) Vertical File.

Raytown Planning and Zoning Commission. "Raytown Comprehensive Plan." October 2002. www.raytown.mo.us.

Raywid, Mary A. "The Accomplishments of Schools of Choice." In *Magnet Schools: Recent Developments and Perspectives*, edited by Nolan Estes, Daniel U. Levine, and Donald R. Waldrip, 31-47. Austin: Morgan Printing and Publishing, 1990.

"Report of the Progress of Desegregation in the Kansas City, Missouri Public Schools 1985-1986 through 2000-2001." State Historical Society of Missouri, Arthur A. Benson II Papers, Box 567.

"Report to the Kansas City, Missouri Board of Education." Citizens Coordinating Committee. State Historical Society of Missouri, Arthur A. Benson II, Box 313.

Resolution Regarding the Current State of Education in Kansas City, Missouri, Commission on Human Relations (March 1973). State Historical Society of Missouri, Arthur A. Benson II, Box 322.

"Resorting to Guards with Guns in the Public Schools." *Kansas City Star*, February 14, 1970. Missouri Valley Special Collections, Schools-Public, Central High.

Revised Statute Missouri Charter Schools. RSMo, Section 160.400.2.

Revisions to Title VI, Department of Health, Education, and Welfare (February 1966). State Historical Society of Missouri, Arthur A. Benson II, Box 315.

Richard C. Hunter Deposition (November 11, 1988). State Historical Society of Missouri, Arthur A. Benson II, Box D162.

Ritter, Sarah. "Accreditation is Only the Start for Kansas City Schools. Here's the Plan for What's Next." *Kansas City Star*, January 11, 2022.

Ritter, Sarah. "After Community Outcry, Kansas City District Now Proposes Closing Far Fewer Schools." *Kansas City Star*, January 11, 2023.

Ritter, Sarah. "Is Plan to Close KC Schools 'Academic Vision' or 'Death Blow'? Neighbors Fear Fallout, *Kansas City Star*, December 5, 2022.

Ritter, Sarah. "'We Don't Understand': Emotional Alums Plead to Keep KC's Central High from Closing." *Kansas City Star*, October 17, 2022.

Ritter, Sarah. "Kansas City Schools May Close, Consolidate Schools After Years of Enrollment Decline." *Kansas City Star*, October 12, 2021.

Rizzo, Tim. "Murder Factory: Part 1: 64130, The Zip Code of Notoriety." *Kansas City Star*, January 25, 2009, A1.

Rizzo, Tim. "Murder Factory: Part 2, Murder Factory: Decades of Blight Leave Zip Code 64130 Reeling in Violence." January 26, 2009, A1.

Rizzo, Tim. "Murder Factory: Part 3: Kansas City Needs to Fight Back and Close the 'Factory,'" January 27, 2009, A1.

Robertson, Joe. "Ambitious School Reform Relies on the Personal Touch." *Kansas City Star*, June 27, 2011, 1A.

Robertson, Joe. "A School by Another Name." *Kansas City Star*, June 28, 2012, 1.

Robertson, Joe. "Calling all KC Hands to Rescue Education System 'On Verge of Collapse,'" *Local Investment Commission*, December 1, 2020.

Robertson, Joe. "Kansas City District will Reconsider Central High School Name Change." *Kansas City Star*, November 11, 2012.

Robertson, Joe. "KC School Board Hires Colorado Educator as Superintendent." *Kansas City Star*, May 1, 2009, A1.

Robertson, Joe. "KC Scores Fall Short." *Kansas City Star*, December 5, 2006, B10.

Robertson, Joe. "Long-term Solution Sought after Central High." *Kansas City Star*, November 11, 2009, A11.

Robertson, Joe. "Meetings to Focus on School Consolidations." *Kansas City Star*, October 4, 2006, B5.

Robertson, Joe. "Ragsdale, Pelofsky Won't Seek Re-election to KC School Board." *Kansas City Star*, January 7, 2010, A4.

Robertson, Joe. "Reform Plan Founders at KC's Central High School." *Kansas City Star*, April 12, 2009, C1.

Robertson, Joe. "Remnants of Magnet Program Persist in KC Schools." *Kansas City Star*, November 2, 2006, A1.

Robertson, Joe. "School Year Brings New Attitude at Central." *Kansas City Star*, August 25, 2008, A1.

Robertson, Joe. "Teachers Defend 'Sick Out' Strategy." *Kansas City Star*, December 1, 2005, B3.

Rodgers, Bruce. "A Good Guy Leaving a Tough Job." *Kansas City View*, November 2, 1990. Missouri Valley Special Collections, Kansas City, Missouri Superintendents, Vertical File.

Rollen, Mike, director. *Kansas City Murder Factory*. IMDb Pro, 2011. 1 hr., 13 min. https://www.imdb.com/title/tt1728241/.

Rossell, Christine H. "The Desegregation of the Kansas City, Missouri School District from Brown to 2000-2001." State Historical Society of Missouri, Arthur A. Benson II Papers, Box 585.

"Rush to Enter High School." *Kansas City Star*, August 31, 1911, 7.

Saatcioglu, Argun. *The Relationship of Public School Closures with Property Values and Crime Incidences in Kansas City Public School District, 2007-2018*. Report Commissioned by BlaqueKC, 2022, Kansas City, MO.

Saatcioglu, Argun and Anthony Snethen. "Preference Compromise and Parent Satisfaction with Schools in Choice Markets: Evidence from Kansas City, Missouri." Educational Evaluation and Policy Analysis 45, no. 3 (2023): 367-98.

"Santa Fe Neighborhood Assessment Report." Kansas City, City Planning and Development Department, City of Kansas City, Missouri (July 2001). Missouri Valley Special Collections.

Scheldrup, John, Regional Representative to the Director, OCR memo to W.P. Hefley, Regional Commissioner, Office of Education, regarding "Eligibility of the School District of Kansas City, Missouri, ESAA Application." May 29, 1973. State Historical Society of Missouri, Arthur A. Benson II, Box 317.

Schirmer, Sherry. *A City Divided: The Racial Landscape of Kansas City, 1900-1960*. Columbia: University of Missouri Press, 2016.

School District of Kansas City, Missouri Executive Summary, "Fiscal Year 2003 Comprehensive Budget." June 11, 2002. State Historical Society of Missouri, Arthur A. Benson II Papers, Box 568.

"School Parents Disturbed by Integration Move." *The Wednesday Magazine* (September 1965). State Historical Society of Missouri, Arthur A. Benson II, Box 314, 12.

"School Plan Termed Racist." *Kansas City Times*, March 18, 1977, B36.

"Schools Here May Hire 100." *Kansas City Times*, April 28, 1966, Schools-Public.

"SCLC Drafting School Plan." *Kansas City Times*, June 13, 1975. State Historical Society of Missouri, Arthur A. Benson II, Box 402.

Sethi, Rajiv and Rohini Somanathan. "Inequality and Segregation." *Journal of Political Economy* 112, no. 6 (2004), 1296-321.

Shelley v. Kraemer, 334 U.S. 1 (1948).

Shelly, Barbara. "Schools Offer Promise and Peril." *Kansas City Star*, January 6, 1999, B1.

"Shots Fired Near Central High; One Wounded." *Kansas City Star*, March 10, 2011, 1.

Smith, Dean. "State Declares Five KC Schools Deficient – District to get Money, Professional Help." *Kansas City Star*, September 21, 2001.

Smith, Deann. "Central in KC will Require Uniforms." *Kansas City Star*, December 4, 2001, B1.

Smrekar, Claire and Ellen B. Goldring, *School Choice in Urban America: Magnet Schools and the Pursuit of Equity*. New York: Teachers College Press, 1999.

Social Explorer Professional. "Census 2020 – Preliminary Data." Accessed August 2, 2023. www.socialexplorer.com.

Social Explorer Professional. United States Census (1940–1960). Accessed October 12, 2013. www.socialexplorer.com.

Social Explorer Professional. United States Census (1960, 1980). www.socialexplorer.com.

Social Explorer Professional. United States Census (1970). www.socialexplorer.com.

Social Explorer Professional. United States Census (1970–1990). www.socialexplorer.com.

Social Explorer Professional. United States Census (1990). Accessed May 15, 2023. www.socialexplorer.com.

Social Explorer Professional. "U.S. American Community Surveys, 2005-2009." Accessed August 2, 2023. www.socialexplorer.com.

Social Explorer Professional. "U.S. Decennial Census, 1970, 1980, 1990, 2000, 2010, 2020." Accessed August 2, 2023. www.social-explorer.com.

Some Questions and Answers: Regarding Citizens Coordinating Committee Policy, Citizens Coordinating Committee (July 1965). State Historical Society of Missouri, Arthur A. Benson II, Box 314.

Spaid, Elizabeth L. "'Magnets' Attract in Kansas City." *Christian Science Monitor*, June 15, 1992, 12.

Sparks, Sarah. "Student Mobility: How it Affects Learning." Education Week, August 2016.

Stankiewicz, Kevin. "Fencing: 'He's a Legend': Vladimir Nazlymov Retires After 19 Seasons as Ohio State Head Coach." *The Lantern*, April 17, 2018.

Statement by the Kansas City, Missouri School District Board of Education (July 1963). State Historical Society of Missouri, Arthur A. Benson II, Box 313.

Stephan, Walter. "A Brief Historical Overview of School Desegregation." In School Desegregation: Past, Present, and Future, edited by Walter Stephan and Joe Feagin, 3-22. New York: Plenum Press, 1980.

"Stewart, D. F. "Warm Farewell Given to Central High Principal." *Kansas City Call*, June 12, 1981.

Stout, Rex and John King. "Background Information on the Problems of Overcrowding and Integration in the Kansas City, Missouri District, League of Women Voters of Kansas City." Missouri (September 1967). State Historical Society of Missouri, Arthur A. Benson II, Box 314.

"Student Arrested After Taking Gun to School." *Kansas City Star*, December 15, 2005.

Study of Human Rights in Missouri, Missouri Commission on Human Rights (1960). State Historical Society of Missouri, Arthur A. Benson II, Box 312.

"Suburban Kansas City Students Are Leaving Magnet Schools." *St. Louis Post-Dispatch*, April 27, 1995, 4D.

"Sues over Home Sale." *Kansas City Call*, December 31, 1949. State Historical Society of Missouri, Arthur A. Benson II, Box 343.

"Suit Asks Schools to Repay U.S. Aid." *Kansas City Times*, May 29, 1975. State Historical Society of Missouri, Arthur A. Benson II, Box 402.

"Suit Says Magnet Schools Bar Black Children." *New York Times*, August 3, 1989, A14.

"Summative Evaluation of the Central Computers Unlimited Magnet High School, 1988-1992." Evaluation Office, School District of Kansas City, Missouri.

"Sunset Glow on Old Central High." *Kansas City Star*, August 31, 1952. Missouri Valley Special Collections, Schools-Public Central High History, Early.

"Survey of Financial Situation in K.C. Schools." *Kansas City Star*, November 9, 1938. Missouri Valley Special Collections, Schools-Public.

Swann v. Charlotte-Mecklenburg Board of Education, 402 U.S. 1 (1971).

Sweatt v. Painter, 339 U.S. 629 (1950).

"System Analysis." Kansas City Public Schools, May 9, 2019.

Szczypkowski, Ronald and Marilyn Musumeci. "New York State Evaluation Study." In *Magnet School Policy Studies and Evaluations*, edited by Donald R. Waldrip, Walter L. Marks, and Nolan Estes, 103-256. Austin: Morgan Printing and Publishing, 1993.

Tabscott, Robert. "Commentary: A Look Back: Early African-American Education in St. Louis." St. Louis Public Radio, September 20, 2009.

Tatel, David, Director, Office of Civil Rights, to Samuel Carpenter, President of the Board, February 22, 1978. State Historical Society of Missouri, Arthur A. Benson II, Box 316.

Tatel, David, Director, Office of Civil Rights, to Superintendent Wheeler, July 7, 1977. State Historical Society of Missouri, Arthur A. Benson II, Box 316.

"Terminate PUSH/EXCEL Program at East High." *Kansas City Call,* March 5, 1982, 1.

"The Opening of the Schools." *Kansas City Star,* December 16, 1895, 4.

"The Spirit of Freedom: A Profile of the History of Blacks in Kansas City, Missouri." Missouri Valley Special Collections.

Thompson, Paul. "Back to School 2016: Q&A with new KCPS Superintendent." *Northeast News,* August 3, 2016.

Thompson, Scott. "Missouri's Statewide BEST Test Helps Shape 'Basics' Curriculum." Special to the *Christian Science Monitor,* August 23, 1985.

"Time to Hire Teachers." *Kansas City Call,* January 24, 1955. State Historical Society of Missouri, Arthur A. Benson II, Box 306.

"To Appeal Housing Decision." *Kansas City Call,* December 23, 1949. State Historical Society of Missouri, Arthur A. Benson II, Box 343.

"Total Student Enrollment, 1955-1984." Kansas City, Missouri, School District, Western Historical Manuscript Collection, Arthur Benson Papers, Box 567.

"Total Student Membership: School Years 1955-1956 through 1999-2000." Kansas City, Missouri School District, Arthur A. Benson II Papers, Box 567.

Transcript of Procedures, March to Protest Resegregation (July 1963). State Historical Society of Missouri, Arthur A. Benson II, Box 313.

Travis, Glenn, Acting Superintendent to Peter Holmes, Director of the Office of Civil Rights, April 30, 1973. State Historical Society of Missouri, Arthur A. Benson II, Box 316.

"Two Kansas City Women have been Arrested, Charged in Connection in Tuesday's Shooting at Central High School." *Northeast News,* February 14, 2019.

United States Commission on Human Rights, *Statement of the United States Commission on Civil Rights Concerning the Statement by the President on Elementary and Secondary School Desegregation.* Washington, DC: Center for Human Relations, National Education Association, 1970.

United States Fencing Press Release, March 2, 1993. State Historical Society of Missouri, Arthur A. Benson II Papers, Box 185D.

United States Government Accountability Office, *K-12 Education: Student Population Has Significantly Diversified, but Many Schools Remain Divided Along Racial, Ethnic, and Economic Lines* (2022).

"Urban Student Characteristics and Urban School Challenges: What High-Quality Education for Every Student Means." Center for Public Education Report (2024). National School Boards Association.

USA Fencing. "Dr. Jeremy Summers Steps Down as USA Fencing Director of Sports Medicine." Accessed June 12, 2023, usafencing.org.

"U.S. Again Halts School Grant." *Kansas City Times*, April 18, 1975. State Historical Society of Missouri, Arthur A. Benson II, Box 402.

"Vandals Rake Central High." *Kansas City Times*, February 24, 1969, 1, 3.

"Van Horn School Group Oppose Bussing Options." *Kansas City Times*, March 28, 1973. State Historical Society of Missouri, Arthur A. Benson II, Box 462.

"Violence Condemned by Central High School Students." *Kansas City Call*, February 20, 1970.

Vopat, Mark C. "Magnet Schools, Innate Talent, and Social Justice." *Theory and Research in Education* 9, no. 1 (2011), 59-72.

Walker, Tim. "A 'Choice' Grounded in Exclusion and Inequality." *neaToday*, August 19, 2021.

Walker, Vanessa Siddle. "Valued Segregated Schools for African American Children in the South, 1935-1969: A Review of Common Themes and Characteristics." *Review of Educational Research* 70, no. 3 (2000): 235-85, 277.

Warner, Mary R. and Mack A. Warner, *Three Year Report: The Quality of Urban Life*, Kansas City Commission on Human Relations, Kansas City, MO. https://eric.ed.gov/?id=ED068594.

Warren, Mrs. Edward C. "Parent Complains of Central." *Kansas City Call*, January 29, 1971.

"Week of Uncertainty at Central." *Kansas City Star*, November 21, 1972. Missouri Valley Special Collections, Schools-Public, Central High.

Wheeler, Hubert, Missouri State Commissioner of Education memo to District and County Administrators, regarding "Opinion of Attorney General John M. Dalton in Reference to Decision of U.S. Supreme Court on Segregation in the Public Schools" (July 1, 1954). State Historical Society of Missouri, Arthur A. Benson II, Box 310.

Wheeler, Hubert, Missouri State Commissioner of Education, to District and County Superintendents (June 15, 1954). State Historical Society of Missouri, Arthur A. Benson II, Box 310.

Wheeler, Hubert. "U.S. Supreme Court Ruling on Segregation in the Public Schools" (March 1954). State Historical Society of Missouri, Arthur A. Benson II, Box 310.

White, Tanika. "Exams to Put KC Students, District to Exam Scores." *Kansas City Star*, April 18, 1999, B1.

Wiberg, Ella. *The History of the Development of Public Education in Kansas City, Missouri*. Master's thesis, University of Wisconsin, 1925.

Williams, Harold, memo to Theron Johnson, July 12, 1967. State Historical Society of Missouri, Arthur A. Benson II, Box 314.

Williams, Henry S. "The Development of the Negro Public School System in Missouri." *The Journal of Negro History* 5, no. 2 (1920): 137-65.

Wilson, William J. *The Truly Disadvantaged: The Inner City, the Underclass, and Public Policy*. Chicago: University of Chicago Press, 1987.

Winn, Stephen. "Effect on Suit Here Unclear to Lawyers." *Kansas City Star*, July 3, 1979, A4.

Wolters, Raymond. *The Burden of Brown: Thirty Years of School Desegregation.* Knoxville: University of Tennessee Press, 1984.

Worley, William S. *J.C. Nichols and the Shaping of Kansas City: Innovation in Planned Residential Communities.* Columbia: University of Missouri Press, 1993.

"Wounded Boy Dies at Help's Door." *Kansas City Star*, June 16, 2005.

Xu, Cynthia Yueting. "Where are All of the Charter Schools Located?" *National Alliance for Public Charter Schools*, December 6, 2022.

Zorn, Eric. "Thug is a Problem Word, Even if It Didn't Used to Be." *Chicago Tribune*, March 3, 2021.

INTERVIEWS

Adams, Gwendolyn. Conversation with Author, September 18, 2012.

Barnes, Jr., Lee. Conversation with Author, November 12, 2012.

Benson, Arthur. Conversation with Author, June 19, 2023.

Benson, Arthur. Conversation with Author, October 23, 2013.

Brooks, Alvin. Conversation with Author, October 31, 2012.

Caruthers, Loyce. Conversation with Author, April 12, 2014.

Collins, Linda. Conversation with Author, October 19, 2023.

Davis, Carmaleta. Conversation with Author, November 13, 2023.

Davis, Jr., Lyle. Conversation with Author, November 7, 2012.

Halim, Marion. Conversation with Author, October 2, 2012.

Jackson, Arthur. Conversation with Author, October 2, 2012.

Kastelein, Jared. Conversation with Author, December 1, 2023.

Lawton, Forestal. Conversation with Author, November 2, 2012.

Madry, Anthony. Conversation with Author, November 14, 2023.

Mahone, Willie. Conversation with Author, October 24, 2012.

Nazlymov, Vladimir. Conversation with Author, July 22, 2013.

Neal, Kayla. Conversation with Author, May 5, 2023.

Norton, Daryl. Conversation with Author, September 27, 2013.

Rainwater, Arthur. Conversation with Author, July 29, 2013.

Shakur, Crystal. Conversation with Author, December 5, 2013.

Shipley, Lynne. Conversation with Author, May 15, 2023.

Slaughter, Christopher. Conversation with Author, September 30, 2013.

Snorgrass, J. Anthony. Conversation with Author, February 20, 2013.

Stewart, Loretta. Conversation with Author, November 2, 2012.

Wilson, Jermaine. Conversation with Author, July 10, 2013.

Witcher, Mikayla. Conversation with Author, November 9, 2023.

Wright, Connie. Conversation with Author, November 12, 2012.

Index

About the Author

Dr. Brad Poos is the Sprint Endowed Professor in Urban Education and Associate Director in the Institute for Urban Education at the University of Missouri Kansas City. Dr. Poos is a career educator who spent his first ten years in K-12 education as both a middle school and high school social studies teacher turned counselor, and who has spent the second half of his career in higher education. Dr. Poos is particularly interested in social history and exploring the lived experiences of everyday people. Dr. Poos has written and published broadly in these areas and has presented his work around the country. He has long been committed to work around equity and justice in education and the community at large.